F♥CK
FEELINGS

Less Obsessing, More Living*

Dr Michael Bennett and Sarah Bennett

*Even if everything's truly horrible

Thorsons

Thorsons
An imprint of HarperCollins*Publishers*
1 London Bridge Street
London SE1 9GF

www.harpercollins.co.uk

First published in the US by Simon & Schuster 2015
This edition published in the UK by Thorsons 2015

10 9 8 7 6 5 4 3 2 1

Interior design by Ruth Lee-Mui

A catalogue record of this book is
available from the British Library

ISBN 978-0-00-814056-4

Printed and bound in Great Britain

For the previous generation, Claire and Dr. Jacob Bleiberg, and Beatrice and Jacob Bennett. Tough lives couldn't stop them from sticking to their values and working hard so that our lives could be so much easier.

And for friend, mentor, and legendary mensch Dr. Ted Nadelson, who taught us that the best way to help people accept what's tough about life is to make them laugh.

There's no "should" or "should not" when it comes to having feelings. They're part of who we are and their origins are beyond our control. When we can believe that, we may find it easier to make constructive choices about what to do with those feelings.

—**Fred Rogers,** *The World According to Mister Rogers: Important Things to Remember*

contents

what's your goal?

Most people read self-help books, or come to see shrinks, because they can't solve their problems after trying very, very hard to do it themselves. This is true whether they feel depressed, anxious, ill-treated, burdened with self-destructive behaviors, hurt by an unhappy relationship, too fat, too thin; you name it. They come expecting advice or treatment that will reduce symptoms, ease painful feelings, strengthen self-control, or mend broken relationships. Basically, they want a cure. These expectations are stoked by the public faces of therapy, particularly those telegenic, first-name-basis self-help gurus like Drs. Phil, Drew, Laura, Nick, etc.

*F*ck Feelings* offers a more realistic approach from a medically trained, practicing psychiatrist who, over a forty-year clinical career, has treated hundreds of patients with intractable mental illness, bad habits, and troubled relationships—Dr. Lastname. That was the alias used by your authors—Dr. Michael Bennett, the aforementioned Harvard-educated psychiatrist, and his daughter Sarah Bennett, a writer who spent years writing sketch comedy at the Upright Citizens Brigade Theatre in New York—as we developed our collaborative technique at our website, fxckfeelings.com.

Observing the difference between what people expect from therapy and what they are actually likely to achieve, I, Dr. Bennett, came to believe that people use the very act of coming for help—and their overbelief in a cure for their problems—to deny the fact that there is much about life, others, and their own personalities that is beyond anyone's power to change. They would rather see themselves as failures or as partially developed seekers who cannot properly begin their lives until they have found an answer that has so far eluded them. Clinging to the belief that they can be cured, they want to know what they or any prior therapists did to block them from achieving their treatment goals. Unfortunately, many therapists, eager to help patients realize these wishes, support their false hopes. I am not one of them.

*F*ck Feelings* explains that, in most cases, you have not failed and do not need to try harder or wait longer for improvement to begin; instead, you need to accept that life is hard and your frustrated efforts are a valuable guide to identifying what you can't change. After urging you to accept whatever it is you can't change—about your personality, behavior, spouse, kid, feelings, boss, country, pet, etc.—the *F*ck Feelings* approach shows you how to become much more effective at managing life's impossible problems, instead of vainly and persistently trying to change them. If you're willing to accept what you can't change, we have many positive suggestions for improving the way you manage the shit on your plate—beginning with not wasting time repeating what hasn't been working.

Your issue may be the love or hate you wish you could stop, the urge to drink or drug that you wish would go away, the blues you wish you could cure, or the spouse, kid, or parent you wish you could change. By the time you seek help, however, it's usually obvious that something about your wish isn't feasible, but that hasn't stopped you from confusing that wish with a permanent, dedicated, high-priority goal. You can't go forward, or be helped by treatment, until you accept its impossibility, suck it up, and turn your bullshit wish into a goal that can actually be achieved.

Accept whatever is obviously impossible about your goals. Accept that depression is often chronic and incurable, so you can stop blaming yourself for not controlling it. Stop treatments that don't seem to be helping. Embrace whatever positive steps help you to live with and manage your illness or issue. Accept that there are some losses that never stop hurting, so you can stop delving into them, get used to living with a heavy heart, and try to build a better life. Accept that you have some urges for stimulating but unhealthy substances, sex partners, or self-expression that no amount of self-understanding will change. Stop asking why you've got weaknesses and start preventing them from turning you into a jerk.

After challenging advice seekers, patients, and our readers to accept what you can't change, we show how you're much less responsible for your misery than you thought. We teach good, often well-established methods for making the best of things—methods that you weren't using because you were too busy with wishful thinking instead of problem solving.

Obviously, we don't guarantee happiness—quite the contrary—but instead we offer you methods for building strength and pride in your ability to deal with the inevitable misery of a tough life. It's not that we're against happiness, just against holding yourself responsible for making it happen when it can't. In our world, feelings don't rule, many things can't be changed, and acceptance of limits, not limitless self-improvement, is the key to moving forward and dealing effectively with any and all crap that life can throw your way.

So, no, we can't tell you how to repair a long-broken relationship with a difficult parent, reform a bad boyfriend, or get respect from your boss, but that's only because nobody can. The only book that can actually teach you how to change how others think is a lobotomy manual. Instead, we can show you how to look past the disappointment, resentment, and/or neediness that result from those issues so they can be managed realistically.

With the right limits, you can have a peaceful relationship with a difficult parent, and with the right standards, you can avoid bad boyfriends altogether. And with realistic expectations, you can get your work done in spite of a bad boss, or better yet, find a better one. Instead of false promises or happy endings, we provide concrete steps for getting past unavoidable bad feelings so you can do your best with what you actually control.

This book is also filled with fun sidebars and tables, like this one, so that I, Sarah, can amuse myself:

Bad Wish	Good Goal
Be my best me!	Learn to accept that "me" isn't the best, and that that'll do.
Learn to love myself!	Love the effort I put into putting up with myself.
Never drink again, ever!	Never stop working hard to resist delicious alcohol.

Given life's cruelty and unfairness, *F*ck Feelings* believes profanity is a source of comfort, clarity, and strength. It helps to express anger without blame, to be tough in the face of pain, and to share determination without sentimentality. On the other hand, we don't tolerate the reverent use of truly obscene f-words, like "fair" or "feelings."

Each chapter addresses the usual wishes people have when they hope to solve a common problem—like loneliness, bad self-image, or conflict—and explains what part of these wishes are impossible to achieve. Using several composite case examples, we show you how to define the limits of what's possible, create realistic goals, and devise businesslike procedures for achieving those goals. We remind you, repeatedly, because you need to hear it, to respect yourself for how you deal with bad luck, not for the overall quality of your luck. We also include information on how to find off-the-page therapy that might work for you.

So while other self-help books guarantee the path to happiness, *F*ck Feelings* guarantees that said path is nonexistent; furthermore, convincing yourself that there is such a path will actually lead you to feel like a true failure, instead of an unlucky hero. What *F*ck Feelings* can promise you is that there is no situation in life that can't be endured if you can keep your sense of humor, bend your wishes to fit reality, restrain your feelings, manage bad behavior, and do what you think is right.

To those who want one of the many famous, overoptimistic Dr. Firstnames to tell them the secret to being happy, we say, fuck happy. Fuck self-improvement, self-esteem, fairness, helpfulness, and everything in between. If you can get over that, you can get real and get to a realistic solution, and yes, you can get it from this book, and from a real doctor, last name and all.

chapter one

fuck self-improvement

Buying a self-help book is usually the second-to-last step to surrendering to a crisis of self, the last step being therapy and the first step being a gym membership, or at least a Zumba DVD or a pamphlet for the Learning Annex.

Dedication to improving yourself is admirable—and if you're Oprah, unbelievably lucrative—but what separates this book from your average work of Deepak Chopra is that we can tell you, up front, that being prepared to make whatever sacrifice is necessary to improve yourself doesn't mean you can do it. You can't somehow get taller once you've stopped growing; there are limits to your physical strength and intellectual ability, no matter how rigorously you train; and, odds are, you have done too many drugs to ever be president.

Eventually, striving to improve yourself brings diminishing returns and prevents you from accepting yourself and living with what you've got. That's one reason self-improvement efforts have to take into account your limits and competing priorities. Otherwise, it's less self-improvement, more self-sabotage.

The same principle applies to controlling bad habits and other weaknesses. The reason twelve-step programs urge people to accept the uncontrollable nature of addictions is not because they're *never* controllable but because, given human weakness, they're never *fully* controllable. There's always something that can, at least temporarily, overwhelm human control and cause us to do things we'll regret, and believing otherwise only makes us more foolishly vulnerable to that possibility and more self-critical when it occurs. Life sucks, our control sucks, but it's not personal. There are limits to what you can do to change yourself, and recognizing these limits is essential to managing bad behaviors, bad pieces of your personality, even bad taste in shoes.

Indeed, the more you study dysfunctional behaviors, the more convinced you become that most of us have weird brains, and those who appear not to just haven't exposed their own brains to the kinds of stress, relatives, or Japanese animation that will reveal their mental dysfunction. The prevalence of unique, genetically associated dysfunctions is certainly consistent with Darwin's theory that individual differences, even dysfunctional ones, improve genetic diversity for the species and enhance its chances of surviving unforeseeable future threats. If genetic diversity is a good thing for the species, however, it's often a disaster for the individual, who gets to carry all kinds of odd instincts and impulses in his DNA that cause trouble and are hard to bear.

Neuroscience seems to show that many emotional and behavioral problems we thought were caused by bad parents or trauma are also caused by wiring that isn't reversible. This explains why self-improvement is hard and sometimes impossible, even when we're strong-willed and well guided. In other words, we're often fucked.

On the other hand, while there's much pain in incurable dysfunction, the joys of self-improvement are overrated. Strength and confidence may give you a wonderful feeling and a license to walk around in a cape and tights, but big fuckin' deal. Real confidence comes from knowing you've used what limited strength you have to do what's important. If your strength isn't great, and as a result you have to strain harder, you deserve even more credit, assuming you've got the values to do something worthwhile.

If you accept that self-improvement has its limits, then you can begin to discover the nature of these limits, which you need to know if you're going to manage them well. So the goal of pushing your potential isn't just to improve your performance but to improve it as much as you reasonably can, given your resources, while discovering what your limits are. That way, you'll know how much help you need and how much to compromise when you can't do everything yourself.

Addiction isn't the only self-destructive behavior that seems like it should be controllable but isn't. Eating disorders, hair picking, hoarding, and procrastination are similar in that they seem like bad habits that should improve with steady effort and strong willpower, but are actually very hard to change. It's no one's fault, not even your mother's. The only conclusion to draw is that many people have less control over their basic behavior than they deserve, and that it's often hard to know how much responsibility they should bear for their actions.

Of course, just because you can't always make yourself stronger or even correct your weaknesses, you still have to try. If your goal is to be a good, decent person who carries out his responsibilities, you're never off the hook. The fact that you're flawed and have limits to how much you can improve or even control yourself means that you just have to work harder to get as close as you can to where you want to go. You should never hold yourself accountable for results you don't control, but always for the strength of trying.

Many requests for help spring from an expectation for self-improvement and a denial of the fact that it hasn't yet happened in spite of many failed previous efforts to get help. This chapter—and really, life—is about how to realistically assess your ability to get better, cope with the pain of accepting what you already know, and turn your knowledge of your limits into a useful plan of action. No matter what shape your life is in, what step of the ladder you're on, or what drives you to buy this book.

Taking Back the Reins of Your Life (After a Stampede)

Since humans control very little besides their DVR queues and their opinions about Miley Cyrus, it's not surprising that we often feel like our lives are slipping into chaos. Sometimes it's because you're actually losing control, sometimes because someone close to you is spinning out, and sometimes because whatever you don't control feels far more important and overwhelming than what you do. In any case, the goals you wish for when you're feeling out of control, as listed and described in the following three examples, are rarely realistic and will often make your helplessness worse.

The trouble is, of course, "out of control" usually means just that, and no amount of sweating, seeking, and therapizing is going to change the fact that life reserves the right to throw more shit at you than you can possibly handle. Accepting the way life sometimes becomes—or at least feels—uncontrollable, however, need never stop you from managing damage or speeding up recovery.

Feeling helpless doesn't mean that everything is going to turn out badly or that you're doing a poor job with your life. If you can ignore the terrible meltdown feeling and take credit for how you're handling the problem, rather than getting carried away or feeling too responsible, you'll have much to be proud of and many more options to consider.

Here's what you can't really control but feel you should:

- Income (or lack thereof)
- Relationship status (or lack thereof)
- How other people feel about you, without magic or the power of hypnosis
- Your offspring, after they've exited your body
- Your ability to refuse the gravitational pull of a "party-sized" bag of pretzel M&M's/any and all booze/your phone after all that eating and/or drinking when your deadbeat ex is still a text away

Among the wishes people express are:

- To regain control they thought they once had
- To figure out how to get close family members to control themselves
- To stop feeling helpless all the time

Here are three examples:

I've always been hardworking and good at doing sales, and I married someone whose love I thought I could count on, so I really don't understand why my life seems to be coming apart. After getting laid off from my old job when the company was sold, I had to take a lower-paying job with a new boss who hates me. Meanwhile, my wife decided her feelings for me were gone and that she couldn't stay married to someone she doesn't love, even though I thought we had built a really nice life together. Now every day feels like a death march and I can't stop crying. I'm the biggest loser I know, and the pain won't go away. My goal is to regain control of my life.

My son has always been a nice kid, but he's always been too good at finding trouble, and even now that he's twenty-five, he just can't seem to get his life together. We tried hard to get him extra help when he was in school, but he never did homework and quit college after a year. We think he drinks too much, but he won't admit it, and the girl he hangs out with has no job, too many rings in her face, and an ex-boyfriend in jail. My husband and I dread the day when she announces she's pregnant with our grandchild. My goal is to finally find out what's the matter with our son so we can empower him to get control of his life.

I'm the world's biggest phony. People at work think I've got it together but they don't know that I'm a nervous wreck who has trouble holding down lunch, can't sleep for three days before every presentation, and is always obsessing about the stupid things I just said and wish I could take back. I'm a mental case who just pretends to have it together, which makes me feel even more out of control. My goal is to have a life that doesn't feel like a train wreck.

It's hard to believe there are ways to classify chaos, but when it comes to losing control of your life, there are different kinds of feeling fucked. Some people get sucked into a bad-luck, no-fault meltdown that, if taken personally, can destroy a good person's belief in his values and motivation. Other people become helpless by proxy, usually by watching a loved one who's unable to get themselves straight, while others feel like they're living on the verge of a meltdown without realizing just how effective they are at staying away from the edge.

In any case, just because you feel out of control doesn't mean you should have been able to prevent it. Instead of searching for mistakes or weaknesses, judge yourself realistically, in terms of what a good person can actually do in a bad situation. Even if your situation is due to a foolish mistake, learn from it and stop blaming yourself for bad results you don't control, whether they involve your job, kids, or mental condition.

If you do blame yourself for the mess you're in, simply because it happened on your watch, you'll weaken and distract yourself at a time you need to be stronger. If you dwell on second-guessing yourself and believing you deserve punishment, you'll have more trouble figuring out the smart thing to do, giving strength to others, and tolerating painful feelings without panicking.

Once you've separated your overwhelmed feelings from a realistic assessment of your own performance, however, you can build self-respect and get to work on managing life. You'll have more strength for rebuilding your work and relationships, setting limits on out-of-control kids, and tolerating anxious feelings without doubting your capacity to ignore them when necessary. In the end, you'll have more respect for the times you kept trucking through a meltdown than the times you were confidently cruising along because everything was going your way.

Quick Diagnosis

Here's what you wish for and can't have:

- The praise, salary, or family you deserve
- Peace, love, and happiness (aka, financial security)
- The knowledge that your present is right on track
- Confidence in your ability to keep it there

Here's what you can aim for and actually achieve:

- Create reasonable standards for what you can actually do, given your Muggle status
- Respect yourself for meeting your standards
- Survive pain, fear, and distress and give yourself credit for doing so
- Not let pain change your values, basic course, or determination

Here's how you can do it:

- Look for pre-meltdown red flags that might have warned you in the past and could warn you next time
- Ask yourself whether you could reasonably be expected to do anything different
- Rate yourself for work effort, honesty, and the value of your priorities
- Assuming you deserve better, find a friend or therapist who can remind you that you've lived up to your values and that the helplessness and humiliations have nothing to do with you, regardless of how you feel
- Check with a psychiatrist or therapist to see whether there are behavioral techniques and/or medications that might reduce anxiety or depression, if they're extreme

Your Script

Here's what to tell someone or yourself while you're feeling hope-lessly fucked-up.

> Dear [Me/Family Member/Fuckup I Can't Help But Care About],
>
> I know you feel like [the royal "we"/you/our fuckup son] is on the verge
> of [insert mistake or potential tragic experience], and life feels like
> an unholy disaster. The truth is, however, that life often sucks and
> sometimes I can't expect to feel other than [insert classier, more dire
> synonym for "shitty"], especially given issues in the past regarding [bad
> luck/anxiety/your many addictions and world-record unemployment].
> So don't take it personally and do take credit for whatever good things
> you were doing, even if they were totally ineffective at fending off this
> mess. Take pride in doing a good job, regardless of bad [luck/genes/
> associates/mental pain] and don't stop.

Did You Know . . . What Is the Real Secret of *The Secret*?

The Secret, by Rhonda Byrne, is a self-help tome in which the essential the-sis is: if you put your desires "out into the universe" (which is to say, if you think about what you want), then the universe will give you what you want.

The Secret says, if you're fat and poor, it's not because you have a crappy job in a terrible economy, or because, after another day working a job you hate, you treat yourself to a deluxe cheeseburger with an extra side of Crisco. It's because when you stand on the scale in your efficiency apart-ment, you're thinking, *This sucks, I am fat and poor*, not, *Hey, universe, I am thin, rich, and wonderful*. Oprah's a huge fan of *The Secret*, as are those out there who credit it for doing everything from getting them better jobs to ridding them of cancer.

In reality, notions like the one put forth in *The Secret* have come up over and over through the ages, often claiming to be extensions of spiritual ideas that are exactly the opposite. The real secret, of course, is one that you don't want to hear and would never shell out your money to learn because it doesn't feel good, which is exactly why you're better off hearing it: whatever good or focused thoughts, wishes, or prayers you put out there, shit happens and it won't be fair, no matter how many collages you make.

The more you *project* your wishes, the more futile life seems while you continue to wait. The worst thing that can happen is that your wish actually comes true, because that's when you think you've discovered *The Secret*, but haven't. Then, since it's your nature to have more wishes, it's only a matter of time until you run into a brick wall of disappointment, which is now your fault, because you've failed to do *The Secret* properly. No matter how much you deserve it, you can't always get what you want, and that's life (unless you're Oprah).

Go ahead and wish, pray, and focus—they help you to know what you want, particularly if it guides you toward keeping your priorities straight and working hard—just don't take it personally when you don't get your reward. And watch your Crisco intake.

Getting to the Root of Your Problem . . . and Tearing It Out

It's not clear when people started equating solving emotional issues with retracing your steps in order to find your car keys, but if you retrace your steps to uncover the ultimate source of your problems, you won't usually find it. On the plus side, you might find your sunglasses.

What people hate to consider, even after root seeking has been getting them nowhere for some time, is that, sometimes, it just doesn't work. There are lots of problems we'll never know the answer to. There's nothing wrong with looking for answers that might actually exist, but, when the search isn't bearing fruit, there's a strong possibility that answers aren't to be had, and obsessing about finding them is a distraction to figuring out where the real keys are—and what you're going to do next.

People prefer to believe that, with enough fact gathering, insight, and the heart-to-heart sharing of honest, heretofore suppressed, and probably embarrassing emotion, any problem can be sourced and solved. In fact, knowing why you've got a bad habit usually gives you no ability to stop it, and the search for deeper knowledge sometimes serves as an excuse for waiting until it's easier to stop, which it never is. So getting to the root of your problem is often antitherapeutic, and, at worst, a giant waste of time.

Or, if therapy hasn't solved a problem, you wonder whether it's been intense and long-lasting enough, or if you've been sincere enough, or if your therapist is skilled enough. If the problem involves a relationship, you wonder if you've worked hard enough to express painful and nega-tive feelings—which again, surprise, often makes things worse.

Here are telltale signs that your quest for a deep solution—or Holy Grail— must end:

- The amount of searching you put in is inverse to the amount you have been able to change your problem
- Your friends, kids, and pets have made it clear that the subject of your past/problems/bullshit is closed
- Your therapist has been less blunt than your friends, kids, and pets, but is clearly falling asleep
- You've revised the past so many times, your déjà vu has déjà vu

Among the wishes people express when they feel there must be an answer to an unsolvable problem are:

- To figure out what happened that caused them to lose the control they once had
- To find out why they can't do something when they've always been good at doing something similar
- To understand why they can't stop being drawn to doing something bad

Here are three examples:

I don't understand why I started drinking again after ten years of sobriety. I had no desire to drink—going to bars didn't bother me, nor
did having liquor in the house or being around friends who were drinking. Then suddenly I was tense over a problem at work, and I figured I
should be able to control myself after all these years, so I had a drink.
It was fine, I had only one, and kept to a one-per-day limit until a week
later, and now, three months later, I have no control over my drinking
and I'm back to square one. My goal is to figure out what happened to
me and why.

I don't know why I avoid finishing certain tasks at work. If something
involves talking to people, and I can get it done quickly, I'll work hard
until I'm finished, but if I've got to fill out a lot of forms and no one is
looking over my shoulder, I let things slide until I'm really in trouble.
I've always been like that and my desk is piled high with papers that
I'm afraid to look at. I don't know whether it's because I'm afraid to
succeed or afraid that I'm living out my father's prediction that I'd be
a fuckup, but it's crippling my life. My goal is to figure out whether I'm
lazy or have a psychological issue that prevents me from succeeding.

I'm always attracted to the wrong kind of guys, and it always ends
poorly, mostly with me getting dumped, sometimes with me getting
either physically or verbally abused along the way. A therapist told
me I choose men who remind me of my father, who was a charismatic
sweet-talker who dumped my mother when she was pregnant with
me. I think that's a fair assessment, and it's time for me to find a better
sort of person, but no matter how hard I try, I keep on dating assholes.
My goal is to figure out why I'm so attracted to Mr. Wrong and how to
get more attracted to someone nice.

Whenever we're perplexed by weaknesses that don't make sense,
questioning why is as helpful from the mouth of an adult as it is from
a four-year-old. If you can't understand why you've started drinking

again after ten years, or can't get work done when you've done it before, or can't find a better guy when you know what you're doing wrong, you have a right to wonder why. Asking the question more than once or twice, however, is a Job-like move that may help you express frustration, but will not help you overcome it.

What neurobiology has taught us is that every action we take depends on multiple unique subcapacities, and all it takes is for one of those subcapacities to be weak or broken, and our ability to function is compromised.

If you resume drinking, it's not because you're a weak person, but because drinking triggers something in your brain that says, "I've got to do that again." If you have trouble with paperwork, it may be because your brain has trouble translating or using written symbols in a specific way (numbers, maps, English). If you can't change whom you're attracted to, you may be directed by a part of your brain that, whether it was programmed before birth or a few years later, can't be changed now.

So the answer you'll get from your maker, when you finally meet Him or Her and get to ask why, is the same one you got from your mother when she didn't know the answer and didn't want to waste time— "Because I said so, now go make yourself useful."

Of course, knowing there's no root answer, or that, at the very least, it's unobtainable, doesn't relieve you of responsibility for dealing with a problem; it just spares you having to take an exam on its origins. Depending on how obsessed you are with a Faustian quest for knowledge or how avoidant you are of messy, painful tasks, you will or won't like putting the quest aside, accepting the uncertainty of not understanding a problem's roots, and nevertheless dedicating yourself to managing it.

Having given up on the false hope that deep understanding would make it possible to solve your problem, gather motivation by reviewing your reasons for imposing change on yourself and your life. Doing it to please someone or to look better are not motivations that tend to last; instead, decide for yourself whether change is necessary for you to be the kind of person you want to be. Then, if you find good reasons rooted in your values, remind yourself frequently what they are so that you can ignore pain, frustration, and humiliation while seeking to strengthen your management of yourself.

Instead of trying to figure out your problem, use your best tools for managing it, be they finding a rehab program, an organizational coach, or a group of girlfriends whose opinions on jerks you trust. Having given up the quest for a deep solution and the urge to ask questions, find the motivations that matter and learn how to take action.

Quick Diagnosis

Here's what you wish for and can't have:

- A clear understanding of what's wrong
- Complete control over your problem
- An easier way of dealing with your problem, now that you know its origins
- A reliable way of treating and preventing it

Here's what you can aim for and actually achieve:

- Know as much as anyone knows about a problem while accepting your inability to know more
- Accept the pain and confusion of having to deal with a problem you don't understand
- Find deep motivation for not letting a problem change your priorities or values
- Not let confusion or humiliation interfere with your determination to manage it

Here's how you can do it:

- If you don't figure out the answer after checking the Internet plus two experts, stop trying

- Don't reopen your efforts unless today's headline proclaims new knowledge of your issues specifically
- Stop asking why and start asking how
- Prepare a plan of action contingent on your knowing nothing but what you know now

Your Script

Here's what to tell someone or yourself while you're totally unable to understand the reason for or source of a problem.

Dear [Me/Family Member/Spouse/Overly Logical Friend]:

I know it's hard to understand why a [positive adjectives] person like me should have a problem with [addiction/politics/attraction to morons] but I do, and, to date, treatment with [three analysts/ kabbalah/Judge Judy] hasn't given me an answer that makes a difference. I've decided that ignorance is okay, but my problem isn't, and that from now on I need to do everything I can to improve and manage my behavior, just to be the person I want to be. So I will be open about my problem [in meetings/press releases/tweets], welcome observations about my behavior [with/without retaliating], and track my progress over time [in my computer/Facebook/a secret journal that you should burn if I die]. And I will not give up.

Becoming a More Positive Person

Negative feelings, particularly anger, self-pity, and envy, are painful to feel and also to hold back, since unleashing them makes you a jerk who's a drag to be around. It's like having to hold in a full bladder all the time, except it's your mouth, and if you let it go, it could release things so hurtful, mean, and unjustified that you'd prefer having a wet crotch.

So when it comes to becoming more positive and less negative, many people would like to cleanse themselves of negative feelings, remove the temptation to act like a dick, and ease the strain of con-stant self-monitoring and self-restraint that often makes them tense and cranky and causes them to be dickish despite themselves.

Unfortunately, many things that promise relief from negative feel-ings aren't good for you and won't really make you a better person, even if they make you feel better. You can be justified in attacking someone, physically or verbally, but the satisfaction it brings is lim-ited; it often leaves you with a bad feeling in the long run and gets you more involved with someone you'd like to stay away from.

You might also try to become more positive by withdrawing from whatever causes you to feel negative, but that's not so hot if it re-quires you to shed responsibilities, abandon people who need you, or dull down your personality. You may wind up with a serene smile but you may also have betrayed your own standards of behavior.

That's why your primary goal is not to get rid of negative feelings and feel better, but to block them from controlling your behavior while you continue to act like a decent person.

Don't stigmatize negative feelings; even pacifists, yogis, and nurs-ery school teachers get road rage under the wrong circumstances (e.g., in downtown Boston). Some people have bad tempers or are chronically grouchy while others are stuck in situations that hap-pen to hit their weak spots and drive them nuts. Either way, if you chastise yourself for having nasty feelings when you really can't help it, you usually make them worse. After kicking yourself, you're that much more likely to kick someone else.

Besides, your nasty, demonic side may be part of the spark that makes you creative, funny, and energetic. While that side may not be easy to control or live with, you can try to use that negative energy in good ways. Becoming more positive doesn't mean becoming sweetly angelic, but rather, decently demonic, or at least decent enough that your friends don't all tell you to go back to hell.

Here are signs that your nasty side is taking over:

- Instead of driving with your hands at ten and two, you've always got one middle finger at twelve
- The glass isn't half-empty or half-full, it's just a toilet
- You think the "stand your ground" laws were invented just for you
- You often use the phrase "I'm just being honest," then say something that just makes you sound like an asshole

Among the wishes people express when they want to improve themselves by reducing bad feelings are:

- To stop hating someone (spouse, child) who doesn't deserve it
- To be less angry and more kind in general
- To stop pining for what's lost and get over it
- To stop being controlled by fear

Here are three examples:

My father-in-law is not the worst person in the world, but I can't get over the feeling that I hate to be in the same room with him, and I have to, because my family lives with him right now. We could never afford to live in a nice house otherwise, and it's great for our kids, but in the meantime, he sits in the living room every night, watching his TV, bossing his wife around, spouting his hateful political rhetoric, and insulting me at every opportunity, and I want to kill him. Complaining to my wife doesn't do any good because it just makes her feel helpless, and then she defends her dad's behavior and I feel worse. I wish he were dead. My goal, if you don't know a hit man, is to stop hating him.

It's been two years, and I haven't been able to get over my divorce. My ex was an asshole who betrayed me terribly and I know I'm better off without him, but for whatever reason, it still hurts. I really loved him for a while there, and I still can't get over the memories or stop tearing up when I think about him. The kids, who are teens now, are doing better than I am and ask me when I'm going to start dating again, but I can't imagine a time when I'll ever be interested. My goal is to get over loving him and feel better.

I wish I wasn't so insecure. I'm always shy and I get very nervous before networking events, which are a requirement for my work, and my least favorite part of a job I otherwise love. I shake and break out in hives. My brother has always been more confident, but I can't really blame my parents, because they've always encouraged me. It's my own fault. I thought it would go away as I got older, but I'm thirty, and it's just as bad as ever, particularly when I get promoted and have to meet new people even more. My goal is to be less nervous and instead have some confidence in myself.

If people could control the way they feel, then persistent negative feelings would be a legitimate sign of failure and a target for self-improvement. Also, nobody would cheat on their spouses, enjoy scary movies, or eat their weight in frosting, but that's neither here nor there.

Since negative feelings are just a fact of neurology and genetics, it's what you do *with* them that counts. The people in these examples are more successful than they think, because success here is not measured by whether they feel better, more loving, less angry, etc. It's measured by all the good things they are doing and have done in spite of the negative feelings they can't get out of their heads.

There's probably a positive, evolutionary reason for having negative feelings you can't get rid of; they may warn you of danger, give an extra bite of sadness to your songs or poetry, or help you stay attached to your tribe. Whatever advantage they provide, it may have been more helpful in a jungle than in the big city, but either way, if it helps the species survive, it tends to persist, regardless of how much pain it causes you as an individual.

Assuming you're going to have to live with negative feelings, develop standards for behaving well in spite of them. No, you shouldn't expect yourself to force smiles so much that they break your face and scare children. You should, however, invite feedback about your behavior from those you trust, so you can be confident that your actions and words don't hurt people or interfere with your positive strategic goals and, most important, make you act like an asshole.

If you're self-critical about your negative feelings, you may be tempted to live with people who dislike you as much as you dislike yourself. Naturally, this could set off a vicious cycle that brings out your worst behavior and justifies continuous self-punishment. Instead, seek people who aren't much bothered by your negativity and who appreciate your positive side. You may be frustrated by their lack of understanding and attention to your supposed worthlessness, but the results will be better for everyone in the long run.

Whether you are forced to live with hate, yearning, envy, or fear, respect what you do with your feelings, not what they do to you. Don't let them distract you from your usual goals of avoiding unnecessary conflict at home, making a living, and being a good friend.

The more you remember your goals and respect your restraint, the less power your negative feelings will have to shape your actions and reduce your self-respect. You can't control your negativity, but you can keep it from controlling you.

Quick Diagnosis

Here's what you wish for and can't have:

- An improved heart free of hate, envy, fear, and general ugliness
- A way of managing relationships that will prevent or resolve bad feelings
- A way to love the ugly feelings right out of yourself

Here's what you can aim for and actually achieve:

- Build standards that are not distorted or compromised by negative feelings

- Act decently in spite of the way you really feel
- Respect the way you act decently when you feel malicious, bravely when you're frightened, determined when you're tired, etc.
- Bear the pain of living with ugly feelings rather than attacking yourself for having them or attacking others to escape them

Here's how you can do it:

- Get to know your inner asshole so as to reduce the likelihood it becomes outer
- Every time it gets control, emerge with new lessons about your standards and the triggers that get you to lose control
- Avoid those triggers as best you can, even if it means a longer drive to work that avoids the freeway
- Find accepting friends and an accepting coach

Your Script

Here's what to tell someone or yourself when you have ugly, nasty thoughts and feelings.

Dear [Me/Family Member/Guy Who Cut Me Off],

I can't deny that I have [angry/envious/completely vicious] feelings for [you/my child/my fuckhead boss], but I have other feelings as well, and my feelings don't matter as much as doing the [work/taxes/college application/right thing] without [insert act of rage], and this I can do. I have doubts about my ability to use [yoga/psychoanalysis/watching Too Cute] to achieve more positive feelings, and I am not sure I would like to give up my list of hated [relatives/celebrities/salsas at Chipotle] or be more blissed out and less wrought up than I am. Let me know if you think I have acted badly. Otherwise, I believe my current method of managing my feelings is best for me.

Did You Know . . . That Trying Too Hard to Control Nasty Feelings Can Make You Even More Nasty?

Negative feelings, like the Mafia or LinkedIn, only increase their nagging pull the more you try to break free. If you try to eradicate them entirely by punishing yourself, doing penance through good deeds, and influencing others to do the same, you might think you're on the path to salvation and that good is winning over evil.

The problem is that, to those who are truly obsessed with eradicating evil, it's infuriating to meet people who won't join the cause. You wind up filled with so much of that same ol' familiar hatred that you want to tell them in a most strained, cheerful-yet-pissed, singsongy, scoldy manner that you would love to stab their faces with the foot of a bar stool.

So beware the excessively virtuous, who never raise their voices except in anger at bad people, whose oversized smiles give you the creeps and show too many teeth, and who use the same, overly cheerful, sugary-sweet tone to speak to adults and children. Helping others is the only thing it's okay for them to talk about, and they're ready to help everyone, especially the unappreciative, disgusting idiots who never appreciate their efforts, never heed their advice, and irritate them so much, they have to act even sweeter. So if they offer you help or advice, be a smart idiot and politely decline before running for your life.

Stop Fucking Up

There are few things as frustrating as feeling too disorganized, unmotivated, and/or unfocused to accomplish even the smallest task. You can blame a noisy work environment, the wrong colored pen, or the need to watch TV in a timely, spoiler-free manner as the source of your distraction for only so long until you start blaming yourself.

Procrastination, avoidance, and disorganization cause delays and failures that provoke shame, criticism, and even legal issues. If you're at the point where you're amazed you finished reading two whole paragraphs before watching *Game of Thrones*, then this section is for you.

Some people with these problems may act as if they don't care, or take pleasure in creating expectations they can't meet and then lying about them, but in reality, they usually care deeply but have become accustomed to cover-ups, apologies, and endless self-defense. They often hate themselves and declare themselves secret self-enemy number one, knowing they're at fault even when they always seem good at blaming others.

The brighter and more capable they are, the more certain they are that their bad behaviors represent bad choices and a failure to accept and discharge responsibility, and that they could do better if they were better motivated, more reliable, and more honest. Often, their parents, teachers, and supervisors agree that accepting responsibility for their failures seems like the necessary first step toward recovery.

While accepting that you *have* a problem is in fact the universal first step, accepting *responsibility* for having it is not. Brain wiring can cause well-motivated, smart people to procrastinate and drop the ball, and nature gives them no choice. The fact that you're not responsible for having a problem, however, never relieves you of responsibility for working with it and finding ways around it, and often requires you to overcome deeply ingrained bad habits and attitudes. It's impossible to change your instincts or make distractedness, impulsivity, and scattered thinking go away; you can, however, become a good manager of the impulses to procrastinate, avoid, lie, and cover up.

Then again, most "faulty" brain wiring, like that which makes tracking and finishing tasks difficult, is probably helpful in terms of Darwinian survival in situations that don't involve sitting in cubicles or writing term papers. Having a mind that shifts attention quickly or persistently stays off topic may actually help in chaotic situations where you need to spot someone sneaking up on you. It also seems to empower salesmen; in fact, it's hard to find a salesman without ADD. Distractibility is not so hot, however, when you're staring at a monitor, or really anywhere but in sales, the jungle, politics, the jungle, etc.

So don't hold yourself responsible for irresponsibility when it comes to being a slacker, assuming you don't really want to be one. Push aside the shame, assess yourself objectively, and learn what's necessary for good management. You can't change your brain, but with the right tricks, extra time, and determination, you can get stuff done, no matter what's on TV.

Here's how you can tell you're not to blame for your brain:

- There are several "to do" lists in your pockets, more than one of which includes "organize 'to do' lists"
- You're better at saying "I'm sorry" than a Canadian, and do it more often
- A lost schedule probably wouldn't matter, as it was with the "to do" lists
- The only way to get you to a meeting on time is to tell you it's an hour earlier than it really is, and then you need to be walked there with horse blinders on

Among the wishes people express about improving their disorganization and dysfunction are:

- To be more responsible
- To stop forgetting appointments
- To stop avoiding work
- To appease someone who wants them to stop avoiding work
- To figure out how to face the pile of shit on their desk before the boss sees it and shits on them

Here are some examples:

I don't know why I've always been a fuckup, but I'm pretty sure the boss is going to fire me, even though he's my dad. I underachieved in high school, even when teachers went out of their way to encourage me and offer extra help. Now I'm working for my dad and I don't want people to think I'm there just because I'm his son, but they're right, because I never get tasks done. I hate screwing up and apologizing so much that sometimes I can't bring myself to come to work in the morning, which just makes things worse. My goal is to grow up and make better choices.

I hate to admit it—in fact, I never admit it—but I'm a liar and can't stop myself. I started lying about my homework when I was little, even though I always got caught, but I just couldn't control it, even after I was punished and publicly humiliated. In college I told my parents I was doing fine when I'd stopped going to classes, and it would have saved them a fortune in tuition if I'd just told them the truth and dropped out instead of waiting to get called out on my bullshit and kicked out of school. Now I'm living at home and I sometimes look for work, but I have no hope for the future. My goal is to be an honest person I wouldn't despise.

I have no excuse for how little I've done with my life. Everything I've tried, I'm interested in for a year or two and then I stop being interested and, before long, find something newer and shinier that I'm sure I'll want to make a better career out of. That, of course, lasts for a short while before something even newer and shinier appears to lure me away from my last job, and the cycle repeats itself. I should be motivated to follow through on one career path because I need the money and I'm not getting any younger, but when an idea gets into my head, there's no room for logic, perspective, or anything else. My goal is to settle on one career path, any path, before I'm so old I should retire.

If you had a problem with, say, constant barfing, you wouldn't settle for feeling like a loser while resigning yourself to a life spent within ten feet of a toilet or in reach of a paper bag; you'd see a specialist, quit gluten if you had to, or at least become a master of puke jokes. That's why the first job as a chronic fuckup is to put aside shame and blame and find out if part of the trouble is a weakness in your mental equipment.

Most people avoid this step because it's painful to know that something about you doesn't work right, but doing so will save energy you're wasting on self-blame and apology and will give you ideas about better things to do than kicking yourself.

Incidentally, the line between bad mental equipment and bad be-havior is often blurred by the fact that bad mental equipment usually causes people to behave badly. This is either because they're innately more angry and impulsive than they can manage, or because they become bitter about their inability to stop themselves from fuck-ing up, which ups the anger factor even more. So the fact that some fuckups act like Assholes (see Chapter 9) doesn't necessarily mean they've made worse choices than the better-behaved fuckups, or that they have more control over their choices. It just means they struggle more and their behavior may be even harder for them to change or control.

If you can tolerate the humiliation and helplessness and admit that you're an out-of-control fuckup, it frees you from expectations you can't possibly meet, promises you can't keep, and appearances you can't maintain; it liberates you from the ensuing cycle of endless failure. It doesn't free you, of course, from your standards or your determination to be as least fucked-up as possible given your new, self-acknowledged fuckup status.

As soon as you accept who you are, think hard about the standards you want to live up to and less about looking normal, pleasing au-thorities, or competing with others. Use those standards to manage your inner fuckup by redoubling your efforts to learn whatever you really care about and manage bad behavior.

Rely on your own standards for defining hard work, reliability, and self-reliance, and use your gifts to achieve them in your own way. If your career happens to lack prestige or follows an unconventional, restless path, don't criticize yourself. Respect yourself all the more for having found a way to meet standards using equipment you didn't choose and given habits that are hard to break.

Remember, fucking up doesn't mean getting bad results; it means not doing your best with what you've got. As long as you've developed values you believe in, and have reason to think you're doing your best to work at living up to them, you'll always be a success, even if learn-ing you've got a wacky brain is hard to swallow.

Quick Diagnosis

Here's what you wish for and can't have:

- On-demand concentration and focus
- Not acting stupid
- Good results whenever you work hard and deserve them
- Not feeling scared shitless before you can start working

Here's what you can aim for and actually achieve:

- Define for yourself what's necessary to get done
- Find your own ways for doing and delegating what's necessary
- Know you've done your best, regardless of result
- Take pride in your ability to work with what you've got

Here's what you can do:

- Test yourself, or get tested by a neuropsychologist, on information-processing problems, and give yourself a Myers-Briggs test to gain a feel for your permanent personality traits and the strengths and weaknesses that go with them
- Get help from whatever teachers and coaches are most positive about you and have the best tricks for helping you perform better
- Avoid friends who understand you but nevertheless overreact to your fuckups because they're too much like you, and embrace friends who, even if they don't understand your fuckups, aren't terribly bothered by them
- Try medication if nonmedical methods aren't enough
- Find a spouse who's good at doing your taxes

Your Script

> *Dear [Me/Family Member/Guy I've Disappointed, Let Down, or*
> *Royally Screwed],*
>
> *I know you feel I've [fucked up/dropped the ball/ignored my deadline/*
> *deserve my trial date and possible jail time]. Let me assure you,*
> *however, that nothing is more important to me than [doing a good*
> *job/keeping my commitments/not disappointing you/staying off*
> *MSNBC's Lockup] and that I am now doing my best to [figure out*
> *what happened/make amends if possible/never screw up this bad*
> *again]. I know that one reason for the problem is that I cannot [insert*
> *basic skill, like time-telling or direction-following], but I'm aware of*
> *that weakness and have developed systems for preventing it from*
> *interfering with the job. I will learn from this experience and continue*
> *to try to fulfill my commitments. [Insert long, sincere string of*
> *apologetic words, followed by silent prayer.]*

Curing Yourself of Addiction

No matter how much evidence accumulates that our potential for addictions of all kinds (controlled substances, sex, edible substances,
Internet, horrible people) owes more to causes we don't control, like
our genes, than those we do, we continue to experience addictions as
moral failures and respond accordingly. Usually, that response means
hiding the addiction and condemning others who have it—at least if
you're in politics.

We don't control the genetic factors that make some people more
vulnerable than others to chemical dependence, or the ADD that
makes some people more impulsive, or the childhood experiences
that make us yearn for bad relationships and avoid the unfamiliarity
of good ones. It's just easier to act like we do so we have someone to
blame, instead of admitting we're all helpless specks in the universe.

Once you can accept that life, in fact, sucks, and the tons of bad stuff to be born and/or stuck with is distributed unevenly, unfairly, and undeservedly, recovery from addiction becomes much less impossible.

In other words, getting unaddicted, or even just less addicted, does not begin with self-criticism, punishment, or hoping that urges to do bad things will ever go away, but with acceptance of the fact that they're there, you need all your strength to deal with them, and you can't waste it on self-blame, false hope, or despair and self-pity.

Some people believe your best opportunity for change comes after an addiction causes you to "hit bottom" and lose everything you value. The trouble is, there's a vicious cycle to addiction that increases your dependence on bad things as you lose your hold on what you value. The worse you feel about life and yourself, the more you think of nothing but immediate relief or pleasure. Addiction can be a bottomless pit that sucks you down harder the farther you fall, leaving you with an addiction as bottomless, and as appetizing, as a salad bowl at Olive Garden.

Some people believe that conquering addiction starts with your becoming aware of the anger and pain your addiction causes loved ones, and if you've been unaware, of course this knowledge helps. Often, however, an intervention doesn't teach anyone anything new, and the best way to get rid of the guilt your addiction causes others is to get even more fucked-up. Then you find yourself getting sober for others instead of for yourself, which allows you to hold them responsible for keeping you sober, and justifies getting high again when they disappoint you.

Trying to make bad impulses go away, or to scare or cry or communicate them into submission, usually doesn't work and may actually increase your neediness and drive you back to your addictions. Long story short, most of what you've seen on *Intervention* doesn't fly in real life.

Instead, improvement begins with acceptance of the permanence of what's wrong and a realization that there are, nevertheless, good reasons for pushing yourself to manage flaws that will never stop being a painful burden.

As everyone in recovery knows, there's no moment of victory and absolute, eternal sobriety. Success over addiction means knowing why being unaddicted is worthwhile, and trying as hard as you can to stay that way, no matter how harsh the truth of your past, present, or future may be.

Here are the signs that you're addicted and stuck:

- You want to understand the root of your addiction (see above)
- You feel constant shame from always letting others down
- You refuse to see your addiction as a problem, even though it's gotten you fired, dumped, arrested, etc.

Among the wishes people express when they need to stop an addictive behavior are:

- To end their substance abuse and/or self-abuse, period
- To get others to understand that they don't have a drinking problem, it's everyone else who's got a thinking problem
- To figure out whether they're really addicted or just a big fan
- To find the elusive middle ground of use between sobriety and addiction

Here are some examples:

I've gone through detox three times and I just can't stay sober. The only place I can go after treatment is back to my family and a marriage from hell, but my kids need me. I start out with lots of determination and a list of meetings, and I just get absorbed by the stress of conflict with my wife and caring for the kids, and by the end of the day I'm grabbing for the hidden bottles. I don't have time to go to meetings and there aren't any near where I live. My goal is to find the strength I just don't have and no one has been able to give me.

My husband tells me he doesn't have a problem with addiction because he never has a hangover or misses a day of work, but he's quietly plastered by dinner and useless after, which is when the kids really want to spend time with him. It's true, he's a quiet, mellow drunk, but he's just not good for much after the second glass. He says he's better than his own father, he's a good provider, he works hard—and so he has a right to relax at night, so I'm just making trouble by giving him a hard time. My goal is to figure out whether he's addicted and how to get him some help.

My wife was angry when she found out that I spend hours every evening looking at porn and playing video games online, but I don't see what's wrong. We have a good sex life, I'm not unfaithful, and there's no harm in it. She says I can't see how much of my life I'm wasting online, how it's taking away from other areas of my life, and that I need help. I think the only thing wrong is that she's mad at me because she's overreacting to my looking at sex on the Internet. My goal is to get her to see that there's nothing wrong.

Before even attempting to decide whether you're addicted to a substance or destructive behavior, define for yourself what those things mean. You know what your family says, and what AA pamphlets say, and even what your dealer says, but unless you take time to define addiction for yourself, everyone else's opinion is bullshit (especially your dealer's).

In fact, most people who struggle with addiction don't necessarily have medical withdrawal symptoms (although, if you do, that's significant), or get arrested, or become the subject of an intervention. So aside from the major signs of addiction, your definition should include all the ways a behavior or substance prevents you from doing your job, being a decent person, and avoiding unnecessary risks.

What you want to examine then, even by asking friends and family when necessary, is the impact your possible addiction has on just those factors: quality of work/security of employment; your own definition of being a good friend or partner; and your physical health (safe driving, safe sex, safe liver, etc.).

Most important, consider whether your possible addiction is getting in the way of being a decent person (with "decent person" defined as someone who does their work, doesn't drive drunk, isn't an insufferable idiot, etc.).

You can even pull a Hasselhoff and ask for a video recording of what you're like under the influence if you don't remember or doubt the objectivity of feedback. Weigh in the opinions of others but ignore their feelings, because this isn't about changing their minds, arguing with them, or pleasing them. It's about whether your behavior compromises your ability to live up to *your* standards.

If you remain in doubt, gather more information by trying to stop using whatever substance or behavior you may be addicted to, observing yourself for a month while abstaining, and seeing what the difference is. Don't talk yourself into or out of recognizing an addiction because of the way you or anyone else feels about it, just gather facts and measure your behavior against your own standards.

If you decide you need to change an addictive behavior and can't do it with willpower alone, finding the right AA meeting can connect you with a huge resource. AA tells you that you become stronger the moment you admit you can't overcome addiction on your own, an admission that, among its twelve steps to recovery, is the first. It also encourages you to disown responsibility for what you don't control, so that undeserved guilt won't prevent you from improving your management of what you *do* control (see: the Serenity Prayer). AA isn't a perfect fit for everyone—some find it too rigid or even cultlike—but because it's free, easily accessible, and pragmatic, it's always worth trying first. If meetings alone don't stop your addictive behavior, seek out a more time- and activity-encompassing treatment, like four hours per day of therapy with professionals (called an intensive outpatient program) or all-day therapy (called day or partial hospital treatment) or all-day therapy while living at an institution (residential rehabilitation).

If you believe that your responsibility for taking care of others prevents you from stopping an addictive behavior, think again. Yes, some people carry huge responsibilities, but what makes it hard for them to help themselves is their help-aholism, or inability to put a boundary on their obligations. They can't help others and think of their own needs at the same time, which means they give too much, get tired and empty, and lose control. As they get better at managing addiction, however, they also get better at managing other needs, including the need to give, so sobriety pays extra dividends for the person who can't stop giving.

If you're trying to get help for someone who doesn't yet want it, keep in mind that such help seldom is effective, because it doesn't work when someone is attending treatment for you rather than for themselves. Instead of taking responsibility for another person's recovery, give them tools for auditing themselves, as above, and challenge them to use those tools to decide for themselves whether they need sobriety and help.

Don't give priority to their happiness or lack of it. Ask them whether they have priorities that are more important than happiness, like safety, health, and the quality of their relationships. If so, then they must ignore happiness and control behaviors that are doing them harm.

The spirituality that helps people help one another to manage addiction does not require a belief in God. It requires a belief that there's more value in doing good, and being the kind of person you can respect, than there is in feeling good.

Addictive behaviors make it very hard for you to control all impulsive actions aimed at pleasure and quick relief of pain, and they prevent you from getting strong. Good management helps you build your own values and gives you the strength to ignore pain and do what, after much reflection, you've decided is right.

Quick Diagnosis

Here's what you wish for and can't have:

- Happiness/relief when you deserve it
- Freedom from fear about life's dangers and the responsibility to protect yourself

- The ability to rescue others from addictions
- Sometimes, the ability to stop your own addictions, at least without tons of struggle

Here's what you can aim for and actually achieve:

- Judge your sobriety and self-control objectively
- Manage behaviors you want to change rather than attack yourself for having them
- Ignore shame, and respect yourself for what you're trying to achieve
- Value a good effort, regardless of results

Here's how you can do it:

- Define your standards for sober behavior
- Decide how much effort, shame, and frustration are worth enduring for the sake of change
- Accept the limits of your responsibility for having addictions so you can take more responsibility for managing them
- Get help from people who are doing the same thing but are further along, be they friends or fellow addicts at AA or NA meetings

Your Script

Dear [Me/Family Member/Beloved Bartender/Anyone Affected by My Addiction],

I know you've urged me to get [help/lost/out of town] because of the effect my [insert addictive behavior, from booze to online poker] has had on your [car insurance/credit rating/reputation]. I assure you that, in addition to regretting the effect of my behavior, I'm also sorry about the [insert verb related to blatant dishonesty] that has worn out your trust. I cannot promise to stop the behavior that has made me act like such a [insert synonym for "dickhead"], but I will try to stop it and

*also be honest about it. Please let me know if you think I am [slipping/
sounding sleazy/getting back that old self-absorption] and I will use
your input to get stronger, one day at a time.*

Did You Know . . . That Your Shrink Talks about You?

Like so many of those born and raised in Brookline, Massachusetts—the
home to 2 percent of the world's psychiatrists, which is a factoid I'm almost
positive my mother didn't make up—I am the product of two shrink parents.
Upon discovering this fact, most people ask me questions I can't answer or
take seriously; I can't tell you if my childhood was weird, because I didn't
spend time with another set of parents to compare it to, and I won't tell you
if it means I'm crazy, just as I wouldn't ask the child of two lawyers if that
means he's an argumentative Asshole stereotype.

Nobody seems to ask me the one question I can answer rather definitively, which is, yes, your shrink talks about you, and not just to her shrink,
who is Peter Bogdanovich, because *The Sopranos* isn't universally accurate. If the fact that your shrink shares feels like a violation, it isn't, neither
literally nor technically; it's perfectly aboveboard for any medical professional to discuss their patients as long as they don't disclose any identifying specifics (name, address, etc.). Your secrets may not be safe with your
shrink, but your identity is.

That might sound contradictory, but the people my parents would discuss over family-style takeout from Caffe Luna—from the severely mentally
ill patients they treated while working in a public hospital to the anonymous
people that would walk up the back stairs to my father's home office—were
not discussed simply as people. This is not just because their names were
never mentioned but because my parents would discuss their patients'
problems and diseases, not their lives, and there's a world of difference
between trying to suss out a diagnosis and dishing juicy gossip (for one, the
latter is fun to overhear and the former is boring, even if you're not a child
just waiting for dinner to end so you can get your homework done before
must-see TV).

Because mental illness is a less tangible disease than diabetes or

cancer, people forget that psychiatrists, or at least the ones who raised
me, approach your problems the way any other good medical doctor would
their patients' ailments; unemotionally, efficiently, and passionately enough
to get a second opinion, even if that colleague is also a spouse. People also
fail to realize that their problems are like snowflakes; not because theirs are
unique, but because, aside from a few nearly imperceptible details, theirs
are akin to millions of other ones just like it that, during February in New
England, at least, are fucking everywhere.

  If you're lucky, your shrink isn't talking about you as a first-date anecdote
or to make another, even crazier patient feel better, but with her spouse,
surrounded by her uninterested children—who are patiently waiting for her
to clock out—in order to determine what treatment would suit your anonymous self best.

The urge to self-improve is universal and always carries a potential for
dangerous self-destruction if we promise to change ourselves before
taking into account what's fixed in stone and will remain so, regardless of the sincerity of our wishes or what well-intentioned friends,
self-help books, and novelty mugs say. If we can learn to limit our responsibilities, and hopes, to what is actually under our control, then
hard work will always pay off and we will always have a chance to
succeed.

  Use your experience and common sense to define the limits of
what you can change, however unhappy that makes you feel. Then,
when you define tasks for yourself, you can be confident they'll be
realistic and achievable and that your effort will be meaningful. Put
doing good over feeling good, and you will get good results.

chapter two

fuck
self-esteem

People think self-esteem is the hallmark of good mental health, but, given the number of people who base their self-worth on having good looks, a positive outlook, money, or just luck, that assessment doesn't mean much. Donald Trump has more than enough self-esteem, but if what's going on on top of his head is a reflection of what's going on inside, then his mental health is in trouble.

Indeed, people who feel good because of something they really don't control are the first to feel like failures when their luck sours and they lose whatever they thought of as their claim to fame. Add to this the way advertisers encourage you to think their product will make you a winner—sexy, beautiful, fashionable—and you have reason to classify self-esteem, as it's usually experienced, as a dangerous drug that should have a black box warning.

Further proof of the risk of overvaluing self-esteem is offered by those people who have too much self-esteem and see themselves as superior and exceptional (see sidebar on page 49). They're the ones who have little awareness of their ability to act like jerks and cause unnecessary harm. They are proud of their ability to be honest and speak out about truths that others are too polite or timid to talk about; they believe in themselves to the point of self-worship, and, most important, they're usually Assholes (see chapter 9).

The Gospel of Self-Esteem would argue that you can't stand up for yourself until you love yourself enough, thus making self-esteem an essential vitamin to take before you can gain control of your life and do what you think is right without being overly influenced or intimidated by others. This gospel can be read in psalms of Oprah, Tony Robbins, and even the most holy, RuPaul.

If this were true, however, many people who are anxious, shy, or compulsively self-doubting would be doomed to a life of passivity and paralysis, and clearly they aren't. People who have done terrible things wouldn't be able to move forward until they found some way to redeem themselves, which if you've seen an MSNBC weekend *Lockup*-athon, is clearly not true. A lot of people would be stuck in a rut, lacking the self-esteem to do things that would make them like themselves and thus give them self-esteem.

Fortunately, you don't have to have self-esteem to value things in life apart from wealth, good luck, and good feelings. When shy people find the strength to deal with people because they're determined to make a living and support themselves, or when an ugly person socializes because of a wish to be positively involved with others, or when a mean-drunk alcoholic tries to get sober, they're acting according to their idea of what's good, and their actions build self-esteem, regardless of how bad they feel about themselves or whether they succeed.

Doing what you believe is worthwhile is the only source of real self-esteem, even if doing so makes you feel inferior, exposed, and ashamed in the short run. Loss of self-esteem in the service of good values is no sin; self-esteem arising from good feeling is no virtue.

That's why people who are extremely unlucky, like those in my practice with severe mental illness, need never feel excluded from the supposed healthiness of high self-esteem. They may be chronically disabled, preoccupied with voices in their heads, careless of their appearance, and unable to work. If, however, they find a way to help one another, or do something useful with whatever abilities they have, they can and should have as much true confidence as people who are normal or gifted. Indeed, they should have more, because their challenge is greater and their achievement that much more awesome.

Fighting the Loser's Curse

The funny thing about needing to feel better about yourself is that it often starts with feeling that you are worse off than someone else. You can take a look at your accomplishments and feel like you're on top of the world, but it only takes one guy who's doing better to bring you back down to earth and right into the dumps.

Like other mammals that live in packs, we note whether our status is more or less than that of our equals, with a default value-calculator that bases worth on attributes over which we have limited control, like physical attractiveness, happiness, intelligence, and strength. In other words, we are hardwired to grade ourselves by comparisons and qualities we can't actually do much about.

Meanwhile, you can have many other positive qualities—carefulness, loyalty, patience, etc.—that you *do* control and that are less superficial indicators of character and self-worth. Unfortunately, they're qualities that, according to your instinctive internal-value calculator, come up as a zero.

Calculator aside, many people can't take pride in the qualities they see in themselves because their standards are too high or their pond is too big and there are too many fish bigger than they are. Sometimes the qualities in their self-inventory, like intelligence, beauty, or strength, are substandard, weak, or obnoxious and, worst of all, limited. The horror.

It's natural, then, to wonder how you can possibly feel better about yourself when you don't like what you see, what you see may actually suck, and what you don't like is probably not going to get better.

Some people would answer that you should love yourself

unconditionally, either directly or by imagining yourself as loved by a deity or by your fellow deity-worshippers. Unfortunately, while boosting self-love in this way may make you feel better and act more confidently, it won't stop you from acting like a jerk or overdepending on the support of your congregation and its leader, so this method may lead to Koran burnings, Kool-Aid parties, and other bad behavior that feels good because you've disconnected your sense of value from your own ideas about good, bad, and common sense.

Other people argue that you can feel better about yourself by finding what you enjoy and/or are best at, and devoting yourself to it, which would be perfectly good advice if it was something everyone could do. The sad truth is that some people don't have any talent or interest, and sometimes life circumstances don't allow them to develop whatever life talent they have. So while it's certainly worthwhile to try to develop your talents and seek fulfillment, it's dangerous to say you should be able to make it happen and thus make yourself responsible for producing a solution you don't control.

Instead, accept the fact that sometimes you can't and won't feel good about yourself. That's no reason, however, for stopping yourself from doing good things and writing off your feelings of low self-esteem as an unimportant by-product of a hard life, perfectionism, or subpar personal equipment.

As long as you do your best to be independent, be decent, and live up to your values, you'll have more reason to respect yourself and actually feel good than if you were super smart, rich, and the fittest of the herd.

Here are telltale signs that feeling better is not an option:

- You've been doing a good job search every day, but you still can't get an interview or afford to eat food that doesn't come from a can
- Plastic surgery is outside your budget, and besides, medical experts say your schnoz is beyond help
- Your doctor talks about fibromyalgia and refers you to a pain specialist
- RuPaul says you need to love yourself before you love someone else, but at this point, you've given up and just—gasp—hate RuPaul

Among the wishes people express when they just can't like or re-spect themselves are:

- To change what they don't like about themselves
- To have therapy make them like themselves
- To figure out how to get their confidence back
- To purge themselves of self-hate

Here are three examples:

I've never liked myself or, to tell you the truth, been very likable. I know it just sounds like I'm putting myself down, but the fact is, I'm not especially good-looking, my grades in school were always average, and I'm a klutz who was always chosen last on any team and hates sports. Now I work at a boring job, live with roommates because I can't afford to live alone, and date occasionally. I'd actually become comfort-able with my status in life, but as the years go by and nothing changes, I'm starting to get restless. My goal is to figure out how I will ever, ever be a winner when there's nothing about me or my life that seems interesting, attractive, or just plain worthwhile.

I'm glad my marriage has ended, but I just can't seem to get over my divorce. I miss having a husband and the greater financial security and support I had when there were the two of us. The kids are good and they're doing well, but I can't seem to recover my confidence; I'm over my husband, but I won't feel like I've moved on until I've found some-one else and become a wife again, which won't be easy since I'm no longer young and good-looking, and most men my age are no longer single. The only guys who want to date me seem to be creeps who are actually already married or just want to be with an older woman. My goal is to find the confidence I used to have, so I don't drive people away and doom myself to a life of mediocrity.

In my twenties, I had confidence in myself and things were really going my way; I got a series of raises and promotions, girls were interested in me, and I was basically considered a hot property and likely to succeed. Then, a few years ago, I got a new boss who really didn't like me, my career stalled, and I wound up having to take a dead-end job just to pay the bills. I know that if I were really competent I would find my way back to the fast track and get my career started again, but the economy has tanked and I just can't make it happen. I've gone from star to peon in two years and it's hard not to feel depressed. My goal is to get back my groove.

It's hard to feel like a winner if you're poorer or less accomplished than your friends, making less money that you used to, and seeing no prospects for doing better in the near future. By this logic, if others are winning, that means the loser must be you.

As a society and as individuals we buy into these measures of self-worth, in spite of knowing that bad luck is measured by being poor or alone or losing whatever you had, and that it happens to people who in no way deserve it. The nasty vicious cycle that threatens us all is that, if we let bad luck make us feel like losers, then feeling like a loser generates its own kind of bad luck. Either you protect yourself from taking bad luck personally, or taking it personally brings you down further.

In reality, many people who feel their lives are going nowhere or sliding downhill are actually doing a good job with an unfair mess, trying to do honest work, take care of relatives, and be good friends. They feel like they're failing life's trials but, in fact, they're not, nor have they let low self-esteem drive them into addiction, self-absorption, or bitterness. Indeed, soldiering on when you feel diminished, lonely, and out-competed takes great strengths and is one of life's ultimate accomplishments.

Having no hope of finding a partner is a major source of deep feelings of failure, yet it often happens to people who are not making social mistakes, neglecting their actual assets, or suffering from nothing other than a lack of confidence and decent selection procedures. It's great when there's a simple fix, but often there isn't, because life is sometimes a social desert for people whose looks, age, skills, or other burdens put a wall between them and the society they're stuck in and with. Plus, if they blame themselves and tolerate bad dates and nonaccepting friends, they wind up worse.

If, on the other hand, they maintain a faith in their own capacity to connect, despite long periods of isolation and loneliness, and stick to their standards, they are more likely to get across the desert eventually and find the socially compatible oasis they deserve.

So forget about the goal of feeling good about yourself. Enjoy bursts of confidence when you can and take credit for your hard work, but beware making confidence a goal, because that implies control, responsibility, and blame when you can't make it happen, and it's wrong and cruel to blame yourself when you're stuck with a hard life, crap luck, or some deadly combination of the two.

Instead, assume you're stuck with shit and ask yourself what a good person should do in your situation. A good person is not someone who is trying to be happy, because that's not possible, but someone who is trying to do right. Make your plans as concrete, realistic, and businesslike as possible, with numbers and timelines. Then monitor your progress, grading yourself according to how you do, not how you feel. You may seem to do little more in a month than get your work done, feed the kids, and make a few phone calls. If, however, you're doing everything you can reasonably expect yourself to do, in spite of poverty, loss, social isolation, and all the other dispiriting feelings that can drag down your soul, you're right on course for success.

It's hard not to compare yourself to others, but try instead to set your own standards, taking into account what you know you're capable of, and refer to them often. You might not always feel like a winner, but you'll never lose.

Quick Diagnosis

Here's what you wish for and can't have:

- Some ability that doesn't suck
- A friend or lover anytime before you die

- Just one reason for confidence and optimism
- Dreams that might actually happen
- The ability to look in the mirror or back on your life without horror

Here's what you can aim for and actually achieve:

- Do your best to survive
- Act as if you like yourself
- Keep busy and distracted
- Avoid adding to your troubles
- Change your underwear in the hope that it will change your luck

Here's how you can do it:

- Replace "should have" and "could have" with "just can't" and "it is what it is"
- List the daily activities you consider necessary for work, health, survival, and nurturing a personal life
- Grade yourself daily, as if you were evaluating a friend
- Give extra points every time you treat yourself or do something positive during times when you feel like a loser who deserves nothing
- Get a dog (cats are an acceptable substitute, but it's not exactly confidence building to have a box of shit in your house)

Your Script

Here's what to say to someone/yourself when you feel trapped, stuck, and totally below average.

Dear [Me/Beloved Pet/The Ceiling],

I know I lack self-confidence, related to my lack of [skills/cash/ education/good looks] and inability to [feel more self-confident after I see my therapist/take antidepressants/read self-help books]. However,

I haven't let it drive me to [insert illegal and/or addictive activity], at least not yet, and I'm still taking care of business. I'm still confident in my ability to ignore how confident I [don't] feel while I wait for my luck to turn.

Did You Know . . . About the Scourge of ESE (Excessive Self-Esteem)?

If you've never heard of ESE, you're not alone; this devastating but, until recently, unrecognized condition afflicts a large number of people who, until now, were thought to suffer from nothing more serious than bad hair and an inability to respond to humor.

It was previously thought that LSE, more commonly known as "low self-esteem," was the more dangerous condition, because it prevented people from developing the confidence required to make friends, influence people, and become a motivational speaker. Or at the very least, get laid.

It turns out, however, that most LSEs learn how to function quite well in spite of persistent self-criticism and self-doubt, whereas those with ESE are unaware of their offensiveness and resulting broken relationships, and so don't seek help. Their overconfidence in everything they do, from their terrible decisions involving relationships to their incomprehensible fashion choices, are, sadly, troubling only to those around them. They can continue in life with intricate facial topiary and numerous (mostly illegitimate) children they can't support, still thinking they're God's gift and deserving of their own reality TV shows.

Meanwhile, health care professionals who encounter a flood of clients traumatized by their relationships with ESEs have mistakenly thought the problem was their clients' own low self-esteem. From a treatment standpoint, it helps a little to feel better about yourself, but it would help humanity a lot more if those suffering from ESE adjusted their self-admiration to more reasonable levels. Until this disorder gets the recognition it deserves by the medical and/or Oprah-centric communities, we all have to protect ourselves from this unfortunately-not-silent killer.

Unleashing the Power of Persuasion

Of the many things you're supposed to feel for yourself before others can follow suit—i.e., love, admiration, even lust—confidence is among the most misleading. The idea that if you believe in yourself, you can persuade others to follow your command, is sold to us near the end of many movies when the unlikely hero finally takes the crown. Sadly, what's true for Luke Skywalker is rarely true for the rest of us.

People often believe that, with enough training, fitness, or self-hypnosis, they can gain the ability to influence others, sell goods, get clients, get votes, get laid, etc.—all of which depends on the strength of their self-belief. If anything interferes with that self-belief, they become obsessed with trying to figure out how to release the magic or undo the damage, a process that can become a self-critical, self-centered spiral into the dark side.

In reality, persuasiveness depends on, and can be harmed by, factors that are beyond your control, including anxiety, depression, and other illness. Just because you're successfully persuasive today doesn't mean you will be tomorrow, and believing that recovering or maintaining this ability is all up to you just worsens your feelings of failure.

In addition, many people just aren't articulate and never will be. We love to see shy, ugly people transform into great, persuasive performers and politicians—in what other universe would *The King's Speech* become a movie?—but the fact that we have to pay to see it at the movies, or get a personal intervention from God, tells you that most of us are who we are and have to work with what we've got.

Certainly, you should work hard, train well, and do what you can to build and rebuild your confidence. If, however, your influence is nevertheless waning or just wan and unimproved, don't self-destruct on self-doubt. Be prepared to admit, after trying all the usual remedies, that maybe there's nothing you can do to get it or get it back, so there's no point in ruminating about what you did wrong. You can still believe in yourself, as long as you believe that your flaws and misfortunes are part of the package.

Don't blame yourself for an accidental encounter with self-doubt, because there's still much to be done. It may not be as easy or as much fun to win someone over as it would be if you were silver-tongued, but having a silver tongue is not the only way to be effective.

In any case, don't try to control your confidence in your power of persuasion, as much as you would wish for it. Instead, use whatever other methods you can find, even if they're not interesting or fun, to get the job done.

Here are signs that the Force of Persuasion is not with you:

- When you try to dress for success, people ask if you're going to a costume party
- Your words come out as if you're speaking a foreign language
- Your listeners respond as if you're speaking a foreign language
- The harder you try to project confidence, the more you get treated like poop

Among the wishes people express when they yearn for the power to persuade:

- To find the confidence to release their inner persuader
- To move the world with the strength of their words and beliefs, or at least move a date, key family members, or important clients
- To stop overthinking and trying to defeat themselves
- To understand where their mojo's gone
- To trick themselves into thinking they're great so others will follow

Here are three examples:

I used to be able to hold my students spellbound, but ever since my stroke it's hard to keep their attention. My speech is clear and my memory is solid, but my words don't flow and sometimes I get nervous and blush, which never happened before. Then I doubt myself, which

just gets me more off my rhythm, and I start to notice they're fidgeting and bored, and it's even harder to get back on track. My goal is to
figure out how to get back my ability to lecture to my standards or let
myself down and retire.

If I wasn't her son (and only child), I bet I could get my mother to stop
drinking. I'm always nervous about how she's going to respond, so I'm
always hesitant and apologetic, instead of telling her why she needs to
quit. It's depressing that I can't get through to her, but with Dad long
gone, I don't know anyone else she'll listen to. My goal is to get the
confidence to speak to her effectively and get her sober.

There are three guys at the dealership I work at who know less about
the cars than I do, but they sell them better because they really think
they're hotshots. I've studied the sales material carefully and know it
cold, and I sell enough cars to keep my job, but I hate getting beat by
guys who are just better at bullshitting than I am. My goal is to get the
confidence to be a better bullshitter or get better at bullshit so I'll have
more confidence, get the bonuses, and never feel screwed over again.

Just because you lack persuasive abilities for one reason or another, or find them unequal to the task at hand, doesn't mean that
you *should* be able to be more persuasive and should keep trying
until you are. There's a certain point—let's call it the desperation fulcrum—at which pushing yourself to be more articulate makes you
repetitive, boring, and overeager, driving people further away from
your point of view.

Unfortunately, practice doesn't make perfect; at some point, after
you've consulted advisers, tried exercises, and analyzed obstacles, it's
time to accept that the problem is what it is. If you keep on looking at
improving persuasiveness as the goal of a failed quest, life will seem
increasingly negative and hopeless, and the fulcrum point will move
ever closer with each new negotiation.

If you accept your problem as an unfortunate dysfunction you've
done your best to fix, then the failure isn't personal. You've done a

good job pushing your limits (even if they pushed right back) and it's time to look for alternatives.

Remember, persuasiveness is one of those abilities that can do both good and harm. It can get you sales, votes, and deals, but it also gives you the power to take advantage of others or use negative emotions to get their support, and this may turn into mini–*Wolf of Wall Street*, damaging your reputation (and eternal soul) in the long run. Even if you get them to do things for you that they wouldn't for someone else, their motivation will disappear if they think they don't have your attention.

In any case, there are ways you can achieve your goal even if you don't have the ability to persuade. One is to follow a commonsense procedure for weighing decisions as if you were the person you wish to persuade. Instead of pushing their emotional buttons, pretend you're a coach or adviser responsible for reviewing all the reasons for or against a decision, taking into account consequences and your clients' values.

Whether you're trying to sell them a car or sobriety, use plainspoken expertise, not flash, to explain the risks and benefits you believe they face. Know the pros and cons well enough that your confidence in your knowledge shines through, and if you still can't close on the sale, you won't feel the urge to keep nudging, or to reproach your own unpersuasiveness, since you'll know you did your best.

So don't despair if you can't summon persuasive powers. You may long for the unique pleasure and power of being a wheeler-dealer or orator, but assuming that your main interest is in getting the job done, there are other ways to do it and feel good about your accomplishments instead of desperate about what you just can't do.

Quick Diagnosis

Here's what you wish for and can't have:

- To get people other than your mother to pay attention and take pleasure in listening to you

- To get people to do what you want for financial, sexual, or generally selfish benefit
- To win people over with the natural charisma you do not have

Here's what you can aim for and actually achieve:

- Offer people a fair summary of the pros and cons of a possible decision
- Persuade people that you're more interested in enhancing their choices than imposing your own opinion
- Be a knowledgeable, good listener
- Keep your emotions to yourself
- Take satisfaction in meeting your own standards rather than moving others

Here's how you can do it:

- Develop due diligence procedures for listing the risks and rewards of any decision, including purchases, partnerships, and partying
- Do your research and gather information about decisions you wish to influence
- Present yourself in terms of your interest in finding a good solution, rather than forming a close relationship or winning a contest
- Learn to present information accurately and concisely, even if you're boring and not funny
- Judge yourself on whether you've followed your procedures, rather than on whether someone did what you wanted them to do

Your Script

Here's what to say to yourself or a skeptical relative, client, or customer when you're trying, and failing, to sell your point.

Dear [Me/Suspicious Client/Stubborn Relative],

Regardless of my own opinion, I'd like to help you [make a decision/ spend a lot of money/pass an exam/get your head out of your ass] by giving you a brief rundown of the [pros and cons /fact and fiction/ details I know backward and forward]. If you happen to have strong [insert emotional noun] about this situation, I hope you will weigh them objectively while considering their likelihood, and add them into your overall equation.

Good versus Bad Things upon Which to Base Your Self-Esteem

Good Things	Bad Things
Sticking with a job you need even though your boss deserves an ass-kicking you can't provide	Quitting and telling your boss to go fuck himself because nobody tells you when you can and can't take a day off to see the new *Fast and Furious* movie
Biting your tongue when you'd rather bite someone's head off	Getting the last word when that pregnant lady tried to steal your seat on the subway
Finishing last, knowing you gave all you had	Being the thinnest woman in your spin class, especially after finding a bike next to the fattest
Taking care of business when you feel like a total loser	Getting higher than Pluto for an entire weekend shift without getting fired or even pulled over
Working your hardest and finishing in a day what used to take you an hour	Having a gold iPhone. It's so shiny!

Standing Up to Bullies

Another big reason people put confidence on their wish list of missing and much-desired attributes is the wish to face down intimidation and humiliation in personal relationships, whether it's from a boss, parent, or spouse. While calling such intimidators "bullies" seems like an awkward thing to do once you've graduated beyond the school bus and playground, the title still seems fitting even if in adulthood the wedgies and swirlies are strictly psychological.

No matter how old you are, when someone insults and intimidates you, you think long and hard, over and over, about what you could have said or done in response. Unless you can also think of how to make a time machine, however, this mental exercise just makes you feel more helpless and less prepared for next time.

Like any animal under attack, you may respond instinctively and say or do something before you have a chance to think. For instance, you may go out of your way not to show fear because it might expose weakness and encourage further attacks, or you feel responsible for defending yourself if you're criticized for something you didn't do. In any case, being bullied makes you yearn for strength, verbal ability, and . . . confidence! And probably a gym membership.

The fact is, however, that many people get relatively inarticulate when they're anxious, and very few people are good at the art of speaking up in the face of authority without getting into trouble. Nevertheless, they imagine they could stand up for themselves if they had more self-esteem, like the movie hero responding with a condescending smile to the bad guy's sneer and pointed gun.

In reality, standing up to intimidation and facing down bullies is a bad goal. It would feel delicious if you could do it (which is why we love to watch such scenes on TV), but retaliation carries all the risks of road rage: losing your original purpose and direction and risking injury, guilt, and punishment for the unintended harm you cause. You've got other goals and obligations to pursue, and fighting battles with people you don't like and aren't going to change seldom makes sense, even if they're smaller than you.

The truth is, fighting back isn't the antidote to humiliation and intimidation; it's more often an accelerant. Instead, give thought to values and consequences.

Ask yourself whether the fight is worthwhile and winnable by considering risks and worst-case scenarios and keeping your mouth shut to give yourself time to think. Nobody likes to be bullied or humiliated, but once you're out of the school yard, the consequences for standing up to bullies are much worse than detention and a black eye, like, say, fines and prison.

So strengthen your resolve, not your muscles, and learn to beat bullies by remembering what's important, and that humiliation isn't.

Here are signs that a face down is not a good idea:

- You're not a black belt . . . or you are a black belt
- He's richer, stronger, better connected, and has better lawyers
- You have better things to do, like get through the day and not ruin your life
- You know that your confrontation won't change anything in the long run, except maybe your employment status or the shape of your nose
- You're throwing around terms like "send a message," "unfair," "can't let him think that," etc., and you're not a Blood or Crip

Among the wishes people express when they want to avoid or end humiliation are:

- To be as amusingly insulting as Dorothy Parker and Winston Churchill
- To be as good at verbal self-defense as their bully is at humiliation
- To control anxious or deferential feelings that cause helpless paralysis
- To get someone to back down

Here are three examples:

My neighborhood was a happy place for twenty years until a crazy guy moved next door and posted No Trespassing signs on the fence between us. He accused me of dumping leaves into his yard and glared at my kids, who are careful not to bother him. He would point a video camera at them and my wife whenever they played in the yard. At first I tried to reassure him, but recently I've told him he has to stop, and he's gotten even weirder. The police tell me they can't do anything unless he physically threatens us. My goal is to get him to back off and not have to worry about him all the time.

My boss is often nasty and demeaning, though he thinks he's just being professional. He'll call me out during a meeting because something wasn't done, even though he either didn't tell me he wanted it or didn't give me enough time. If I protest, he treats it like I'm giving him excuses or he just changes the subject. When I've tried to discuss his leadership style with his boss, I get told that's just his way and I shouldn't be so sensitive. I feel trapped and intimidated. My goal is to stop my boss from being abusive.

My husband is a know-it-all who gets overbearing when he's drinking, but never admits it when he's sober. He's a good provider, and I don't want to break up our family, but we all tiptoe around him when he starts to drink, and it's oppressive living with him. My goal is to figure out how to stand up to him so I don't have to feel like a mouse.

Sadly, not all protest is effective, and if you've witnessed most recent American political protests, whether they involve hats with attached tea bags or giant puppets, you know that protest can have unintended consequences, like making you look ridiculous. If this were a fair world, a brave protest would expose every bully to appropriate ridicule and/or cause him/her to reexamine and correct bad behavior. In this world, however, protests often strengthen and empower your enemies, especially if somebody takes your picture.

Your goal then isn't to stand up to trouble, but to determine what, if anything, you can say or do that won't stir up trouble even more. Whether a bully is crazy or just touchy, criticism is more likely to trigger irrational attack rather than thoughtful dialogue.

In the case of a crazy bully, you may have no choice but to accept an ongoing risk of being humiliated, intimidated, harmed, and/or fired and knowing you can't stop it. That said (and your tears wept, and chagrin spat out), think of your other options.

Knowing that you can't reduce these risks should motivate you to look elsewhere to live, work, etc. If you try too hard to fight a battle you can't win, you'll be too worn-out to leave. Instead, if you know the battle is unwinnable, smile politely until you're gone.

Of course, every now and then you'll discover that you actually have more power than you think and the bully's power rests on nothing but hot air and your own fears. Most times this happens, however, you can't celebrate a simple victory by telling the bully to get lost because s/he is stuck in your orbit (close family, neighbor, etc.) and both your celebration and new power must be wielded quietly to encourage good behavior.

It's not fair, but if you've been alive long enough to own books with "F*ck" in the title, you know that not much is. Besides, if it's any consolation, a truly crazy bully doesn't even know why he's coming after you in the first place, because that's the nature of crazy. You can always move on, but he'll always be stuck in his own insanity.

Aside from considering departure options, the other way to protect yourself, especially if a bully is irrational, is to wall off your negative, helpless emotions and feel proud of your ability to make the best of tough situations. Whether you're getting zapped by your boss at a job you can't afford to leave or by a husband under comparable circumstances, stop sharing how you feel and start negotiating, beginning with whatever you're accused of doing wrong.

Talk proudly about whatever you've done right and positively about whatever your bully, if he or she has flashes of reasonableness, does right. Regret disagreement, conflict, or disappointment and express hope that it will get better, without apology or blame. Look confident and stand proud, regardless of how you feel. Build a boundary that lets the bully know that you value his opinion, but still judge yourself by your own standards, which, in this case, you've met. As long as you haven't let fear and anger compromise your behavior, you can disagree without having to defend, persuade, or continue conversations that you think are destructive.

Unfortunately, as you know, many bullies, due to some combination of physical, financial, and psychotic strength, can't be stopped, in which case winning means doing what's necessary to survive until you can get out. To others, it may appear as if you're bowing to intimidation, compromising your principles, and giving in to weakness. What you know, however, is that you have more important priorities than avoiding humiliation and that you have the strength to tolerate humiliation whenever you think it's necessary.

As long as you haven't let fear and anger compromise your behavior, you can disagree without having to defend, persuade, or continue conversations that you think are destructive. Whether or not your protest is heard, you know where you stand, and you've kept your pride intact.

Quick Diagnosis

Here's what you wish for and can't have:

- Victory over unfair aggression
- A fair outcome (forgive me for using this horrible f-word)
- Freedom from undeserved criticism
- Control over your reputation
- R-E-S-P-E-C-T

Here's what you can aim for and actually achieve:

- Keep your cool under fire
- Learn to choose your battles
- Respect yourself regardless of disrespect from others
- Find the least humiliating option that's necessary to bear
- Take pride in your ability to eat shit when necessary and smile

Here's how you can do it:

- Shut up until you're ready to speak; don't yell or act out because you're angry or tired
- Gather information about whether you can win
- Assess yourself and respect your self-assessment
- State everything positive you can about yourself, your persecutor, and whatever has been or could be good about your relationship
- Regret disagreement and conflict without expressing responsibility or apology for it

- Take action when you've decided it's worthwhile, not because your feelings tell you to
- Until you can move on, bear the pain

Your Script

Here's what to say to a bully/yourself when you feel falsely accused, mocked, or disrespected.

Dear [Me/Relative/Boss/Assailant],

I value our having a [insert positive adjective to describe kindness and nonviolence] relationship and am sorry you are [unhappy/ angry/dissatisfied/threatening legal action/urging me to make painful physical moves]. I believe in the values of [hard work/good neighborliness/brushing after every meal] and have examined my own behavior to see if, as you've suggested, it needs [improvement/cranial-anal insertion/self-sexual engagement]. I can't agree, but I believe we continue to have much to gain from working together and hope things will go better in the future.

Did You Know . . . That Prince Is an Inspiration to All?

You don't have to enjoy Prince's music (although you should) or agree with his political or religious views (you probably don't want to know) or even want to quote his words in your own book (please look up the very-apt lyrics to "Let's Go Crazy" since we can't afford to reprint them) in order to appreciate the man who was born Prince Rogers Nelson.

That's because Prince is so much more than a Lilliputian juggernaut of talent; he's an icon to anyone who feels different, loser-like, or generally doomed to outsider/failure status. True, he has an outsized and admirable talent, but what's most inspirational about the Purple One is not his musical success but his determination to make music and pursue other forms of self-expression (dance, wardrobe, articulating the sound of crying doves) simply because that's his artistic mission, and in defiance of so much easy ridicule.

Despite being mixed race and of decidedly minimal height (five foot two), Prince believed in himself and his own talent so strongly that he began writing and performing his own songs as a teenager and put a shirtless portrait of himself on his second record. Admittedly, he had the talent to culturally dominate the 1980s, managing to do so from not-cultural-mecca Minneapolis and while wearing a pirate shirt with a bandmate dressed in surgical scrubs; but he also had the determination to do things his way, regardless of how or whether the public responded. Given that he was a tiny, barechested "not a woman, not a man" with a quasi–Jheri curl, that response could have been cruel indeed.

So if you've ever been tormented by self-doubt and wished you could be better looking, taller, or less inclined toward platform shoes so you could believe in yourself more and maybe accomplish something, look to Prince, and trust that you too can be a massive weirdo and stay true to your vision and mission without having to forgo your dreams of acceptance.

Overcoming the Stigma of Disability

Given the way we equate poor performance, damage, and abnormality with low self-esteem, it's not surprising that the goal of people with disabilities, be they physical or mental, is to gain confidence by reducing their disabilities, keeping them hidden, and reclaiming normality as soon as possible. Sometimes, they seek out special challenges—some positive, like running a marathon, others less positive, like running away from treatment they're sure they no longer need—to prove that they have the strength to overcome all obstacles and get their confidence back.

What's dangerous, however, about taking too much responsibility for controlling a disability is that disabilities usually come with an even-higher-than-normal vulnerability to unforeseen shit, and thus prevent the less able from ever having full control. As a result, if your self-esteem depends on the state of your recovery, you will waste energy fearing and then feeling personally responsible for slips, setbacks, and relapses that even the most capable person doesn't have a handle on.

You may stop treatment that might otherwise help, or hide symptoms in order to keep up appearances at home or at work. The state of your illness will dictate your self-esteem, which means you will become your illness, rather than a person who happens to have a disability. You won't be someone living with a disability, but someone whose disability *is their life*.

Instead, accept what you've already learned: that your disability will come and go and you'll never control it completely. Educate yourself about it, become an expert manager, and use treatment whenever you think it's necessary and without regard to your yearnings to be normal. Fight the shame that comes with being ill by sharing as much with others as you think is appropriate according to your own standards of privacy, not the culture's stigma.

Since you can't rid yourself of your disability, fight to manage it so that it affects your life as little as possible. Don't take pride in looking normal, but in how well you cope with abnormality, tolerate the burden of your illness, and get as much as you can out of life. Living with a disability is in itself a marathon, not a sprint, so take pride in the small accomplishments that make up your every day.

Here are signs that your disability is getting the better of you:

- No one knows you have it, and if you can help it, no one will
- You're afraid of what will happen if it gets worse and you're not prepared
- You can't imagine feeling good if you don't look and act normal
- You can't imagine telling anyone about your disability unless you're very sure of their support

Among the wishes people express when they feel stigmatized by disability:

- To be in control and look normal
- To not rely on medication and never go in the hospital again
- To avoid losing control
- To maintain performance in all areas of their lives
- To find treatment that will give them the above

Here are three examples:

I don't want to tell anyone at work that the doctors think I'm bipolar because it would freak them out. I'm not even sure lithium is necessary anymore, because it's been a long time since I was sick, and I know that people would think I was crazy if they knew I was on it. I'm not sure I know what bipolar means and I know the diagnosis spooks people. My goal is to keep quiet about the illness, gradually get off meds, and see if I can be normal.

I feel embarrassed going out after work and always being the designated driver who never drinks. They know I'm sober because I believe I'm an alcoholic and sometimes they make sly jokes about it. I've been sober for three years, I don't feel like drinking, but I know I'd feel a lot more confident if I had an occasional drink. My goal is to get my confidence back and try to be a normal person instead of an alcoholic.

I look pretty well put together and I'm attractive, so I get asked out a lot, but I can never feel comfortable with guys. I was abused by my uncle, and it's left me with tons of anxiety about guys and sex. I'm ashamed to talk about it because it makes me cry and I feel like a head case. My goal is to straighten myself out so I can date and have sex and lead a normal life.

Of the many twelve-step aphorisms we like to borrow in this book, "you're only as sick as your secrets" seems most apt in this instance, or maybe something more like "you're only as handicapped as your hidden issues."

It's human nature to want to hide your disabilities so you can protect your confidence, pretend you can count on steady performance, and prevent others from knowing or exploiting your weaknesses. Playing pretend, while fun for children and kinky adults, is usually self-destructive in everyday life.

Since hiding or undertreating a disability usually makes it worse, your job is to accept it, regardless of embarrassment or self-disappointment. That's the only way to become realistic at assessing its impact on your life, one day at a time, and become expert at managing it. Learn when you need extra rest and when to tolerate the risks of treatment, then educate your boss and family about your problem so that they know how to help and understand your periods of relative dysfunction.

It's true, some people may not accept your disability—especially if you don't—and thus hold you responsible for underperforming; they're the ones who will believe you're lazy, exaggerating, or bothered by mental issues (and they don't mean illness). As much as their opinion may matter to you, don't waste time and energy hiding from their scrutiny or trying to change their opinion. Stand by what you've learned from your own experience, which is that your disability is real, you're doing your best with it, and you don't want to argue or spend too much time with anyone who doesn't agree. The people who matter can forget about your handicap, and the people who don't can go fuck themselves.

Yes, you may have to find another job or limit the acceptable topics you can discuss with a family member. The alternative, however, is worse, which is that you're constantly hiding, explaining, and apologizing, all of which interferes with your ability to manage disability and respect yourself.

People can't respect you for how you are managing your disability or help you deal with it until they know what it is, so if you don't tell them, they'll wonder what they're doing wrong or why they can't help you, and your fear and shame will infect them. Letting them know what's wrong is never a confession; it's a proud statement of achievement and intention, and if they care about you, they'll have your back.

As usual, the self-respect that comes from believing you're normal and can expect to stay so is a fragile illusion. Instead, build self-respect on accepting your abnormality and knowing you're competent to make good decisions about it, regardless of what others think or how severely it limits you.

You may win no competitions, but you should take pride in the tougher task of getting something done when there's lots of pain and no glory. So let go of your secrets, fight shame with twelve-step and other aphorisms, and give priority to your spiritual growth, whether you do it by steps, religion, specialized ramp, etc.

Quick Diagnosis

Here's what you wish for and can't have:

- The strength and recovery your hard work entitles you to
- Delicious, boring normalcy and averageness
- Outstanding accomplishments and reliable performance to offer your friends, family, and employer
- Confidence in a future when you can count on being in good shape

Here's what you can aim for and actually achieve:

- Know how far you can push yourself without causing relapse
- Know whom to call and what treatments to try in case of relapse
- Take pride in your performance, regardless of how it compares with others'
- Accept no nonacceptance
- Assemble a circle of approving, helpful people

Here's how you can do it:

- Educate yourself about your disability and the risks and benefits of treatment
- Don't let fear or shame stop you from doing what's necessary to treat it and lead your life

- Educate people about your disability, your needs, and your standards for dealing with it
- Select friends and employers from the accepting
- Do not make it your responsibility to convert the nonaccepting
- Audit your performance regularly in terms of what's possible, day by day

Your Script

Here's what to say to a nonaccepting person who thinks you could do better.

Dear [Me/Relative/Boss/Disability Examiner],

I value your opinion about my [performance/efficiency/seemingly endless sick time], taking into account the [pain/unnerving tremor/ fatigue/drooling] that my disability may impose [regularly/ unpredictably/every St. Swithin's Day]. I take pride in knowing the limits of my disability and using treatment well to keep myself as functional as possible. I've heard your concerns, but I believe I'm doing well, considering [do NOT insert explanatory details, it's too defensive] problems I've experienced and discussed with my doctor, but wish to keep private. I expect to be able to do more as my recovery continues.

Did You Know . . . Life Is a Special Olympics?

Many people believe Olympic competition is particularly meaningful because it draws together the best of the best in the whole world and validates their excellence using the most advanced measurement techniques available. In their minds, there is no achievement equal to being an Olympic champion (at least until that year's games are over and they forget that ice dancing ever existed).

The reason we often say, and truly believe, that life is a Special Olympics isn't because we mean to degrade the achievements of those involved in the actual Special Olympics or those games in any way. It's because the actual Olympic games aren't really a fair fight; some countries have more money than others, some athletes get the better performance-enhancing drugs, and everybody cares a lot less about national glory than springboarding a win into a sneaker endorsement.

In real life, many losers work harder than winners, because there is much about winning or losing that is unfair. The competition that should attract more attention and respect, if we thought hard about what it meant, is not the Olympics but the Special Olympics. The person who chooses to compete, knowing their equipment is inferior and unreliable, deserves more respect than the lucky and gifted, and more medals.

Saving Your Kid's Self-Esteem

If there's one responsibility that parents take seriously, more than making their kids wear helmets just to breathe or considering a full hazmat suit to be the only suitable protection against the sun, it's shielding their children's self-esteem.

You may not be able to teach a child math, baseball, or music, but you haven't really failed unless he or she comes out of childhood without good self-esteem. This overvaluation of self-esteem may be responsible for the ESE epidemic (see above), beginning with kids who actually believe they are the most perfectest special snowflakes who can be presidents of the universe and solve all the problems that exist with one smile from their precious, angel faces that were crafted by Jesus Himself in His heavenly garage/woodshop.

Unfortunately, your ability to control your child's self-esteem is even worse than your control over your own. You can provide lots of love, good nutrition, a functional parenting partnership, and reasonable schooling and security, and still not be able to protect her from having a rough time academically or socially or from just being a very nervous, perfectionistic, self-hating little weirdo.

It's scary to have kids, knowing how easily things can go wrong and how little your love can do to protect their self-esteem. We'd much rather watch movies about the redemptive powers of love, be they wielded by a parent or stern inner-city principal, to rescue a kid from misery and self-hate. Measuring your parenting effectiveness by your child's lack of self-esteem can make you feel like a failure, which will probably make you an ineffective parent, even if you were pretty good to begin with. But at least now you and your kid can bond over feeling like shit.

The domino theory of good self-esteem would lead you to believe that if you can help your child become competent in math, sports, etc., self-confidence will follow, which will help social skills, which will cause success, wealth, happiness, and amazingly good luck, which will make you feel successful after all. On the other hand, if anything gets in the way of one of these dominoes that happens to lie outside of your control, the last domino will never tip into success, leaving your mission as a parent forever unfulfilled.

We know why parents impose this global responsibility on themselves; it hurts to watch your kid feel like a loser and not be able to help. Nevertheless, it's part of the parenting job description for many unlucky parents. Sometimes, no matter how much you adore your kids, your love just doesn't get through and they don't like themselves. So your job, though it may sound heartless, is to do your best to build them up, remember you've done your best, and then go do something else. Otherwise, you'll burn out and do your kid and yourself harm, instead of surviving to help another day.

What makes parents most awesome, however, is not the power of love, as wonderful as that is. It's the power to love when love is doing no good, not take your kids' suffering personally, survive, and keep on loving. It's the loving parents of self-hating kids who are genuinely the most amazing, specialest snowflake parents of all.

Here are signs that you have little power over your kid's self-esteem:

- Your threats have as little impact as your praise
- Finding a punishment or reward that matters is really hard
- You have trouble getting an answer, a laugh, or even a grunt to any invitation
- You can't find a topic of common interest besides silence
- You can't get a good suggestion from the kid's shrink, who hasn't heard so much as a grunt, either

Among the wishes people express when they want to protect their kids' self-esteem are:

- To figure out what's wrong
- To get through to their kids with their love and admiration
- To help her do better and/or get away from bad friends and drugs
- To find a treatment or therapist that will help

Here are three examples:

I know my fifteen-year-old daughter lies because she never wants to admit she hasn't done her homework, even though it's obvious she hasn't. Still, she lies every goddamned time, even though her lying gets her into tons of trouble, and then she feels awful when teachers who have tried to help her just give up and tell her she's let them down. I've punished her and I've been understanding, I go to meetings with the teachers and get her tutoring, but nothing works. My goal is to get her out of this cycle of doing poorly, lying, punishment, and feeling like a total failure.

My son has been a mess since his girlfriend dumped him a year ago when he was a high school sophomore, and we just can't get him out of it. He's seen a shrink, tried antidepressants, and nothing works. He stopped going to school for a month but he's been going now; he just isn't able to learn very much and he won't answer the phone. I check with him to make sure he's not suicidal, but beyond that I don't know what to do. My goal is to help him recover.

Simply put, my daughter is big. My wife and I have tried everything to help her without making it worse—our house only has healthy food, we have her doing physical activities after school, we've talked to our pediatrician a million times—but even at her thinnest, she's still both heavier and taller than the other girls in her class, and the teasing has been terrible from boys and girls alike. She cries all the time and we're terrified that she's going to hit puberty and start cutting or starving herself. My goal, with my wife, is to protect her from bullying by helping her become less bully-able.

The best way to help your kid with his self-esteem is to help him limit his responsibilities, just as you must limit your own. This seems like anathema to many parents, who feel the only way to develop their kids' strengths and gifts is to load them so full of responsibilities and activities that they have to schedule pee breaks. Limiting responsibilities also seems overly permissive to parents and teachers who are trying to help kids manage inner monsters, outer peer pressure, or just hormones.

The fact is, however, that kids and adults often have limits to their self-control, and pushing responsibility across this limit breaks, not creates, confidence.

If you give yourself unlimited responsibility for your kid's happiness, you can never be successful, and the same applies to him. If he takes full responsibility for finishing his work well, controlling his behavior, being a good kid, being happy, *and* not being judged or bullied, he may well wind up hating himself for flaws or just situations he can't control, particularly considering how little it takes to mess up something on that list above.

Your mandate, to him as well as yourself, is to do as well as you can and certainly to recognize your flaws and work on them, but also to understand that certain problems may not be solvable and that doesn't make you a failure. For kids in particular, certain problems that may not be solvable this year may be solvable in the future as their brains grow and mature. In any case, acknowledging limits is necessary for restricting the damage of caring too much about flaws and failures that can't be helped.

So don't look too hard for bad choices, either yours or his. Be careful to note the things he does well and the things you've done right as a parent. Don't assume he's unhappy or doing poorly because of something you didn't notice or didn't take care of. The only thing you may have done wrong is having unprotected sex with your spouse wherein the one wonky egg or gas-huffing sperm won the day, thus transmitting some difficult genes that are hard to live with.

Just because educators are there to help you on your quest to improve your child's self-esteem doesn't mean they don't share your sense of overresponsibility and thus the need to search for what and who's to blame for whatever's wrong. Meetings start out friendly, but then get tense as everybody finds faults in the other guy's performance. Don't go down that road or react to teachers who are caught up in that negative process.

The best way to team up with teachers, instead of being sucked into polarizing discussions about what should or could have happened, is to note what they're doing well for a problem that many people haven't been able to solve. Give them the same protection from blame as you do your child and yourself.

Of course, embrace reasonable responsibility for trying to control whatever you think *can* be controlled; there are rules for bad behavior that you can enforce with incentives, even if no one knows how your child will respond, and there are procedures you can follow to track homework and provide extra help. There are also procedures for setting limits on bad impulses and eating disorders. If they don't work, get advice and try something else. In any case, stop frequently to take pride in your efforts, your child's efforts, and the strengths you take for granted when he's doing well. For instance, notice what your child does well in spite of obesity, not just what goes wrong because of it.

By recognizing your efforts as a parent, regardless of results, you can prevent frustration and helplessness from poisoning your parenting and your hope for your child's future. At least until he's eighteen, when the law says your kid and his self-esteem are no longer your responsibility.

Quick Diagnosis

Here's what you wish for and can't have:

- Power to shore up your child's confidence
- Confidence in your own ability to protect your child from depression and self-dislike
- Access to treatment resources that will do the above
- Knowledge that things won't go sour tomorrow

Here's what you can aim for and actually achieve:

- Get to be a pretty good parent
- Know what you can and can't do for most problems
- Get reasonable professional help and judge whether it's worthwhile
- Know when pretty good parenting and other help just aren't enough
- Keep up morale when nothing is working

Here's how you can do it:

- Through reading, watching others, and/or your experience with your parents, create standards for being a pretty good parent that don't depend on anyone's being happy
- Using the same methods, develop reasonable procedures for managing tough problems

- Accept the notion that kids can suffer lots of misery, including not liking themselves, even though everyone is doing their best to do their job, including your kid
- Always remember the good things you and others are doing, despite a bad situation
- Never assume that a lack of progress means that someone has failed to do what they could have and should have done
- Never assume that your child's lack of self-esteem is a personal failure or that it necessarily requires more work and attention on your part

Your Script

Here's what to say to yourself or a worried third party who wonders why your kid is so unhappy and lacking in self-esteem.

Dear [Me/Relative/Teacher/Shrink/Angry Social Worker],

I share your concern about my child's [misery/bad grades/bad behavior/status as a human black cloud] and have for some time. I think my spouse and I and [insert list of professional helpers] have come up with some good ideas about how to help him/her, and some have worked, but not enough. Right now we're considering a new [psychotherapy/home-based care/change in meds/military school]. We see some positive signs, but it's still touch and go. We appreciate the good help we've received.

No matter what popular psychology tells you, don't pay too much attention to self-esteem, as nice as it is to have (and as often as the plea for you to like yourself comes with a pitch for a product to help you do just that). Develop your own objective methods for determining whether you or someone you care about is doing a good enough job and rely on the facts to tell you whether you should hold yourself responsible for whatever is going wrong. In almost every situation you can think of, there are commonsense procedures for defining a good-enough effort and seeing how you measure up, given whatever it is you don't control. Then, regardless of whether your self-esteem is too low or too high, you can figure out how to make the best of bad situations, take pride in your effort, and have confidence in your ability to do the right thing. You can like what you do with your choices, even if you don't love yourself.

chapter three

fuck fairness

Seeking justice and valuing fairness are supposed to be ideals worth pursuing, especially if you believe books by politicians, movies starring guys in capes, and shows involving law and/or order (not limited to *Law & Order*). Unfortunately, while justice makes for a good motivation in fiction, it's a dangerous goal in real life.

Since movies, TV shows, and a politician's ramblings are mostly fantasy, they can get away with depicting a world that is fundamentally just. The world we actually live in, however, is basically unfair, so seeking justice can become an excuse for pursuing unattainable dreams while ignoring important but much less satisfying obligations, like getting to work, making a living, and doing all the boring stuff, like taking out the garbage and paying the cable bill, for which capes are totally unnecessary.

Admittedly, experiencing personal injustice leaves lasting scars and a strong desire not just for revenge but for that better fantasy world where unfair acts aren't allowed.

That's why the need for justice and fairness is not just a philosophical notion but a deep craving that easily blinds us to consequences and the existence of other priorities. We spend our leisure hours watching criminal things happen to innocent people, just because it satisfies a deep need to see the bad guys get identified, kicked, and permanently trussed in the end.

A willingness to make sacrifices for the sake of justice is what turns you into a crusader and martyr, caped or not, but the fact that most cartoon crusaders often wear masks, uniforms, and generic faces points to another side effect of justice lust: it erases your individuality. Whatever your responsibility to friends, family, parenting, and self-protection, pursuing justice rationalizes self-endangerment and thus imposes a lower priority on all the other things that make you you.

Given the amount of evil you can cause by pursuing fairness, you should know better than to trust your instincts when you feel a strong need to right a wrong, nail a villain, or, worst of all, get closure.

At least force yourself to think of probable and unintended consequences, so you don't wind up, say, hurting two of your children while punishing whoever hurt your third. Then redefine your goal, so that it's not to pursue justice or punish unfairness but to accept the unfairness of the world, bear the humiliation and helplessness that go with it, and then seek to do the most good.

You need to know when to accept the fact that you've been fucked and know when fighting will get you further fucked and the only way to make life fair again is to move forward and treat others fairly yourself.

Defending Your Right to Live in Safety

There's a certain kind of person—usually middle class, sometimes conservative, always in Florida—who feels that they have a right to live in safety, free from fear. This is an illusion not shared by less lucky people, many of whom are the very people who end up shot by the safety-entitled, often in Florida.

The danger of believing in your right to security, especially when faced with danger and lawlessness, is that it can draw you into either slow, unwinnable conflicts, or sudden, regrettable acts of rage. You're safer knowing, from the beginning, that you can never count on safety, rather than having the illusion that it's something you're obligated to fight for. You'll be much better at knowing when to suck it up, shut up, and/or duck and live for a better day.

The other risk in believing in your right to safety is that you feel you have a right to blame someone if you're threatened or harmed. Sometimes, in the course of seeking help against your perceived threat, the called policeman arrives on time, the authorities place responsibility fairly, and you either wind up protected or compensated. Most times, however, the timing is wrong, the facts get distorted, and the process of pinning responsibility and getting restitution is prolonged, expensive, and possibly futile. Such ordeals also may then stimulate your tendency to ruminate over could-haves and should-haves and blame yourself. It's better to avoid the issue of responsibility, get restitution when it's available, and think of other things.

Instead of expecting to be safe, assume that every life can, with sufficient bad luck, turn into a war zone—your new neighbor could turn out to be a nut, you could park your car on a sinkhole, you could have a perfect bill of health and get hit by a rogue bus—and fighting to restore your safety may attract more danger and ruin your life.

If you can accept the fact that you live in a jungle, however, you may not sleep as well at night, but you'll be more alert to danger. Then you'll do what you can to preserve your safety, regardless of whether it requires retreat, humiliation, and victory for your enemies. And you'll avoid blame, regardless of how frustrating it is to keep it inside, unless you're really lucky (or at least have an excellent attorney).

You might like yourself better if you could enforce your safety with your own strength, or at least your own firearm (Florida). You deserve more respect, however, when you recognize things are beyond your control, and make whatever tough, humiliating, weaponless steps are necessary to minimize the danger.

Here's the safety you should have as a right, but don't:

- No fires, burglars, or dangerous intruders after you turn off the lights and lock the door (and set the alarm and motion-sensor lights and land mines)
- Safety from vengeful crazy people once the authorities are on the case
- Freedom from any/all car accidents as long as you drive carefully, change your oil, and obey the speed limit exactly
- Prompt assistance from friendly and professional cops if you've done nothing wrong and talk politely

Among the wishes people express are:

- To figure out why they can't make themselves safe without fleeing or otherwise putting their life at risk
- To get through to authorities who are either failing to protect them or siding with the person who is threatening them
- To figure out what they did wrong to let themselves be harmed
- To figure out how to get closure after an event that leaves them feeling violated and terrified

Here are three examples:

My husband's ex is mentally ill and really can't help herself, but ever since she had a breakdown after going off her meds a few months ago she's been determined to kill him because voices in her head tell her he's possessed by devils. The last time she was hospitalized, she was trying to burn down our house when I woke up and smelled smoke. No real damage, but now she's about to get discharged, and she always stops her meds as soon as no one is watching. Right now she sounds perfectly sane, so the police tell me there's nothing they can do. I know she'll be crazy again within six months and no restraining order will stop her then. I have no intention of giving up my job or moving out of our home. My goal is to get someone to stop her and not have to give up the home we've built for ourselves and our kids.

My boyfriend is a sweet, loving person, but he gets violent when he's drunk, and sometimes he hits me. I forgive him because I know he's trying to stop, which is especially hard for him since both of his parents are alcoholics and his childhood was pure torture. My friends tell me I could get hurt if I don't leave him, but I know they're just saying that because they're my friends and don't know or understand my boyfriend like I do. My goal is to figure out a way to support him and get him help, so we'll both be safe from his violence.

After getting mugged by a burglar I interrupted when I came home early, I changed the locks and installed an alarm, all of which should have made me feel strong and empowered and all that shit. Instead I have nightmares, I'm afraid to answer the doorbell, and every little noise makes me jump and hyperventilate. I've recovered physically but I can't get over my fear; it's so bad that sometimes I get anxiety attacks in the middle of the day and can barely do my job. My goal is to recover my sense of security and get back my old self.

Joan Didion famously said, "We tell ourselves stories in order to live," but people don't just tell their autobiographies; they're prolific in their own fan fiction as well. Such fictions, also known as lies, are also integral to all of our lives, and one of the biggest lies we often tell ourselves is "everything is going to be okay."

We nurture this illusion of safety so we don't have to live in a constant state of panic, but sometimes wishful thinking makes us fool ourselves into believing we can reform either someone dangerous or our own dangerous thoughts after a random, overwhelming trauma.

The facts are, however, that we can't count on safety even when we're careful; neither can we stop feeling fear once it's got hold of us, and sometimes we have to give up all we own and flee.

In any case, it takes careful thought to be realistic about safety, avoid exposure to danger for the wrong reasons, and stop blaming ourselves for the harm and losses that occur when safety is impossible.

When a relationship is unsafe and you don't know when or how you might be attacked, a lawyer is usually your best therapist, because knowing your actual risks is the best antidote to both unreasonable fears and wishful thinking. Just don't look for a lawyer who will listen, hold your hand, and sympathize with how unfair it is that the police and courts can't really protect you. Lawyers charge too much for you to use them for sympathy alone, and besides, it would be a waste of time for everyone involved.

Instead, look for a lawyer who will tell you what will really happen; help you estimate your risk exposure after doing everything you can to preserve your home, relationships, etc.; and encourage you to do what's necessary, however unfair it is that you have to do it, to protect yourself.

Don't make the mistake of looking for a shrink who is well meaning and foolish enough to try to help you work out your relationship with a dangerous person, because pursuing such a goal can stir up and stimulate a psyche set to explode.

If you have a loved one who is dangerous but wants to control it, urge them to find a shrink who won't waste time figuring out why they're so angry, but will just help them put a lid on things and keep it there, regardless of the pain inside, while you stay out of it.

Even if you've done the right thing, don't expect to feel good. No one controls their reaction to trauma, which may linger for years. Certainly, you should try standard PTSD treatments, like medication and cognitive therapies, which sometimes help. Remind yourself, however, that whether or not you continue to have anxiety attacks and phobias, you've done the right thing and you're not to blame for your current condition.

Accepting the fact that you can't protect yourself or your family from crazies or the fear they inspire doesn't ever mean you've been defeated. It just means life is full of crazy dangers and you're a success as long as you get the message and act accordingly, even if you have to cut off your right arm in doing so.

Indeed, every day that you venture out of your house, do your usual job, and endure fears and symptoms, you're a hero, and in a nonfiction way.

Quick Diagnosis

Here's what you wish for and can't have:

- Safety, security, and control over same
- Guaranteed preservation of your closest relationships, job, home, etc.
- Exorcism of demons in those you love
- Restoration of your peace of mind

Here's what you can aim for and actually achieve:

- Find the best compromise between safety and your other priorities in an unsafe world
- Reduce the risk of violence by walling yourself off from dangerous people, even those close to you
- Strengthen your survival skills and help your family survive
- Become strong enough to pursue your usual life in spite of humiliation, loss, anxiety, and fears that won't go away

Here's how you can do it:

- Judge your risk by what is likely to happen, not by what you wish will change
- Gather information from experts about what you can actually do to reduce your risk
- Discard wishful thinking and do what's necessary
- Manage the pain of loss and persistent fear without feeling like a failure
- Take pride in your survival efforts and what they require

Your Script

Here's what to tell someone/yourself when you're feeling endangered.

Dear [Me/Family Member/Dangerous Family Member/Ex/Nut Job Who's Forced His Way into Your Orbit],

I hate to think that the danger of violence means we can't find a way to [work things out/avoid legal action/prevent an explosion], but that's something you or I can't control, regardless of what we do. I'm therefore going to [take whatever action is necessary/leave town/go into witness protection] to put an end to the risk and allow both of us to move on. I believe we should stop communicating and will not accept [insert any type of communication here, including carrier pigeon].

Did You Know . . . That Judge Judy Is an American Hero?*

Retired family-court judge Judith Sheindlin, aka Judge Judy, makes tens of millions of dollars every year for doing one of the least appreciated jobs in the world: going on television and telling foolish people that they are wrong, that they can't get what they want just because they feel it's owed to them, and that adult men cannot wear ripped dungarees.

Judge Judy has been broadcast in syndication for years, and even though her message and delivery haven't changed much during her run, her worth and popularity only seem to increase. It might seem unclear why viewers can't get enough of being reminded not to play house and sign a lease with someone if you're not married, or that an oral contract is bullshit, or not to cross your arms because you're in court, dummy, but the fact is, as humans, there is a part of us deep down that refuses to acknowledge how unfair life is.

That means every time Judy tells someone she can't get back all the money she lent her baby daddy, or tells someone she doesn't care how he feels because this is court, not therapy, it's always a mini-revelation. She

*This book was completed before the release of Amy Poehler's excellent memoir/call to arms, *Yes Please*, in which she also uses the phrase "Judge Judy, American Hero." As such, the similar phrasing is due to a genuine, shared admiration for a legal heroine, not a theft, intentional or otherwise, and we hope Ms. Poehler understands (or just reads this book; she's great).

does more than settle small-claims cases; she is the oracle of the big truth. When you see the happenings in the courtroom of Judge Judith Sheindlin, you see a true hero at work.

Getting Closure After Childhood Abuse

Child abuse is a particularly heinous crime because kids are helpless and defenseless against it, the effects stretch on forever, and if you really care about helping kids grow and become strong, then watching them harmed is truly heartbreaking. Not only is it instinctive for us to punish child abuse; we want to eliminate abusers from our world, and in a most painful manner.

But sometimes, punishing an abuser may harm a victim more than it helps, while making it harder to reduce abuse in the world. For those abusers who are easy to manage—the drunken parent who never does it again once he's outed—jail does no good while destroying the family's financial security and, most important, making it more difficult for victims to recover. The prospect of punishment may also deter reporting by family members who fear its effect on the family.

Some would argue that it helps recovery to have victims confront their abuser, or at least see their abuser confronted by authority. In fact, a kid's feelings of responsibility for the condition of his or her parents and other adults aren't easily erased, even by validating the much greater responsibility of parents for kids.

Unfortunately, recovery from abuse usually requires long-term retraining rather than catharsis, and guilty feelings of responsibility and the destructive urges that go with them tend to linger long after kids have grown up and escaped the coercion of their past.

So don't expect to overcome child abuse by gathering courage to confront your abuser. Feeling validated and knowing that he's exposed and punished may not improve depression, despair, and loneliness. What does help, however, is to learn how to value yourself and fight self-destructive urges.

So the long-term symptoms that arise from child abuse—depression, anxiety, PTSD—may or may not be helped by confrontation, direct or indirect. Indeed, they may not be curable by any treatment. What is most important, however, is that the abuse victim understands that he is not responsible for causing or clearing up symptoms, but for living a meaningful life in spite of them. That's the only sure way to stand up to child abuse: by living a full life in spite of it, not defined by it, as a healthy adult.

Here's what should happen to the victims of child abuse but often doesn't:

- Healing from anxiety, depression, and self-hate
- Reduction in feeling overly sensitive to and responsible for the feelings of others
- Comfort with close relationships, sexual and otherwise
- Confidence in the ability to protect oneself

Among the wishes people express are:

- To stop anxiety, depression, and self-harmful urges
- To break the pattern and stop choosing friends and partners who are abusive
- To feel happy, confident, or normal
- To get closure on their experience

Here are three examples:

My father stopped abusing me after I told the school social worker, and now I'm seeing a therapist who is trying to help me with depression. The therapist thinks I don't want to see my father punished because I'm trying to protect him, but I'm also worried about what will happen to the family if he's in jail and we're broke. My mother can't work, and I have older siblings who were never hit and will have to drop out of school if my parents can't help pay. My goal is to figure out what will be best for my recovery and how to find treatment that will help.

It turns out my daughter was abused by her stepfather when he was drinking and I didn't know, and now I feel terrible. She was seeing a therapist because she was cutting herself, skipping curfew, and hanging out with a much older drug user who was clearly taking advantage of her. I've told her I'm sorry, and that I was so busy trying to keep things going that I was blind to what was really going on, but she's as angry and depressed as ever and I just don't know what to do. My goal is to help her recover from this horrible trauma, for which I feel responsible.

I was molested by a family friend whenever the two families spent a lot of time together when I was a child, and now, ten years later, treatment has helped me realize how inappropriate it was and how much I hated him for it. When I told my parents, they were shocked and very supportive, but they're close to this man's entire family and they don't want to say anything, particularly now that he's old and unwell. I've told them if they won't, I will. My goal is to make sure this can't happen again, strike a blow for honesty and openness, and help my own recovery.

There's an all-or-nothing quality to the anger experienced by survivors of abuse that, while perfectly understandable, is very hard to change and manage. Whether you turn it on others or yourself, it leaves little room for trust, hope, or compromise and is pure poison for relationships with others and your desire to live. The anger is as powerful, destructive, and erratic as a *natural* disaster, except the cause is anything but.

Focusing that anger on the abuser seems like the obvious choice—he certainly deserves it—but doing so doesn't make the pain go away. It may also hold false promise for relief and healing that, when broken, could make the pain worse.

You may feel comforted by a therapist who joins you in your

anger against your abuser and other people in your life who treat you badly. As time goes by, however, you have to ask yourself whether it's really helping. Your feelings may be validated, but your long-term goal is not to hate your enemies, regardless of how hateful they are, but to find friends who are basically trustworthy and learn how to manage extreme feelings, whether you're trying too hard to be liked or getting too angry when you're hurt. Make sure your therapy can provide you with tools and good coaching for that difficult task.

A good way to educate yourself about remedies that help you manage extreme feelings is to read the curriculum for a cognitive/behavioral treatment called DBT (dialectical behavior therapy). It provides ideas, exercises, and values for training yourself to respond constructively when you feel hate and despair. It doesn't make those feelings go away, unfortunately, and frustrating them can temporarily make them worse. The fact that you've prevented yourself from doing something destructive, however, like hurting yourself or blowing off a friendship, can protect you from re-traumatizing yourself and, in the end, give you a better life.

If you're the parent or friend of someone who happens to have the extremely negative feelings that result from abuse, advising her on how to manage feelings is much more helpful than trying to ease, or take responsibility for, her pain. If you feel responsible, think carefully about what you actually controlled and apologize, but don't let guilt get you to blindly encourage and tolerate venting, accusations, and mean behavior.

Instead, remind yourself that neither you nor she deserves pain and that she has to learn to manage it, or it will cause more pain. Familiarize yourself with DBT or some other cognitive/behavioral approach to managing negativity, and encourage her to do likewise. Then remove yourself from negative conversations and try to focus her in a positive direction.

If you wonder whether disclosure to family will help, don't do it for catharsis. Instead, add up the positive and negative consequences. Of course disclosure is necessary if it's the only way to prevent further abuse (or if you're a legally mandated reporter). Otherwise, it may stir up a hornet's nest among friends and family who can't tolerate the truth and can thus cause further isolation and conflict for the victim. What's important is not airing the truth and punishing the criminal (especially if s/he can no longer hurt anyone else), but getting as much support and understanding as you can from those who have it to give.

Not all abuse victims are troubled by negative feelings, but most must carry some burden of pain, anxiety, and mistrust that doesn't disappear, even with good therapy and loving friends. When they can endure those feelings and nevertheless find a reason to live, love, and restrain negative impulses, they've truly overcome their trauma. The negative emotions may still be powerful enough to linger, but positive actions are what matter.

Quick Diagnosis

Here's what you wish for and can't have:

- A world in which abuse doesn't occur
- Freedom from pain, trauma, doubt, self-hate, and yearnings for bad people and bad substances
- Reliable healing through catharsis, intense support, or anything quick
- Healing through punishment and a slow and painful revenge

Here's what you can aim for and actually achieve:

- Improve safety
- Get better at controlling self-destructive behavior
- Gain perspective that is less distorted by negative feelings and close relationships
- Gain hope in a better future

Here's how you can do it:

- Report and stop child abuse whenever you encounter it
- Discuss methods for evaluating how you're doing and what's important for you that are not reactive to intense negative feelings or the opinion of others
- Practice methods for staying in touch with your goals and values when you're flooded with negative feelings
- Find coaches and supporters who can reinforce your progress
- Take pride in what you've accomplished, despite continuing pressure to despair and hurt yourself and your relationships

Your Script

Here's what to tell someone/yourself when you're feeling abuse-related fear and despair.

> *Dear [Me/Abuser/Person Who Has Disappointed Me But May Not Be Abusive/Indifferent Jerk],*
>
> *I feel as if life is [insert synonym for "bullshit"] and the people I care most about don't really respect [what I have to give/me, since they've used me like a Wet-Nap at a clambake], but I know my childhood left me with horrible feelings and even more horrible taste in friends. I will continue to avoid [drinking/drugging/hanging out with Assholes], attend meetings with like-minded people, keep on working if I can, and review the exercises that remind me about what I value in life and myself.*

Getting a Square Deal

Getting your due, in spite of most people's inflated expectations of what they deserve, is a reasonable goal only if you're under the age of seven. Children often use fairness as the main argument for both getting what they want and avoiding what they don't want, and it's also why their arguments often end in tears.

It would certainly be a better world if you could count on

getting what you deserve if you stand up for yourself and appeal to the right authorities. But facts are often impossible to confirm, and authorities have the same weaknesses as everyone else, so it's no wonder that fights about fairness escalate fast. When parents are the authority, they can just tell kids that life isn't fair. When adults accuse other adults of unfair behavior, it implies they're bad, and the nastiness that results is usually much worse than a time-out.

A righteous strike for fair wages may push your job overseas, or getting your spouse to understand your point may win you a cold shoulder and weeks of couples therapy. The amount of passion you *feel* for getting what you deserve, however, should tell you it's a dangerous wish and force you to think twice before adopting it as a goal and making it a cause.

Instead, if you haven't gotten anywhere after you've done your best to push your case, check out the attitudes and past actions of the people who stand in your way. Almost always, you'll find their words and actions reflect values that are not likely to change and will not allow them to agree with you about what you believe is fair. If you argue that your ideas about fairness have greater moral weight than theirs, you can expect them to respond similarly. Ultimately, the more you're right, the more they'll hate you.

So instead of having a tantrum, stop damaging your case and discover whether it's possible to make a deal using different incentives than guilt and fairness, or whether no deal is possible and you have to accept the pain of feeling screwed. Sure, the latter choice feels supremely unfair, but as grown-ups, we accept that that's just the way life can be.

Life never guarantees you a square deal, but you can be a good, realistic dealer in an unfairly chaotic marketplace if you assume that no one necessarily sees things the way you do, no matter how obvious the truth appears, and that getting what you deserve is a lucky event, not a right. You might have good reason to feel badly treated, but you can't be stopped from giving yourself a time-out to regroup, then making the best of a bad deal.

Here's what should happen to you if you deserve a square deal but don't get it:

- Eventual victory if you know your rights and express them with confidence
- Protection by higher authorities (Human Resources, courts, Jebus) from fuckups by lower authorities
- Satisfaction of wearing out your opponents by being persistent and right
- Confidence that comes from getting what you deserve, especially when it's from the clenched fists of the undeserving

Among the wishes people express are:

- To get a system they believe in to work for them
- To get no more than what they deserve, and no less
- To make the system work better for everyone
- To get the boss to see what's fair

Here are three examples:

I was promised a promotion eighteen months ago, but it clearly hasn't happened. Meanwhile, a guy who's old buddies with the boss has moved ahead instead. I've had terrific performance reviews, though I think my boss was bothered when I raised an ethics concern that he didn't think we should worry about. Now I'm wondering whether I should speak to HR or share my concerns first with my boss. My goal is just to get ahead and get the promotion he knows I deserve.

My husband says he needs to spend time with the guys every night because he works hard to support his family and will go crazy if he can't blow off steam, but I work too, and he leaves me alone with the kids every night. When I tell him it isn't fair, he tells me I'm nagging and that's another reason he's not home in the evening, because he doesn't

like my nagging or the pressure I put on him to be Superdad. My goal is
to get him to see that he's not doing his share as a husband or parent.

My parents treat my brother like he can do no wrong, and they're always urging me to spend time with him and try to build him up. In
truth, he's an alcoholic and fuckup, but I love him and would like to see
him get ahead. What drives me crazy, though, is the way my parents
take my success for granted and give me a hard time whenever they
think I've made my brother unhappy. Sometimes I'd really like to tell
them all off. My goal is to have a relationship with my parents that
isn't unfairly distorted by my brother's needs.

Unfair treatment is often paid forward; many times when you feel
someone is treating you unfairly, that person feels she's under unfair
pressure herself, making tough decisions, asking you for something
you should provide, and getting less than the understanding and respect she deserves. It should be a Chinese proverb that he who dishes
out the most shit feels the most like the toilet of the world.

You may be right and have good reason to feel the way you do, but
as long as the other person sees it her way—her feeling of moral en-
titlement is always bigger than yours—you're not going to win. Plus,
arguing about fairness will probably trigger bad feelings and a vicious
cycle of nastiness that hurts everyone around, the weak more than
the strong. Indeed, the more you're right and the more she doubts
herself, the nastier her response will be. That's why expressing yourself about unfairness is a dangerous goal.

Once you know you're not going to get someone else—your boss,
wife, colleague—to go along with your idea about what's fair, shut up
and think. Stop lining up new arguments for why you're right, even
if you think of better punch lines. Instead, mend fences by finding
legitimate ways to acknowledge the other person's right to see things
the way they do.

Regardless of how you really feel, don't imply that her views reflect
selfishness, laziness, or other bad values. Cite good values that, at
least theoretically, may be driving her, so she no longer has to prove

that she's right and you're wrong—you simply have different ways of adding things up.

At that point, there may or may not be other incentives you can use to make a deal. For instance, the boss who would ignore your dedication and find fault with your work might think twice if you told him how much you liked the job, appreciated his mentorship, and subtly pointed out how much you wanted to stay despite the rising market value for your services, as evidenced by a current job offer elsewhere.

When there's no way to get a square deal, disengage from argument and decide whether you believe enough in your own point of view that you don't need validation. If so, ask yourself what you wish to do about it. That's when, without argument, you're likely to look for a better job, tell a partner he can shape up or ship out, or decline pressure from friends or family by saying, simply, you'll have to agree to disagree and let the subject drop. Believing in your standards for a square deal, even when there's no way to get it, is what allows you to create boundaries and take independent action.

Knowing you can't get what's fair and then shutting up about it feels frustrating and demeaning, and may make you feel defeated. In reality, you're simply butting up against the chaotic way good and bad people, using differently structured brains and coming from different cultures, come up with different ideas about fairness.

If you continue to believe in your values, sidestep conflict and shit and decide what you can do with the choices you have, then you'll always get the fairest deal possible, from yourself.

Quick Diagnosis

Here's what you wish for and can't have:

- A square deal for everyone who deserves it
- A fair system of authority for correcting unfair actions by those who don't know better
- Faith in the power of justice to do more good than harm
- The satisfaction of eventual vindication

Here's what you can aim for and actually achieve:

- Build your strength and market value through hard work, if you're lucky
- Find people who share your vision of fairness and have the ability to make decisions
- Treat yourself fairly, apart from what your feelings tell you
- Know when to keep your mouth shut

Here's how you can do it:

- Recognize when your idea of fairness has become threatening to others
- Ease the threat by spreading honest if limited moral approval like manure
- Make deals with whatever you've got to offer, other than a common understanding of what's fair
- Never feel personally defeated by your inability to make things work fairly for yourself or others
- Never stop trying to make things work fairly in the tiny part of the world you control

Your Script

Here's what to say when you're feeling unfairly screwed.

Dear [Me/Ingrate/Promise Breaker/Manipulative User],

I feel as if I'm being screwed over by a [best friend/boss/parent/ partner]'s idea of what's fair, and it makes me want to [insert synonym for "have a tantrum" here]. I know now, however, that they actually believe in the fairness of what they say, which shouldn't surprise me, but I didn't think it was going to happen to me. If our relationship needs to continue for reasons of [love/kids/being unable to afford to leave town or hire a hit man or lawyer] I will mend fences, define fairness for myself, and do what's necessary.

"That's Not Fair!" Quote from a Politician, or from Jacob, the Elder Bennett Daughter's Four-Year-Old Son?

1. Providing fairness to the American people . . . is all we're asking for. My goodness.
2. It's not fair that my brothers get to go and I don't, and also you said I could have a grilled cheese.
3. *I want what I want when I want it.*
4. I'm presenting a fair deal, the fact that they don't take it means that I should somehow do a Jedi mind-meld [*sic*] with these folks and convince them to do what's right.
5. That does not sound like a good plan. That's not fair. That sounds like *no plan*.

1. Politician (John Boehner, *This Week with George Stephanopoulos*, 10/6/13); 2. Jacob; 3. Politician (Eric Cantor's high school yearbook); 4. Politician (Barack Obama, 3/1/13); 5. Jacob

Clearing Your Name

If you're at all familiar with science fiction or fantasy novels, or maybe blues ballads, or even just the autobiography *I, Tina*, then you know that names hold a special power. Mostly, names are a target for mortal attack, presumably because they stand for identity and reputation, and once someone knows your true identity, you're exposed.

There's little that can make you feel as helpless and violated as an attack on your name. Even though there are laws to protect you, it often takes a long time before you can defend yourself and, meanwhile, you're very vulnerable. At least in this galaxy. Just ask Tina Turner.

Frequently, the person who has slandered you really believes what they say, even if facts have been distorted or don't exist. If you haven't checked in with your local anti-vaxxer lately, you might've forgotten that people believe something is true just because they believe it strongly. It's often impossible to prove something didn't happen after someone says, sincerely, that it did. Unless you're lucky enough to have an all-seeing video cam at the right place, you can't prove a negative, and arguing about it just increases the impression that you did something wrong.

If you protest your innocence with sincere anger, you sound like an angry person who might actually have done something scary. Meanwhile, false accusations may trigger investigation, charges, and legal actions that drag on for months or years. Or they may prevent you from seeing your kids or require you to pay for guardians, monitors, and other costly services. The more you make it your goal to clear your name, the higher your risk of widening the hurt.

Sometimes false accusations can cause you to doubt yourself; even though you know you didn't do wrong, it's hard not to feel you did something to make someone mad at you and to wonder what you could have done better, especially when the accuser is family or someone trusted. You wind up focusing on the accuser's feelings and your continued interactions, rather than reassuring yourself that the distortions are his, not yours, and you have no reason to hold yourself accountable for wrongs you didn't commit.

Knowing how helpless you are to feel better and control slander is not comforting, but it can help protect you from making things worse and direct you toward realistic hope, which depends on patience and a willingness to gather information. Most lies unravel in time if you survive long enough, keep good records, and believe in your own standards of right and wrong. To survive, however, you must accept the unfairness of what you're up against and believe that it can happen to good people.

Enduring severe slander is like having cancer. It takes over a large part of your life for a long time and causes you great pain and weakness. Even so, that doesn't mean you've made a mistake or failed to fight a good fight, because whether you have the illness or die from it says nothing about you as a person.

Your having the strength and will to fight, in spite of pain and humiliation, is what says something significant about who you are. And who you are goes far beyond your name and all that it entails.

Here's what should happen to the victims of slander but often doesn't:

- Vindication after a quick investigation, followed by a forgiveness sacrifice
- No devastating costs, literally or emotionally
- An opportunity to tell your side of things and be believed (by parties other than your dog and therapist)
- A chance to preserve your basic rights to have privacy and your business not minded by others

Among the wishes people express are:

- To get through to their accuser, the police, the press, the judge, other relatives, tabloids, and everyone else whose opinion matters
- To prove their innocence without having to wait a long, long time for procedures to unfold and vindication to be achieved
- To not feel horribly punished when they feel they were the ones wronged in the first place
- To protect their kids from a total family meltdown/shit-flinging contest

Here are three examples:

I've always known my wife saw nothing good about me when she was in a bad mood, but I hung in there because I love the kids. Besides, everyone knows she's vicious sometimes but gets over it, and I never thought she meant what she said. So I was shocked a month ago when she kicked me out, changed the locks, and got a restraining order after telling the judge I hit her. The fact is, she hit me and I never hit her, but I was so angry when I marched to the police station to get them to help me that I think they took her side. She won't let me have my tools, I can't work, and I don't know how I'll afford a lawyer. I can't believe how fucked I am. My goal is to get out from under this mountain of lies and get to see my kids again.

My mother says she won't talk to me because I lied to her and wouldn't help her when she had cancer, but that's just not true. She's the kind of person who makes things up and then believes them, and my family should know that. Even so, no one will stand up to her, so she avoids me at family parties, if I'm invited at all, and the years go by. I'm worried that she'll die before we ever have a chance to make up or say good-bye, and the estrangement hurts. I wish I could be sure my family knows that what she says isn't true. My goal is to put an end to this crazy conflict before she dies.

I know my ex was bitter and our divorce dramatic (restraining orders were involved), but I thought he was out of my hair since our finances were settled by the court and he's even remarried. Then I noticed someone was writing anonymous, negative comments about me as a Realtor on every website imaginable (Yelp, various listing sites, etc.). Now I've got prospective clients, referred by other clients, who seem to drop me once they google my name, and I know he's doing it to me. My goal is to protect myself from a vicious attack that is destroying my professional reputation.

When you're wounded by false allegations and unable to retaliate or set the record straight, the biggest mistake you can make is to decide that, because what's happened to you is insane, undeserved, and agonizing, fighting back with truth and sanity is the "right thing to do." Unfortunately, that's like violating the laws of physics and creating order out of a nuclear meltdown, and it's not going to work. You'll double the amount of disorder, given how explosive the situation is to begin with.

Unfortunately, no one can really protect themselves from this kind of trauma. Expressing your outrage will add to the chaos by giving comfort, pleasure, and excitement to your enemy. As the Bennetts' first law of insanity/energy dictates, attempting to force sanity on an insane situation just adds to insanity's power and momentum.

So if possible, starch your upper lip and prepare to communicate calmly and only when necessary. Instead of pretending you don't care, just show self-control and an ability to stay focused on business. Begin the process of documenting your transactions with whoever wants to take your words out of context or get you to say things you regret, so as to create a record of reality. Stay calm, act constructively, and demonstrate that you're the opposite of who you're alleged to be.

Be prepared to state your differences, if the opportunity arises, but not to argue, defend, or persuade. Those who are against you won't listen, and when the need to argue arises, your lawyer understands the ground rules better than you do. Yes, keeping it all inside is hard, but it will be harder if you don't.

If your relationship with your kids is at stake, don't panic. Nothing could be more important, but you've got lots of time to put things back together and you'll do better later on, when the big loyalty battle gets old and the usual divorce issues get settled. If nothing is on your side in the short run, your opportunities may get stronger as time goes by.

Your goal isn't to prove your enemy wrong, but to avoid centering your life on your enemy and his allegations, no matter how aggravated you get or how much time and money you're required to spend on a struggle. Fight to keep your focus on your usual values and to move past whoever is trying hard to hold on to you; it's easy for them to get a grip on you in the beginning and much harder later on.

Remember, the nastiness of a slanderous attack proves how right you were to mistrust the character of someone you may have once been close to and how healthy it is for you to distance yourself. You used to think there was something screwy about him, and now you know he's even worse than you thought. If a persistently strong attachment continues to make the relationship painful, accept the pain and take comfort in knowing that distancing is the right thing to do.

You can't protect yourself from the immediate pain and helplessness of slander, but you can always win in the end by staying focused on your own goals, controlling what you do with your feelings, and working to restore the balance of your life, energy, and universe.

Quick Diagnosis

Here's what you wish for and can't have:

- Quick validation and vindication
- Protection from loss and damage to your finances, reputation, and family relationships

- Control over the damage by persuasion, negotiation, or retaliation
- Relief from outrage and general unbelievable bullshit

Here's what you can aim for and actually achieve:

- Avoid making things worse
- Limit damage, gather allies, and fight if necessary
- Stay focused on your life, as opposed to your defense
- Strengthen your self-control
- Learn from your mistakes

Here's how you can do it:

- Don't let your outrage take over
- Learn how to assert yourself in measured, careful speech
- Identify what's worth fighting for and what you can win
- Don't get panicked by outrage and fear
- Educate yourself about relevant laws and legal procedures and get the best help you can afford
- Take heart in your long-term goals and in your gradual ability to move beyond the reach of the Assholes who are out to get you

Your Script

Here's what to say when you're slandered.

Dear [Me/Unjust Accuser/Those Who Believe Said Accuser's Shit],

I am aware of allegations stating that I [fool around/am a criminally bad parent/don't bathe] and can assure you they aren't true. I don't intend to discuss them unless it's necessary to protect my [livelihood/ time with my kids/now fragile sense of sanity and reality—and even that, only with my lawyer]. Other than to deny them, I hope to avoid wasting time on old grievances and instead focus on the [insert positive noun describing anything but the rumors].

Instant Catharsis!

Unfair scenarios with some fictional justice, so you don't try to find it on your own.

Frustrating Situation	Imagined Justice	Best-Case Scenario
After a few blissful months, the man of your dreams suddenly declares that it's not you, it's him, and dumps you like a sack of dirty towels. You never hear from him again.	Soon after his heartless dumping, he contracts a rare virus that attacks his genitals and gives him the first known case of chronic penis farts. He dies not long after, alone and exhausted, kept awake for days by his constant frontal flatulence.	You spend a couple of weeks sulking in front of Nora Ephron movies, then figure out better criteria for dating, like focusing less on dream guys and more on real-life decent men.
You have an interview for your dream job, kill it, leave totally satisfied/high-fiving all of your interviewers, but then never hear back. You find out later that they gave the job to a guy who's less qualified who's buddies with the boss's son.	Turns out the boss's kid and this new hire are more than buddies, and when they reveal their secret affair to the closed-minded daddy/CEO, he banishes both from the company, which leads to a boycott, which puts the company out of business. The couple marries anyway and opens a successful spa for small dogs in Jersey.	You remember that even though life is unfair and the job should have been yours, the reason you didn't get the job had nothing to do with your skills, which are still kick-ass. You go on to work somewhere else less exciting but with fewer dickheads.

Frustrating Situation	Imagined Justice	Best-Case Scenario
You and your sister have had a tumultuous relationship for as long as you can remember, but after she dies suddenly in a car accident, you realize how much you wish you'd made peace, and how much you'll suffer knowing you'll never have the chance.	While helping to clean up her things, you find a letter from her that says how much she actually loves you, even if she can't stop bickering, and that letter is wrapped around several hundred thousand dollars. You build a large statue in her honor (after buying a big house and a pony).	You remind yourself that your sister wasn't a bad person, and if she had the chance, she'd certainly want the same thing. Instead of focusing on what can't be, you remember the good times you had and the good sister she could sometimes be.

Getting Justice and/or Closure

Sometimes it's hard to get over a great disappointment or loss because of the longing, not just for what's been lost, but for what could or should have been. That's when the pain of mourning isn't just hard to bear but is prolonged by shock over the unfairness of life and the need to seek closure, that great emotional unicorn.

You've been counting on the power of a shared set of moral beliefs, together with your record of good actions, to keep your life and the life of your family and community moving forward. The yearning for closure happens when your heart and your faith in the way society is supposed to work are both broken.

So when someone betrays you, or something bad happens and no one sets it straight, it feels like your world is undone and can't be put back together. It feels like an open wound, which closure would protect from infection by restoring your world to its natural order.

In reality, of course, even people with the same beliefs often see the world differently, interpret the rules differently, and thus wind up betraying one another while feeling it's the other guy's fault. And bystanders and authorities, confused about the facts and having to listen to multiple arguments, can't act decisively and often do more harm than good.

So it's neither surprising nor unusual for things to fall apart in a way that undermines your faith in hard work, sacrifice, justice, and a fair society. What you want is for something to restore your faith, but what you need is a different kind of faith to begin with. You're the one who forged the connection between doing good and getting good back from others and you're the one who has to knock that crazy, dangerous idea out of your head, not keep pushing for relief and vindication that will never come.

It's not just the lingering malaise that's a problem; having faith in the commitment of others to your values is also dangerous because it blinds you to reality and makes you too reactive when something goes wrong. Feeling oppressed by whatever went wrong makes you seek out similar situations, looking for a do-over and a chance to make things right. You look for ways to get even or just to straighten things out instead of accepting what's broken and moving ahead.

Instead, accept life's painful lesson that some people you trust will betray you because, from their frame of reference, it's the right thing to do, or just the only thing they feel they can do. Some people will let bad things happen without doing much to stop or punish them because it's just so complicated. If anyone promised you otherwise, they were wrong and were just speaking for themselves, not the true powers that be.

So if you want to do good, make commitments and be part of a community, but don't expect it to be easy. In fact, given how often your efforts will be undone or treated badly by life—how often your good deeds will get punished—you deserve all the more credit, assuming you do them knowing the shit you're getting into.

And when you do get into shit—shit that you can't help but feel shouldn't have occurred—focus less on what could and should have been and more on what can happen from here on out. Remember, unfairness is very real, and closure is not.

> Here's what should happen to people who can't get over something bad:
>
> - Intervention by an angel
> - Transformation into a superhero, or Superman using his powers to turn back time and make things right
> - Confession on the part of the wrongdoer, followed by a dramatic making of amends for all unfair actions

Among the wishes people express are:

- To get some official acknowledgment of what really happened in order to achieve catharsis
- To see some benefit, instead of endless harm
- To make sense of what went wrong so they can feel peace
- To see something bad happen to bad people so justice is done

Here are three examples:

My last job was almost ideal until the new boss came in; before that I was a happy member of the team. We all respected one another, the work suited me, and everyone knew I was doing a good job. I loved it. Then came the new boss, and it was subtle and unintentional, but he was buddies with the guys and was vaguely creepy with the girls, so he and I had zero chemistry. It was hell, but not in any way I could protest, so I let my contract run out and left. It bothers me though that I had it so good and lost it, and while my current job is okay but boring, I'm haunted by wondering what I could have done differently to hold on to something that was so right for me. My goal is to get over this feeling of not being able to stop thinking about what I had now that it's gone.

After almost twenty years of marriage, my husband left me for his gold-digger secretary. It turned my life upside down because I thought we had a good marriage and were getting along well—I felt I worked hard and made big sacrifices for our family, which included both him and the kids, and to get rewarded by having him leave me for that tramp made the shock just too hard to bear. Now that my husband and I have been apart for longer than we were married, I want to hate him less, but can't figure out how. The kids are fine with families of their own, and I found a career that I really enjoy, but I've barely dated since the divorce and still find it painful when my kids mention going to spend time with their dad and his trashy wife. I don't care about re-marrying, but I hate that my ex still has this hold on me after all these years. My goal is to find the closure I need to finally let go.

It took five years before the guy who killed my brother while driving drunk finally got a trial, but I know they got the right man. Unfortunately, this guy is from a rich family, so he's got a good lawyer who, as it turns out, has gotten him off the hook several times over the years for everything from DUIs to assaults. I go to the trial every day and glare at this spoiled asshole, because I want the jury to know there won't be any closure for me or the family until he's convicted and put away, and there can't be separate laws for rich people and working people like my brother. My goal is to get peace and know that justice was done for my brother.

After a loss that you feel shouldn't have happened, you may well find yourself unable to move beyond grief until you find something to balance out its unfairness, or give it positive meaning. What you actually need, however, is to attack the ingrained assumption that unfair shit doesn't happen.

Rationally, you know lots of bad things happen for no reason. On a subconscious level, your mind will tell you the opposite, and it's your job to talk back instead of getting hung up on closure, which is about as likely as cold fusion or a Cubs World Series win.

Instead of mourning unfairness, improve your ability to do good in an unfair world. You may have lost a relationship that should have lasted, but you did a good job with your part of it (other than, per-haps, choosing the wrong person). You may have lost a great job, but you did well with it when you had the opportunity, and learned something about the kind of boss you should never work for. Challenge yourself to blot "should have" and "could have" from your vocabulary.

Whatever was good about what you lost, think about your contribution to that goodness, rather than trying to figure out what you did wrong to lose it. Whether it was a good job, a good relationship, or just a very happy time, focus on the good things you did to appreciate it while you had it, like making the most of a summer's day, knowing you probably had little to do with the way it ended other than, perhaps, not bringing an umbrella. If someone dumped you when things seemed to be going well, it probably had much more to do with their character than anything you did wrong or had any influence over.

Death can be particularly meaningless and unfair, but don't make it your job to give it significance. For most of us, death is what we have the least control over and it's not what we want to be remembered for. What gives our lives meaning is what we do with our living days, not how they end, so attend to what was good about the life of someone you lost, and your relationship with him, not to what was horrible about his death and the relationship's finish.

If you never stop feeling regret and a yearning for closure, consider it the price of experiencing something wonderful and having the kind of temperament that doesn't let go. Your brain may hit you with should-haves whenever you have too much time to think. So keep busy, and build a philosophy for fighting regrets and yearnings for fairness in a world that just doesn't have it.

Some people will always feel the need for closure, like an itch on a phantom limb, and if you're one of them, learn how to live with the feeling without paying attention to what it tells you. It will have less power over your life if you remind yourself that even if you can't have what it wants, other things are more important.

You haven't lost your ability to do good things with life, even if it never loses its ability to do bad things to you.

Quick Diagnosis

Here's what you wish for and can't have:

- Restoration of your belief that things will eventually work out
- Faith that everything happens for a reason
- Justice, fairness, vindication, world peace, etc.
- Closure, or relief from its opposite, aka waiting for the other bad-luck shoe to drop

Here's what you can aim for and actually achieve:

- To accept the loss of what you thought was yours
- To accept your lack of control over staying happy and keeping the good times rolling
- To develop tools for confronting false assumptions about a good person's right to a good life
- To live with regret without considering it important

Here's how you can do it:

- Confront negative should-have and could-have thoughts
- Think about how you demonstrated your ability to do good things and enjoy good times
- Learn to tolerate regret and need without giving it value or allowing it to control what you do
- Confront yourself with the inevitability of unfair loss
- Reassure yourself of your lack of responsibility for losing what's gone

Your Script

Here's what to say to yourself and others when you yearn for closure.

Dear [Me/Fellow Closure-Seeker],

*I know I can't get it out of my mind that I once had a [respectable job/
spouse/nice car/unshakable sense of safety] and now I need some
way to restore my faith in life and myself. I also know that life [insert
extremely negative verb here] and I've done nothing to deserve this.
If I can't [move to a better universe/get plastic surgery/find a mystic
guru], I will try to accept that I can't protect myself from major shit
and learn to live with whatever bad feeling that leaves in my [head/
gut/bones]. If I need closure, I'll get a zip tie.*

Some people extol the human yearning for a just and fair society; it's
certainly something everyone wishes for and many people adopt as a
goal, without stopping to accept the many, many situations in which
fairness, justice, etc., are impossible. Ironically, defying that reality
is the surest way to increase pain, frustration, and injustice. Accept
unfairness and injustice, without ever giving up on trying to be a fair
and just human being, even if that acceptance may require you to face
your vulnerability, and that of your family, to the chaotic nature of
our world. On the other hand, it will also give you more power to deal
with that chaos and impose your own (very) small measure of order
and justice.

chapter four

fuck helpfulness

Helpfulness is supposed to be a higher form of goodness, but you should know by now that if it feels good (and helpfulness can feel wonderful), it can be dangerous (like that other source of wonderful feelings, heroin).

In fact, altruistic-feeling efforts almost always carry a high risk of making things worse, yet most religious leaders, therapists, politicians, and professional do-gooders talk as if you can never do enough to help your fellow man. Meanwhile, history has too many examples of people with the best intentions—from missionaries to armies to the developers of OxyContin—who end up helping people to death.

The truth is that helpful feelings are what drive us to try to change others, whether it's possible or not, and regardless of unintended consequences. The most strongly motivated and dedicated would-be helpers have been known to kill people in order to protect them from spiritual harm, and if you're taking a life to save a soul, you're probably doing it wrong.

Yes, other people need and deserve our help, and we have a special responsibility to help our families. The fact is, however, that many of us have an off/on switch in our brains when it comes to helpfulness. If it's on, we feel responsible for whatever happens to our helpees and guilty if we neglect to do something that might help; if it's off, too bad, they're on their own, and there's no guilt to worry about.

We avoid in-between commitments because they make us feel more uncertain about what we're supposed to do and whether we've done enough. Unfortunately, most of life isn't in the convenient on/off or black/white decision areas; it's the in-between/gray area where you have to do less and think more. Also known as the place most humans hate the most.

Helping indiscriminately—reacting reflexively instead of thoughtfully—does harm when it's misdirected, misappropriates resources, and raises risks. Yes, it's noble to make sacrifices for the sake of others, but not when the chances of benefit are low and the cost and risk are high. Many helpers, by nature, are not interested in doing cost-benefit analyses; they live to help and despise risk-benefit managers as coldhearted, selfish, and timid. They would readily sacrifice their entire family resources for an incurably sick child, regardless of the impact on the health and welfare of the other kids, whose chances of growing up healthy and safe are diminished with each noble act.

Resist the call to helpfulness and the rush that comes with it unless you're willing to acknowledge its potential to do harm and evil. There are methods for managing this powerful emotion and the dangers it creates, so if you want to be helped to be a better helper, read on.

Easing Others' Sorrow

If one end of the giving scale is donating a kidney, the other is that ol' standby, "making someone smile." After all, if you can't help people in a material way, at least you can try to ease their pain and sorrow. The trouble starts, however, when it's just not possible, and instead of making someone feel better, you make a bigger mess.

Many of us feel compelled to accept responsibility for the happiness of our loved ones, without question or limit, either because we're the responsible type or we instinctively feel guilty if we fail. Which means that when they aren't smiling, we're in tears.

Or we may need to help people feel happy to make ourselves happy, meet a professional goal, give in to a guilt trip, or simply to satisfy altruistic urges. The sad fact of life, however, is that we're often unable to help others feel better, regardless of our motivation, intimacy, and commitment.

There are, for example, people who can't help but always be in pain, whether from grief, physical or mental illness, or even self-destructive actions they can't perceive or stop. If they, other loved ones, and professional helpers can't improve their suffering, there's little chance you will.

The fact that you have accepted responsibility, even when it's for a very good reason, does not mean you have more power to be helpful. It just means you might be making things tougher for everyone, since failing to help will hurt you as much or more than anyone else.

We take on that blame because it's human nature to find someone to blame for our unhappiness, beginning with loved ones—an uncaring mother and painful childhood, or a vengeful ex—and ending with the president or a local sports team. A major reason for marriage, of course, is having someone to blame. But that doesn't actually mean there's a person, be it a parent, political figure, or pitcher, who's responsible for our unhappiness. More often, the real source may be our personalities, our genes, or a lot of shit luck.

Knowing when you can't make people happy, even when you want to with your whole heart, is essential to changing your goal to one that's constructive and achievable instead of dangerous and exhausting. Accept that and you'll end up doing less harm and feeling better, even if nobody else does.

Here are some powers you'd like to have to ease suffering, but lack:

- An ability to make people feel better about themselves, or at least look like they don't want to die all the time
- A list of therapists who are guaranteed to take everyone's insurance and who never allow patients to leave their first session until they're feeling better
- The name of an antidepressant, psychotherapy, or inspirational video with a money-back guarantee
- A knack for making people feel it's someone else's job to make them happy, and that someone isn't you

Among the wishes people express are:

- To find the right words, action, or therapy to make someone feel better after everything has failed
- To get an unhappy person to understand that they've done their best to help her and can't do more, but that she needs to help herself
- To get an unhappy person to change behavior that is causing her unhappiness
- To feel less guilty and powerless about their inability to help

Here are three examples:

I hate how much my seventeen-year-old son is suffering from depression, and how there's nothing I can do to help him. Helping him to feel better is the top priority for me and my wife, but nothing we've done has worked. His doctor says he's depressed, but can't seem to find a medication that will help him, and the therapist he sees says they can't seem to get at the cause. My son weakly jokes that I look so miserable that he's very, very sorry for making me depressed with his depression, but the fact is, I'm just endlessly worried. My goal is to do something, anything, to help my son.

I had a wonderful relationship with my mother for many years, but she's developing dementia, and now being around her makes me feel totally helpless. She's convinced that people are breaking into her apartment and stealing from her and she complains that I'm unwilling to do anything to help her. Meanwhile, she's had a couple bad falls but refuses to use a cane. She feels scared and abandoned and there's nothing I can do. Her lawyer tells me I can't force her to accept treatment or move into assisted living until she's more obviously impaired. My goal is to ease my mother's suffering and protect her from danger.

I'm scared to death that my ex-boyfriend will kill himself and it will be my fault. I know he had periods of depression before we dated, but after I decided to end our relationship, he told me he was suicidal and couldn't stop drinking every evening. I urged him to get help, but he says the only thing that makes him feel better is talking to me. I hate to see him suffer, but I don't want to resume our relationship. I hoped I could use our phone calls to persuade him to stop drinking and get help, but he says they're the only thing keeping him alive. My goal is not to be responsible for his suicide.

If you can't stop feeling responsible for making someone feel better, it can make *him* feel guilty for not getting better, make *you* feel guilty for not making it happen, and drain everyone's resources until you and the sufferer are each other's pain slaves in a misery death-spiral. At this point, assuming you aren't in therapy, the only person you've helped is probably your local bartender.

You'll also wind up angry at the one you want to help, at yourself for being angry, and at everyone else for not being helpful enough. If you don't know when to give up on your happiness-bringing goal, you can get locked into a vicious cycle of anger, guilt, and therapy, either the real or liquid kind. Whereupon you'll find yourself the subject of an intervention as all of your friends try to help *you*, and then the world will implode.

Before allowing yourself to take responsibility for other people's painful feelings, ask yourself whether there's something you can do that will actually help, that you can afford to do (given your other commitments), and that isn't better done by someone else (including the person you're trying to help).

Using these standards, you'll decide whether the person you want to help is doing a good job bearing chronic, incurable pain for which there may be no cure. Instead of feeling like a failure because you can't help, or wondering why he can't do better for himself, respect your joint efforts and the success of living a full life together in spite of chronic pain. Then you can focus more on enjoying your small victories than your greater defeat.

Give yourself even more respect if the person you're trying to help is needy, demanding, and impossible to satisfy. Even when you know that person can't avoid it, you can't help but want therapy yourself after being around them for any period of time. Once you decide on and meet your own standards for providing necessary care, you can protect yourself and your own needs, go about your other business, and then give yourself a medal.

The biggest medal you can win is for trying to help a desperately unhappy person who tells you that you're the only reason they're still alive. Whether you're his ex-lover, child, or therapist, accepting responsibility for saving someone from despair can enslave you if you let it. Unfortunately, the only person who can save the life of a desperately needy person is that person, and releasing his death grip on the ones he loves is the first step toward recovery.

As long as you don't take or give responsibility for life's incurable misery, you're free to evaluate and respect what's more important: whether everyone is doing what they can actually do about it, assuming unhappiness really is unavoidable. Don't be surprised that unhappiness continually promotes negative thinking and self-blame in all involved.

If, however, you remember how much you respect what this person does despite his unhappiness, you can show him how to fight negative thinking and urge him to seek coaches who can build pride by focusing on what he does with his pain, rather than on whether or not he has it.

You may not be able to make him happy, but you can show him powerful tools for preserving his pride, and save yourself and them from the dark, powerful forces that can turn helplessness into pure (sometimes boozy) hell.

Quick Diagnosis

Here's what you wish for and can't have:

- A happy smile on the face of the one you love, like, or are otherwise related to
- Confidence in your ability to make someone feel better
- Belief in the power of the right treatment to solve any problem
- Faith in everyone's ability to feel good as long as they take care of themselves and practice meditation, yoga, a gluten-free life, etc.

Here's what you can aim for and actually achieve:

- Know that you've done what you can to make someone happy
- Tolerate unhappiness without flinching or blaming
- Respect how well people pursue their values in spite of unhappiness

Here's how you can do it:

- Find out what can be done to help and do your proper share
- If behavior change is necessary, be objective about whether it's possible
- Urge treatment only if you think it has something to offer
- Stop treatments that haven't proven useful
- Encourage suffering people to do what matters in life, to the extent that symptoms will allow
- Coach people on methods for fighting negative thinking, using the above values

Your Script

Here's what to tell someone/yourself when you're seized by urges to help the unhappy.

Dear [Me/Family Member/Poor, Miserable Sonofabitch],

I can't watch someone I care about [suffering/weeping/flunking out/ drown in hurt] without feeling there's always something that can help and I should be able to find by [trying harder/visiting Lourdes/ finding money for a psychoanalysis], but I know that's not true. I will try to ease your suffering, if possible, by [being a friend/wearing a rainbow Afro wig/farting repeatedly], but if my efforts don't work, I will not judge you or me as failures. I will respect you for continuing to [shower/take out the garbage/face another day].

Dumb Things We Say to Try to "Cheer Up" the Depressed, and Their More Helpful Alternatives

Dumb	Why It's Dumb	Helpful
C'mon, pull yourself together. Where's your willpower?	Depression is a disease, like cancer, and nobody'd assume you should will away a tumor. Offer sympathy, not blame.	How bad is it today?
How come we don't know what's causing this?	Trying to find the source of the pain won't reveal the cure, just create more blame. Focus on the burdens of enduring pain, not the source.	Are you safe?
It kills me to see you like this.	Making a depressed person feel guilty for your suffering is about as helpful as a punch in the dick. Don't point fingers, offer a hand.	Is there anything you want me to do?
Are you sure you're getting the right help?	Again, this makes their suffering their fault somehow, like they can't even choose doctors right.	Is anything helping much?

Dumb	Why It's Dumb	Helpful
You shouldn't have to live with so much suffering.	A really depressed person finishes this sentence with "so I should kill myself." Be positive by accepting, not highlighting, the unfairness of suffering.	It's a big deal to get through a bad day.

Rescuing the Addicted

We all want what's best for those we love, which is why our first instinct when we see signs of alcoholism or drug addiction is to express worry, argue about whether or not a problem exists, and push for treatment. Rehab is not just, as the interventionists call it, "a gift" but *the* gift; it's the Tickle Me Elmo on every addict's Christmas list.

If we argue too much, or if the addict tends to behave badly while under the influence, we get angry and then feel guilty about that. Everyone can agree that the one thing that can cure both her addiction and our discomfort is the aforementioned treatment, which, like that ointment for the rash you got from a regrettable sexual encounter, will clear everything up right quick.

Unfortunately, however, given the way people usually react to other people's advice, and the fact that treatment often doesn't work, especially when agreed to only to placate others, urging addicts into treatment often backfires.

For one thing, intense urgings usually wind up making the addict (and nonaddicts) feel the problem isn't addiction, it's your feelings, and her goal isn't to evaluate or improve herself, but to make you happy or change your mind. She feels responsible for your feelings, you feel responsible for her rescue, and her responsibility for her own well-being and self-control gets lost in between.

If she agrees to get treatment in order to make you happy, not only is treatment less likely to help but blame for failure of said treatment is more likely to land on your doorstep, leaving you angrier and more helpless than before. In other words, you can start a dangerous vicious cycle by intervening the addict into treatment that often promotes more conflict and drug use than sobriety.

Fortunately, however, there is a better way to discuss sobriety with an addict (or to determine whether someone's drug use is dangerous) than by creating an emotional, or any other, mandate for treatment. It begins with accepting your inability to rescue someone from addiction, an acceptance that is as hard as an addict's accepting his or her inability to control addiction.

It requires you to keep intense feelings, including fear and anger, to yourself. It allows you to be potentially helpful with less risk of doing harm or being harmed. So if you're called on by love or bad luck to rescue an addict, slap yourself and get help right away.

Enroll in Al-Anon or get a good counselor to coach you on how to manage your rescue instincts. Yes, there are probably some good, helpful things you can do, but not until you've learned how to protect yourself from being drained, over- or underdiagnosing addiction, and inadvertently encouraging addictive behavior. Then you can put aside accusations and fears and instead use the dispassionate language of business to describe the problems that need to be improved and what will happen if they aren't.

Control your urge to help and you'll be better able to help someone control their urge to use and give them a truly useful gift: the power to help themselves.

Here are the rescuing powers you wish you had but don't:

- Denial-busting insight that will show the blindest, dumbest addict the extent of his/her poisonous bullshit
- Love that will draw the addict into trusting your vision and getting help for the sake of your future, legendary relationship
- The name of the ultimate intervention clinician with the ultimate power of denial-busting insight (i.e., the bald guy from *Intervention*, although Candy Finnigan would also do)
- The name of a clinic, guru, or spell that, given enough time and money, can guarantee good results

Among the wishes would-be rescuers express are:

- To fill whatever need causes the addict's addiction, but in a healthy way
- To help the addict understand feelings that cause addiction, and thus improve control
- To get the addict effective treatment
- To get the addict to see the need for treatment
- To figure out where everyone went wrong

Here are three examples:

My boyfriend is a great guy and would do anything for me, but I can't get him to stop drinking. I know he had a miserable childhood, and I respect the way he basically raised himself, but he gets tipsy every night to get to sleep, has a glass in his hand after 3 p.m. on weekends, and doesn't realize how angry and scary he can sometimes get when he's had one too many. He's never hurt me, and he never misses work—as he points out to me over and over again whenever I bring up the issue—but I see trouble ahead. I don't think he's ever had a serious relationship before, and I have confidence he'll listen to me if I can get him to see it's important and I love him. My goal is to help him get into treatment.

My brother was always my best friend, but he's been different since he got back from Iraq. He was discharged for using drugs and alcohol, which made him bitter because he's got PTSD (and was probably self-medicating in the first place). Since then he's been in and out of rehab, but it's always a revolving door and he never really gets the help he needs. I'd do anything to see him get better, so I'd like to spend my savings on getting him into a private thirty-day program and then maybe have him come to live with me and my husband, who, as you might imagine, is not crazy about the idea, particularly since my brother stole from us the last time he was here. My goal is to help the big brother who always helped me, no matter what it takes.

My wife nags me to stop drinking, and I know I like to have a couple glasses of wine with dinner, but I'm confident that I never go over my limit and there hasn't been a time in the last ten years when I had a hangover or put myself over the limit when I had to drive. She's pretty sensitive about drinking because she grew up with alcoholic parents, and I don't like to make her unhappy, but I work hard, I love good wine at the end of the day, and it's not something I want to give up just to make her happy. My goal is to get her to see that I'm not an alcoholic so she can feel better and I can keep enjoying the finer things.

Using love or any strong emotion to push an addict toward rehab usually causes nothing but false promises and/or a nasty argument (e.g., quoth Amy Winehouse, "No! No! No!"), so when it comes to trying to help an addict, it's best to manage your emotions carefully.

Trying to nurture a tortured, misunderstood, drunk Shrek who loves you into a confident prince is appealing as a fairy tale but dangerous as an actual game plan. Of the many things that cannot cure addiction, love is one of them, even if it's unconditional and mutual. Believing otherwise and banking on Beauty's curative love actually prevents Beasts from realizing *they* need to learn to manage themselves.

Sheltering a needy drunk when no other place will is another sweet gesture that backfires. Addicts don't deserve the horrible dangers they encounter, but if you don't make shelter conditional on sobriety or ensure your safety in some other way, they won't get better and you (and your marriage, health, and credit score) will suffer even more than they will.

Rescue makes addiction worse until you gain control of your own addiction to being a rescuer, and spell out what's acceptable and safe. Borrow a page from the *Intervention* playbook by figuring out what will oblige you to leave, evict, or divorce an addict if they don't give recovery a try. Spell out addiction-related behaviors that must stop, whether it's stealing, nodding off, neglecting your kids, and all the other shades of the fuckuppery rainbow. Decide what you need to do with your feet, wallet, and brand-new alarm codes, then let the addict know where you stand, with regret, and be prepared to follow through.

Don't skimp on your love, but know what needs to be done to protect it from addiction, including yours to helping. Let your caring motivate sobriety, not stimulate emotional reactivity.

If addiction is just a possibility, and not a well-established disaster, don't overdiagnose or overreact. Instead of asking a beloved suspect to get sober because you care and you're worried, ask him to figure out his own standards for defining problematic drug use and apply it to himself. Avoid debate over how often he has to experience cravings, hangovers, or withdrawal to be in trouble. Instead, ask him whether drug use has interfered at work or caused him to do things he regrets. If he's unsure, ask him to try a few months of sobriety, just to compare.

Educate yourself about treatment and AA. If you think it might help, invest in a big intervention, but keep in mind that, like bar mitzvahs and magic shows, interventions are only for the young, impressionable, and green, at least in terms of usefulness. Even then, treatment's power is limited and depends a great deal on an individual's motivation, so don't assume that more is better.

If treatment fails, urge him to keep thinking about his own reasons for getting sober—not to make you happy, but because he wants to keep living with you—and to use whatever he's found helpful. Even so, don't regard relapse as failure; every day of trying to stay sober, as long as one is trying one's hardest, is a success.

If you can't get an addict help, respect the strength it takes to continue to love someone who is always in trouble, always requires careful management, and may or may not get sober, recover, and grow. If you can control your urge to save an addict while not giving up, however, you may help people recover from addiction and possibly get a yes, yes, yes.

Quick Diagnosis

Here's what you wish for and can't have:

- An ability to get through to someone about addiction, with or without professional assistance
- Faith in treatment
- Progress through spontaneous sharing of feelings
- Freedom from fear of relapse
- Freedom from addiction worst-case scenarios

Here's what you can aim for and actually achieve:

- Accept addictive behavior as possibly unavoidable and uncontrollable
- Limit responsibility and blame
- Manage anger and false hope
- Do your best to help addiction without taking responsibility for rescue
- Know when you have to go and know that you've done your best

Here's how you can do it:

- Discuss tools for thinking rationally about addiction
- Define what has to change for both you and the addict to live under the same roof or under current conditions
- Offer input about ongoing addiction-related behaviors and stand by what you think about their dangerousness or other potential for harm without expressing negative emotion
- Urge an addicted person to check out potential sources of therapy, guaranteeing that a patient search will be rewarded but that he or she may first find many duds
- Rescue yourself if you can, knowing that you can't rescue anyone else

Your Script

Here's what to tell someone/yourself when you're tempted to rescue him from addiction.

> *Dear [Self/Beloved Drunk or Junkie/Person I Once Trusted Who*
> *Pawned My TV to Buy Pills],*
>
> *I would have given my [life/TV/fortune] to save you, but that approach*
> *seems likely to cost me my [life/TV/fortune] and make me [pissed/*
> *broken/broke/very obsessed with the one relationship in my life that*
> *makes me most unhappy and which I can do nothing about]. So instead*
> *I will [check your health insurance/put aside money/change the locks]*
> *and let you know that living with me requires [sobriety/doing your*
> *share/no unreasonable shit]. Of course, various treatments may help*
> *you get there, but that's up to you. Good luck.*

What They Say on Intervention vs. What's More Likely to Be Helpful

The long-running A&E series *Intervention* made a few things very clear: (1) even the gnarliest addict has cute baby pictures, (2) huffing keyboard cleaner is a thing, and (3) most important, speaking to an addict from the heart is the best way to break addiction's spell. While two outta three ain't bad, that last *Intervention* lesson is actually false, since heartfelt pleas often make someone else's addiction your problem when you want to make it his or hers. Instead, bypass hiring a former drunk named Jeff and reserving a hotel conference room, talk to the addict one-on-one, strip away the drama from the content of your concern, and ask him whether or not he's ready to make it his. In the meantime, find old episodes of *Hoarders*, because the therapists on that show may be worse than the interventionists, but at least you'll get motivated to clean your house.

Intervention	Helpful
Your addiction has affected me in the following ways . . .	Your addiction has affected you in the following ways. The question is, which of those matter to you?
I can't keep watching you kill yourself!	You've lost the ability to protect yourself. (Or even wash your hair.)
I love you so much and your addiction is destroying me.	Your addiction will drive away the people who love and depend on you and leave you with a new group of friendly fellow addicts who might rape you when you're unconscious.
Listen to your mother! You owe her that much!	Try listening to your own values and experience. And stop calling your mother when you're broke.
Will you accept this gift [of rehab, or else] we are offering you today?	If you haven't tried rehab before, there's a lot you can get out of it, but it depends on you. If it didn't work for you last time, then ask yourself whether you're ready to try harder. Either way, if you can't examine your addiction seriously, then I have to withdraw from this relationship.

Protecting Victims of Injustice

Everybody loves an underdog, mostly because, at one time or another, everyone's been one. If you're lucky enough to have never felt powerless or mistreated, you probably feel an extra obligation to help the underdog, because helping the wronged is a way for the undeserving lucky to feel less guilty and even the score.

That's why coming to the rescue of the unfairly disadvantaged is one of those equally selfless and self-serving acts; helping a badly treated good guy feels like you're both avenging a personal injustice and making the world a better place. You're helping him, helping yourself, and helping the universe.

Unfortunately, it's often hard to tell a sob story from the real thing, and not all mistreated underdogs are necessarily good people.

Even when you're sure he's a good guy and his mistreatment is real, defending him may do nothing but draw further fire and endanger other good people, including you and yours. In other words, even if you're not taken for a sucker, rescuing good people from injustice may suck you into an impossible situation that can create more injustice and victims, namely you.

Fortunately, you can protect yourself from your instincts for helping victims of injustice, while actually helping victims when it's possible. It requires strength and patience and is often emotionally frustrating. If what you're committed to, however, is protecting victims of injustice when it's actually possible to do so, rather than satisfying your desire to feel like a victim protector, then you can do good while staying out of the (under)doghouse.

Here are some magical powers you'd like to have to protect victims of injustice, but lack:

- A truth amulet that distinguishes noble victims from conniving liars
- An enchanted canary that tells you how many new victims will be created, if any, by your protective efforts
- A sword of justice that defends true victims without causing unintended cuts, sprains, or amputations to its wielder and innocent bystanders
- A Pegasus that flies you away to your next assignment, putting an end to your responsibilities to the victims you've just helped by making you impossible to trace

Among the wishes injustice menders express are:

- To find a method for protecting victims that will be effective and not provoke any counterattack
- To get others to understand that a victim deserves support and respect
- To spread the truth about who hurt whom and why their reasons were bad and the results were devastating and unfair
- To feel like they did the right thing

Here are three examples:

Our new boss is trying to fire one of the best members of our team. He was loyal and helpful to me when I was starting out and deserves better. The boss seems to like me for some reason, but she doesn't like it when I defend this guy, and seems to think that, by defending this coworker, I'm trying to undermine her authority, and I don't want to get myself into trouble. My goal is to find a way to protect a hardworking colleague from getting unfairly targeted with criticism and maybe losing his job.

My family hates my girlfriend, not because she has three kids from previous relationships, but because all the kids have different dads, and she never married any of them. I tried to explain to them that each of those men was abusive, and that, like me, my family should instead see her as someone who has been treated badly and is now flowering because she's finally with someone who loves her and treats her right. She no longer feels like cutting herself and says she's stopped taking pain pills altogether, and I'm so proud of her. My goal is to stop my family from being mean and undermining her confidence.

It's my job as a high school counselor to help troubled kids, whether or not they've had run-ins with the law, and I think the positive relationship I've formed with this one particular kid has been good for him, since he needs the extra attention. My colleagues tell me to watch out because foster kids are always trouble, plus he's had a specific history of getting violent with a series of foster parents, and he broke into his last counselor's house while she was away on vacation. I've gotten to know this kid and I think he just gets blamed for everything because he's had such a tough upbringing that everyone expects the worst. My goal is to give him the trust and confidence he deserves.

The risks of protecting victims of injustice are numerous, including possible violence that can turn you from protector to one of the persecuted. That's why it's your job to assess your risks before getting on your white horse (and possibly galloping off a cliff).

First, find out what happened to the white knights who preceded you into battle. Often, they ran into bad guys who had the big boss and HR behind them, or a damsel in distress who went back to her wicked thug boyfriend, or a counselee who filed complaints. You can try to talk to your predecessors, but it might be hard, as they're likely in hiding, prison, or the grave.

Do your best to check out facts, because, as much as it can give you a headache (and absolutely no catharsis) to hear three contradictory-but-sincere versions of the same story, information is the key to knowing how much help is deserved and what it's likely to trigger. If you know that your coworker has a clean record with HR and that your efforts have a remote chance of saving his job and, most important, won't cost you yours, then rescue away. The odds of those things being true, however, let alone knowable, are as good as a successful quest for the Holy Grail.

Second, do background checks on all innocent victims, no matter how clear their innocence may seem. Without blaming them for their bad luck, explore the possibility that they encounter more of it than most because of weaknesses they can't help, including mental illness and addiction. If that's true, your intervention won't do much to protect them in the long run unless they change their bad habits. Be suspicious of stories that are too bad to be true, especially when they concern serial victims and their tales of woe. Your innocent single mother may be the kind of unstable person who falls in love as quickly and arbitrarily as she falls into hate.

Finally, remember your other priorities. You have obligations to others, as well as yourself, for your independence, safety, and stability, even if those commitments lack the emotional pull of the good fight. Don't enlist until you're sure your protective mission doesn't endanger your other missions at home, because, like the distressed damsel above, your misunderstood teen may turn out to be a jerk who steals your laptop. Since, by definition, Assholes (chapter 9) always see themselves as victims, some victims of injustice will turn out to be Assholes, and it's your job to protect yourself.

Real opportunities to help victims of injustice are limited, but you'll be most effective when you're selective and careful. Respect yourself for doing careful screening, which requires hard work, is often painful, and seldom gives you the thrill of righting a wrong. Even when you can't protect someone from unfairness and harm, however, show respect for how hard it is to endure injustice and still remain a good, determined person.

Given the facts of life's injustice, you do good by honoring victims of injustice who refuse to alter positive moral values and priorities, despite knowing that a rescue party isn't on the way.

Quick Diagnosis

Here's what you wish for and can't have:

- Knowledge of who really deserves protection and will really benefit from it
- Power to protect those who really deserve it
- Resources to protect yourself from retaliation
- The ability to protect people from weaknesses that expose them to repeat victimization

Here's what you can aim for and actually achieve:

- Care appropriately about helping people who have been mistreated
- Develop the skills to assess a complex, righteousness-drenched situation
- Tolerate the fact that you may be able to help no one
- Retain your personal priorities, regardless of protective urges and pressures
- Respect people who endure injustice, regardless of what happens

Here's how you can do it:

- Develop effective methods for fact gathering
- Do careful risk assessments, including risks caused by a victim's bad habits

- Perform careful political evaluations that include the risk of escalation and retaliation
- Offer respect to those who endure injustice, whether or not you can correct it

Your Script

Here's what to say when you're tempted to rescue a victim of injustice.

Dear [Self/Unfairness Refugee/Victim of Nastiness],

Helping you, after you've been unfairly damaged by [your boss/your ex/the town gossip/the IRS/Fox News] would give me great pleasure, but I can't forget that [I've got to make a living/I'm vulnerable to the same kind of crap attack/you have a history of making enemies]. I will find out more about what happened and whether it's likely to happen again while trying to figure out whether I can help and [lying low/ changing my name/winning a Nobel Prize for unassailable virtue/ making it look like it's coming from someone else]. Even if I can't help, I respect your ability to stay focused on the goals and values of your life without being distracted by [bad luck/bad choices/being born under a bad sign].

Brokering Peace at Home

Of all the "-making" professions, from cheese to dress, peacemakers are the only ones to be blessed, and with good reason; a good cheese can be heavenly, but peacemaking has more potential benefit, given that conflict often hurts and tends to escalate in ways that bring out the worst in everyone.

If the warring enemies are sufficiently powerful (e.g., India and Pakistan, Godzilla and Mothra, Red Sox and Yankees), successful peacemaking can be exciting, but can also be dangerous and sometimes prolong conflict. So don't assume every peacemaker is, or should be, blessed, and therefore able to work without a bulletproof vest.

Taking too much responsibility for other people's wars means you wind up feeling responsible for everything they say and do, so before long, you've got their headaches and they've got someone to complain to who feels obligated to listen. Yes, you may have every good reason in the world to wish for peace, but your peacemaking may actually make it easier for hostilities to continue, especially now that their conflict has one convenient, human representative who can neatly receive all grievances and blame.

Peacemaking a long-standing conflict also tends to devalue old grievances that some people feel are worth endless sacrifice, so if they think you're succeeding, they'll go out of their way to make those old arguments seem fresh again with timely discoveries, new evidence, restraining orders, or even another round of violence.

In the end, the one thing on which warring parties may come to agree is that they both hate you. Of course, as long as you're not too sensitive, and survive, you may regard this as a mission accomplished.

So don't try to broker peace because you're good-hearted and want to help people just get along. Before stepping into the combat zone, get your peacemaking urges under control and learn the techniques you need to know before deciding which conflicts are worth peacemaking and which ones you should stay away from.

Learn how to keep responsibility where it belongs, which is never, ever in your vicinity, and if the conflict resembles a pool of quicksand, learn how to make a nice fresh mozzarella instead.

Here are some peacemaking powers you'd like but (probably) lack:

- A calming, charismatic presence that makes everyone eager to win your approval when you ask them to "do it for *me*"
- A strong empathy for grievances that relieves combatants of the need for any other satisfaction, so you can feel the pain right out of them
- An ability to interest angry opponents in the mutual advantages of peace, despite their shared interest in pummeling each other
- Arm strength sufficient to knock heads together

Among the wishes people express are:

- To protect combatants and their family members from the pain of their conflict
- To end rifts that divide and weaken groups and families, so they can function more effectively
- To solve a problem they feel responsible for but can't see their way out of without help
- To get groups to sit down and find an answer to their dispute, no matter how difficult

Here are three examples:

Unlike most kids, I was thrilled when my parents got divorced, because living in a house with the two of them constantly fighting was pure hell. Since their miraculously peaceful divorce, I've enjoyed my time with each of them, because separately, they're very nice and loving people. To this day, however, they still can't be within a hundred feet of each other without a battle, which means I have the impossible task of trying to equally divvy up any holidays, events, birthdays, etc., that involve their grandkids. Both insist that they're getting the short end of the stick and I'm favoring the other parent, but neither will even consider just shutting the fuck up and putting up with each other at the same event for the sake of my kids. Maybe I should ask them to get couples therapy? My goal is to get them to sit down, make peace, and put aside their anger so they can enjoy family events without being excluded.

I've got two smart people working for me who do a great job, but they're always snapping at each other. They've got personality styles that just don't mesh, so each one thinks the other's questions and requests are stupid or exploitative, and then they complain to me. I've asked HR for help, but mediation didn't work. I like to have an open-door management style, but each of them takes advantage of every opportunity to give me an earful about everything the other guy is doing wrong. My goal is to get them to be happy members of my team.

My best friend is nasty and overbearing with her teenage son and I can't get her to see it. She sees him as a disrespectful liar because he often doesn't do his homework when he tells her he has, but I see him as a nice, bright kid with some ADD who lies because he's afraid of her reaction. If I suggest she's overdoing her criticism, she tells me it's none of my business and I'm trying to undermine her as a parent. My goal is to help her avoid making obvious mistakes and traumatizing her son and ruining their relationship.

After giving careful thought to the risks of peacemaking in general (and paying homage to the prematurely deceased blue-helmeted peacekeepers who have gone before you), define goals for your warring parties that are entirely positive, professional, and designed to enhance the happiness and well-being of both sides.

At the same time as you define these goals, be extremely careful not to make yourself a shared target, which is what happens if you screw up and make yourself responsible for easing the terrible, unfair wrongdoing they blame on each other.

Ask each combatant to assess, with your input, whether the cost of conflict outweighs its advantages, taking into account the impact of long-term penalties, retaliation, and unintended consequences. Yes, expressing anger feels more satisfying, sends a tough message to your enemy, and may eventually bring about desired change. But urge people to get real, remember what has actually happened, and anticipate the bad things that will keep happening. Then offer them your help in making peace if and when they decide it's in their best interest.

While it doesn't fit with the positive spirit of your mission, don't exclude the possibility of imposing self-protective limits and penalties if fighting continues; if the United States can impose sanctions on Iran, you can impose sanctions on grandparental visitation and worker performance ratings. That way, you send a clear message that you're sorry they're unhappy and you're willing to penalize their bad behavior if they can't just suck it up already.

Be clear, however, that whatever limits and penalties you impose are an unfortunate necessity, and are not meant to express criticism, superior power, or pressure to change. Should the conflict come to a resolution, with grandparents and employees who find the strength to keep their feelings to themselves, you will be delighted that sanctions can be lifted.

If one party is clearly more aggressive, don't protect the underdog (see previous section), because it will negatively impact the peace process. Instead, point out to the oppressor the many ways that attacking a perceived underdog can backfire, including passive resistance and counterattacks by others who also feel threatened. For example, instead of questioning whether the critical mother in the above case loves and supports her underperforming son, express concern that her vehement way of expressing herself may lead to a stalemate with him and possibly the school. If she comes to agree, you have suggestions.

Spell out methods for reducing hostilities without asking people to give up grievances; you're not asking them to stop hating or mistrusting one another, simply to stop expressing their feelings verbally or in the form of offensive actions. Spell out the behaviors that will allow them to escape penalties, whether imposed by you or others. If they comply, they're not abandoning their cause, just determining that it is not advanced by conflict.

Don't expand your responsibilities beyond your stated offer, regardless of how fervently you wish for peace, because it doesn't help to take sides (or appear to be doing so) and it's exhausting to listen to complaints. You've done your job by offering objective thoughts about the cost of conflict and making it easy to reduce hostilities. To do more is likely to cause harm.

Don't blame yourself or others if you get nowhere; good ideas sometimes take time to sink in, and some people may have reasons for fighting that you can't understand. Don't expect to make peace happen, but respect yourself for doing what you can to give it a chance, and trying to do better than the troops that came before.

Quick Diagnosis

Here's what you wish for and can't have:

- An ability to ease grievances
- Power to enforce a just solution or stop bad behavior
- An ability to reason with people so they'll do what's good for them
- Enough patience to not be upset and annoyed by other people's feuds

Here's what you can aim for and actually achieve:

- Keep your own negative feelings from adding to hostilities
- Find reasons that peace would be less costly than war
- Add to those reasons with your own sanctions and limits, if it's in your power
- Don't take responsibility for the grievances or hostilities of others
- Take care to protect yourself

Here's how you can do it:

- Talk politely, regardless of how you really feel
- Stay positive and concerned, but not enough to listen to complaints
- Sell the specifics of peace, including the painful, tough penalties you and others won't have to inflict
- If people don't want peace, stay out of the way of bullets
- As usual, respect your efforts, not your results

Your Script

Here's what to say when you wish to broker peace between parties in conflict.

Dear [Self/Repeatedly Wronged/Unfairly Traumatized/Folks Who Hate Each Other],

I'd like to help you feel better, but experience has taught me that
listening [doesn't help you for more than five minutes/gives me a
headache that lasts an hour/is for music, not opinions], and besides,
it's more important that you stop [trash-talking/cold-shouldering/
rumormongering/Facebook-flaming]. I've put together a [proposal/
PowerPoint presentation/one-page memo] detailing the pros and
cons of peace and where you can reach me if peace is what you want.
Otherwise, don't call, and know that I continue to wish you well.

Raising the Downtrodden

No matter how much sacrifice charity requires, be it of personal
needs, finances, or just hygiene, there's usually enough pleasure involved in giving to blur the lines between selfishness and selfless-
ness.

Even when people sacrifice their health and well-being, those who
literally give until it hurts find that the pain is its own kind of reward;
humans have a long history of using pain to purge guilt, from self-
whipping medieval monks to self-harming modern teens.

So while most people are content to be rewarded for their good
deeds with thanks, warm feelings, and/or the occasional tote bag,
others find that if getting sick while tending to the sick cures the
shame they feel for being born healthy, then they'll take tetanus over
a tote bag any day.

Unbridled giving may feel good, but good people need to make
tough, less-satisfying decisions about giving that take into account
their own needs, resources, other obligations, and the risk of doing
harm with their gifts. Good giving is equally selfish and selfless, and
is measured not by sacrifice or the pleasure it brings but the objective
effectiveness of your gift.

That's why, when it comes to giving, you need to put together a
plan that reflects your values, including those that unavoidably
compete with one another because your resources are limited. This
doesn't mean it's not good to give to the downtrodden, but it may be
bad if giving compromises your safety, diverts resources away from

those who could benefit more, or sacrifices the welfare of people for whom you have more immediate responsibility.

Fortunately, if you can put aside the great buzz that comes from helping the truly wretched and examine the particulars of each case, you'll see that the risks of giving are not infinite and can be assessed and managed. Ultimately, it's not the amount you give, or the amount of pleasure you get out of it, but the amount of care you put into giving that matters.

Here are powers that you'd like but (probably) lack:

- A major fuckin' Gates/Buffett bankroll
- An invulnerable immune system (and colon)
- A genius for doing simultaneous child care and world saving
- Magic hindsight to assure you that the gratitude and admiration people feel for your efforts is not undermining their respect for their own culture or fueling a backlash of envy and destruction

Among the wishes people express are:

- To dedicate their lives to something worthwhile
- To help people who need it the most
- To help life's worst rejects
- To avoid the meaninglessness of a life of self-indulgence

Here are three examples:

As a Christian, I make charity and volunteer work a huge part of my life; helping people who are poor, mentally ill, and neglected by society isn't just God's work, but work I can feel good about. Recently, though, my faith received a blow when I decided to hire one of the regulars at the church soup kitchen to do a painting job in my house. He's always been friendly, if a little off, but after he left, I found the door to my locked closet had been forced open and some of my wife's jewels were gone. There's a part of me that wants to show him love by forgiving him, hoping that will restore his faith in mankind, and there's a part of me that agrees with my wife, that this guy just takes things and I should call the police. My goal is to do good for people who really need it, without losing the jewelry that represents my love for my wife.

There's nothing about animals I don't like—they're much nicer and more loving than people—so I regularly foster animals for the local no-kill shelter, and I'm always willing to take in and adopt strays or abused pets. My friends have started to complain that they can't come over because dogs and cats have taken over the furniture, and neighbors have complained to the authorities that they can't stand the smell, but I think they're all overreacting because I have multiple cats and a couple of my dogs are pit bulls. My goal is to be helpful and heal the damage caused by human cruelty.

I feel selfish living in a rich country with my middle-class comforts and all the luxuries I could ever want, so it's always been meaningful for me to spend a couple weeks every year doing something helpful in developing countries. I had such a good time the last time I did it, I began thinking of making it a full-time job by finding an NGO I could work with. My boyfriend points out that such a move wouldn't help our relationship (he's happy with his job and thinks giving a bit to charity is enough) or my retirement. My goal is to figure out a way to do something good and important in this world without losing what's important in my life.

The great Boston philanthropist Daniel Rothenberg famously judged the effectiveness of charitable organizations by interviewing their janitors, reasoning that janitors, as the canaries in the coal mine of a business, best reflect an organization's ability to enact its values and keep its priorities straight. In other words, shit flows downhill, so if the guys who clean up shit feel fairly treated, then the organization probably knows how to do its work.

Ask yourself what you owe yourself and those who depend on you, including safety, before you pal around with the terribly infectious and potentially dangerous. Otherwise, if you give for sentimental reasons and without considering those issues, you can expose you and yours to danger with little chance of benefit, leaving your metaphorical janitors up shit creek.

Before assuming that you're not giving enough in life, figure out how many you can afford to help in a way that's bound to be beneficial. If you give to all comers, whether they be people or pets, without first measuring your resources, the only true benefactor will be you, as you'll inherit a shit storm from everyone around you.

Before becoming a full-time giver, also rate the value of your relationships, since you'll have to take time from them to dedicate your energies to your new, full-time cause. Most close relationships require a certain level of involvement and attendance, and if you're off on a giving crusade, your relationships may fall apart as well.

The due diligence list for checking out uplifting opportunities isn't endless or complicated, but it does make it hard to maintain your enthusiasm and virtuous feelings if it leads you to discover that many programs don't measure up or will cost you too much. When it comes to giving, it pays to give a shit about the details.

Being a good person doesn't mean you have to be charitable as an occupation or lifestyle. Being a good person means doing right by friends and family and working hard and honestly to support yourself. If you can keep those standards in mind while also trying to do good in the larger world, you'll come up with rules for giving that allow you to do some beneficial things without becoming a jerk to those who know you, or even those who do your shit work.

Quick Diagnosis

Here's what you wish for and can't have:

- Enough resources to prevent a deserving group from being deprived of benefits you happened to give another group
- Advance assurance that people won't misuse what you've given them

- Confidence that giving to people from a much less-affluent culture won't cause envy or otherwise hurt that culture
- Assurance that you won't give or receive undesirable new bacteria

Here's what you can aim for and actually achieve:

- Prevent harmful or ineffective giving by doing a thorough assessment
- Avoid repeating previous, unsuccessful attempts to help
- Make a huge difference to a large number of people
- Learn how to maximize your impact without wasting resources
- Minimize harm and unintended consequences

Here's how you can do it:

- Decide what's needed most
- Identify those who don't have it and can't get it
- Define an amount that's necessary and enough, rather than what's best
- Maximize the number who get it
- Measure the bang per buck
- Look for unintended harm

Your Script

Here's what to say when you or a loved one wishes to donate services to reduce human misery.

Dear [Self/Spouse/Desperate Beggar/Huddled Masses Yearning to Breathe Free],

I am willing to sacrifice [lots of time/money/my DVD collection] to making the world a better place, but I won't be satisfied by intense gratitude from a small group of people who maybe [didn't need my or your help in the first place/deserve help but offer repayment in the form of rare amoebae/weren't worth losing a marriage or bank account or foot over]. I will take time to assess need and will not be distracted by [loud begging/ sob stories/disheveled appearances]. I will learn how to ration resources, assess impact, and take pride in providing what's necessary and otherwise unavailable to the greatest number for the least negative impact.

Did You Know . . . About the Dark Side of Social Work?

There's an old country song called "Mammas Don't Let Your Babies Grow Up to Be Cowboys," and while it's arguable that mamas should be more worried about their children becoming performance artists or senators than cattle rustlers, one occupation that parents should also be quite wary of is social worker. Believe it or not, your money's better spent underwriting your child's MFA in performance studies than an MSW of doom.

Social work school will train your kids to be the ultimate helpers, and you might think that would make them really, really good kids. After all, they'll listen carefully to what you have to say and show great interest in your feelings, and you'll never have to ask them to take out the garbage, make curfew, or not mess around with drugs. Then again, they'll give the same kind of care to people who are all kinds of messed up with drugs, since they'll also feel obliged to help them—in addition to hustlers, criminals, the garbage man, etc.

That's because what social work school doesn't do is prepare them to say no to bad people, be sensitive to bad instincts in good people, discipline their own giving instincts, and stand up for their own needs. Mostly, it encourages some of the worst habits that counselors of any kind (shrinks included) can have: listening nonjudgmentally, being empathetic, and caring deeply about those in your care. All skills that will set anyone up to get taken advantage of, feed others' bad habits, and fall short of achieving the goals that sent them into social work in the first place.

The sad irony is that social work often takes good people with the best of intentions, pairs them with bad people with terrible intentions, and best-case scenario, robs the good people of their faith in humanity as they realize they've been working very hard to help bad people do worse. The worst-case scenario is they don't realize when they're being suckered and feel angry at the world on behalf of their victim-clients. At least until they get laid off due to budget cuts (as the social workers are always the first to go).

There are, of course, many counselors and social workers who are good at their jobs because they developed smart instincts through experience (not school). Even so, their jobs are often thankless, poorly paid, and grim. Being a social worker, like being a nun or a Walmart greeter, rewards sacrifice with more sacrifice (all three face poverty, crappy clothes, and periods of uncomfortable celibacy). Most of those who don't quit end up with so much contempt for the people they were trying to help that they let off steam by beating children with rulers.

Helping others is a noble pursuit that, without a strong set of independent and protective values, can do much more harm than good, and social work school rarely provides the preparation one needs. You may want your kid to want to help people, but not this way. Teach them to be cowboys instead, and at least you'll get free steak.

The wish to help others is a powerful motivator and source of self-esteem that can be realized on many different levels of human interaction, from helping a relative be happy to ending conflict between those we love to improving the world. At each level, the desire to help can easily backfire if what we wish isn't realistic and if we don't think carefully about risks and consequences. If you accept the fact that helping others is sometimes impossible, you'll become more helpful, even if the most helpful thing you let yourself do, at times, is nothing. True helpfulness often isn't satisfying, but if you've taken the time to evaluate what you're doing, and your values put a higher premium on being helpful than feeling helpful, then you have a right to feel you're living up to your ideals and doing the correct thing.

chapter five
fuck serenity

For those not in the medical field, knowledge of what's good and bad for our health can usually be found in the center of a Venn diagram involving "factual scientific knowledge," "pop culture," and "total bullshit." That's where you'll find such statements as "kale is God's personal salad," "deodorant gives you Alzheimer's (or something)," and in bold letters "stress KILLS."

Therefore, many people feel they should be able to reduce or eliminate stress, along with anger and fear, and achieve more serenity in their lives, both as an end in itself and to promote physical and mental wellness. They regard anger and fear as feelings that can be cleansed through meditation, or the practice of peaceful, giving philosophies, or sweaty yoga, or drinking vegetables, etc.

Unfortunately, like all of life's unpleasantries, stress, fear, and anger are unavoidable, at least sometimes. In some ways, they're beneficial—fear and aggression are basic primal defenses—but whether stress is a force for good or bad in your life, or even both, trying to do away with it is futile, harmful, and a way to set yourself against your basic nature.

If you really want to dedicate yourself to a serene existence, then accept a life absorbed in therapeutic and religious exercises while you either succeed in self-lobotomy or feel like a failure because you can't. The model of such laid-back living is probably Jeffery "The Dude" Lebowski, the fictional character from the Coen brothers' 1998 film, whose keys to a carefree lifestyle appear to be lots of weed, no self-awareness, and not bathing with marmots.

Certainly, you can and should avoid stress if you're not also avoiding your responsibilities; it's good to avoid conflict when you can and hang out with people you get along with, rather than with those who set you on edge. We assume, however, that there are lots of conflicts and relationships that life dumps on you (or in your bathtub) without giving you a choice. Likewise, your temperament dumps feelings on you, like anger and anxiety, without asking your permission or necessarily responding to meditation, exercises, medication, and intensive psychotherapy.

Remember that the actual Serenity Prayer, which is central to twelve-step methodology, isn't a prayer to end stress and anger, but for the clarity of mind and the humility to deal with whatever life inevitably throws at you. You can usually tell when conflict, fear, and negative feelings are unavoidable; that's when you've honestly tried everything, asked for advice, and still feel stuck. And when you start looking for your second therapy and third medication.

Self magazine may tell you that stress is deadly, but dedicating yourself to eliminating it will make you feel like you're not really living at all. Accept that peace of mind is rare, and that, without learning proper management of stress and fear, you can lose your mind entirely.

Stop Hating the Ones You Love

It's easier than most people think not to fall in love with the wrong person; Woody Allen's excuse was "the heart wants what it wants," but so do toddlers, and you don't give every four-year-old a pony.

On the other hand, it's almost impossible to stop loving someone, no matter how awful they are, when that someone is family, practically family, or a fellow survivor of hard times. They're not just friends or partners; they're part of your life.

Certain connections and experiences bond you to a person, so your love isn't a matter of choice and you can't turn it off. Unfortunately, you may also find yourself hating them or hating yourself for the way you respond to them. That, too, is seldom deliberate or easy to stop.

If you're lucky, your reasons for hate are temporary or hinge on a grudge you can give up or neutralize by lowering your expectations; for example, you may hate your parents until you're old enough to see their side of things or realize they couldn't help many of their faults and mistakes. Occasionally, other realizations can also put an end to hatred, like seeing that you have the right to decline an impossible responsibility and thus no longer have to hate the person you formerly felt responsible for or to.

These are the kind of hate-to-love transformations we celebrate and relive in stories because it feels so good to stop hating someone you love and stop feeling like a hateful person. Unfortunately, we also love to relive such moments because they are far too rare.

Most often, it's not in your power to stop hating someone you love, and your efforts to stop hating are likely to make hatred worse. You'll try to talk out issues that can't be resolved, or change character traits (yours and/or theirs), which is the best way to start a fight. You'll feel like a failure, which will make your hatred more acute and harder to keep inside, where it belongs.

If after much effort to resolve your negative feelings, you come to the conclusion that you can't stop hating someone you love, don't despair, because if it's really not in your power to stop hating, there's no point in blaming or hating yourself. Once you accept that anger is there to stay (and only bound to get worse the more you rage against it), you're now ready to think of ways to manage your perma-hate.

Please note, however, that accepting hate is not the same as accepting hateful behavior. It's a sad fact of life that many people can't help loving people they're also bound to hate, but if you can live with hate without acting hateful, you're doing a good job.

Living with hate will never feel good, but anyone who knows how much combustible anger you're currently storing in your brain recognizes how much respect you deserve for your decent behavior. The heart wants what it wants, but the hate wants everything, and if you hate someone you also care about, you need our advice.

Here are some powers you'd like to have to take the hate out of love-hate, but lack:

- A Jesus-like ability to love shitheads and bathe the feet of Assholes
- A sweet temperament like your beloved kindergarten teacher, who never, ever got angry at anyone (but, in retrospect, was probably high)
- The ability to just ignore people who should definitely shut the fuck up
- Access to a family therapist whose judgment and direction are accepted by all as gospel (see: Jesus, above)

Among the wishes people express are:

- To feel less angry
- To get loved ones to stop the behavior they hate
- To figure out why they're so angry
- To discover the secret that allows them to love everyone, even the ones they love-hate

Here are three examples:

My seventeen-year-old kid is a fuckup, a liar, and generally an asshole, so even though I know it's my job to support him, I can't help but become infuriated by his bullshit, and then my anger helps no one. He's gotten expelled from school and he's not working, so you can guess where the money comes from when he buys drugs, which he's obviously using. Not that he always uses the money I have to give him, because every now and then something disappears from the house. Of course, he admits to nothing and lies about everything. I yell at him, and he either looks defiant or scared, but it obviously does no good, and then my wife tells me it's all my fault. My goal is to help my son grow up and get off drugs, but I can't help him if I'm so angry—my wife is right about that—and that's what I need to stop first.

I hate the way my husband gets bossy with our kids. He's not abusive, but he's overbearing and it reminds me of what I disliked most about my father. He's usually a reasonable, responsible guy, and we get along fine when the kids aren't around, but alone time is rare and they won't be leaving home for at least five years. I've tried getting him to change his style, but it doesn't work and the kids don't like to see us argue. So I sit there, feeling resentful, with a sour look on my face, always angry at the partner I have to live with. My goal is not to be so pissed at him all the time.

I believe in honoring my parents, and I certainly love my mother, but she often gets very mean and is really nasty to my father, who is too old and hard of hearing to defend himself. He just gets on her nerves—partially understandable, since he can't hear a word she says—and she lets him have it when he doesn't even know what he did wrong. She is wonderful at justifying her actions to herself. I believe in accepting her, but I can't stop being angry whenever I see her, and that's not who I want to be. My goal is to be able to be around her and my father without always feeling nervous or enraged.

Since the last thing anyone wants to do is hate someone they really care about, it's important to recognize hate is often acquired only after a clusterfuck of bad behavior. If someone's inability to stop doing wrong makes you furious, then feeling less anger may only be possible when she improves her behavior, which is to say, never.

Even after analyzing the reasons for your anger, lowering your expectations, and trying to forgive, you'll probably find your feelings unchanged. It's a Clusterfuck-22, so if your goal is to stop hating and feeling guilty about your emotions, then you know where that leaves you.

Your first job, in these situations, is to try to understand, forget, and forgive, but once that proves impossible, accept your feelings as unavoidable facts and use your common sense to limit the damage. Speak softly but use your big (Roosevelt, not phallic) stick, if you have one, to limit hateful behavior.

Addicts are always selfish Assholes (see chapter 9), but if your son ever gets clean, he might return to his old, not-unbearable self. Until then, declare a list of bad behaviors—like stealing the TV or failing a store-bought drug test—that will require a young adult to spend a night or more elsewhere. You have to accept him as he is without anger, but if he can't accept your rules, then it's his turn to be angry, not yours.

If parenting leaves you angry with your spouse's style, split up your responsibilities, maximize the tasks you do separately, and schedule regular childless time together. If you express your anger, you will probably find it harder to set limits. If you set limits, you'll often find yourself feeling less angry.

If you can't protect one of your parents from the other's meanness, find ways to see them separately, e.g., lunch with mom and hog racing with dad. Whether you're all together or one-on-one, keep the conversation light and steer away from contentious subjects. Withdraw from offensive conversation if you have a nearby locked bathroom you can retreat to and think it will help protect you and/or reduce the nastiness. Don't discuss your feelings. Let your actions reflect your most constructive response to bad behavior.

Never lament hateful behavior or hate-filled chemistry as unnecessary or evidence of a dysfunctional family. Instead, celebrate the success of your ability to manage difficult relationships while avoiding open conflict.

You can't help having hate in your close relationships, but you should respect your ability to make them work, even if it's in a difficult, entirely fucked-up way.

Quick Diagnosis

Here's what you wish for and can't have:

- A heart untainted by hate
- A family with no Assholes
- A new temperament
- A spouse with no traits you dislike

Here's what you can aim for and actually achieve:

- Control your mouth
- Be confident in penalizing bad behavior
- Live with hate without hating yourself

Here's how you can do it:

- Use standard methods for chilling your anger
- Accept managing love-hate as part of a good person's job
- Use all opportunities to stop bad behavior and/or reduce your exposure to it
- Never get discouraged by having hateful people in your life or hate in your heart
- Respect good hate management

Your Script

Here's what to tell someone/yourself when you're tortured by hate for those you love.

Dear [Me/Family Member/Intimate Enemy],

I wish I wasn't so angry at my [parent/spouse/kid] but I've tried [family therapy/exorcism/high colonics] and I can't get rid of the [anger/filth/evil thoughts/inner tension]. I will not take responsibility

for the [insert synonym of "excruciating psychic pain or those who
cause it"] but I will become amazingly good at managing difficult
people and keeping them working together.

Accepting the Inescapably Annoying

Unless you find yourself in Guantánamo or a North Korean labor
camp, the worst kind of torture you can expect is being obliged to
spend time with someone, due to family, work, or just geography,
whom you hate enough to murder with your bare hands. Even Dick
Cheney would admit that the experience is more painful than an "en-
hanced interrogation technique."

It's one thing if the person you're stuck with is an Asshole (see
chapter 9), but it's even worse if you find yourself annoyed by someone's harmless habits and wanting to do violent things to the perfectly
innocent. That's when you'll feel like you're locked in an interrogation
room with Dick Cheney himself.

You want to feel like a nice person who wishes people well, not
a stressed, irritable, and hypertensive jerk, but when you're around
that special someone—and, alas, you often have to be—darkness fills
your soul. You can't change him, but you feel there should be a way to
change yourself.

It's true, some kinds of intolerance and irritability may be resolved
with insight or self-acceptance. If you find yourself irritable about everything, you may be depressed, and treatment can help you get the
symptoms under control.

At some point, however, you'll have exposed yourself to all the insight your psyche can bear and found that most focused annoyances
are both part of who you are and whom you're forced to sit next to for
long periods of your life. Trying to find a way to immunize yourself
against petty or even grand annoyance is just one more way to force
yourself into being someone you're not.

Asking people to be less annoying, of course, usually backfires, because they don't believe they're doing anything wrong. Asking people
to change isn't always futile, but if their annoying habits are part of

their personality, it can be one of the best ways to start a bad fight and cause hurt feelings. Improving communication is good for cellular companies, not for people looking for a good technique for reducing irritation.

Figuring out why someone gets to you is supposed to make you more tolerant, but what you'll find is that the reason you dislike some of their traits so much is because they're the same ones you hate in yourself, which, no surprise, is not a valuable insight. It will just make you more irritated with that person, since they now serve the dual purpose of annoying you and making you annoy yourself.

Instead, prepare to live with pent-up irritation, regardless of the number of people who tell you it isn't good for you, your blood pressure, and your soul, and accept that you can't let it out or snuff it out. You won't be out of the woods, but you will be out of the depths of the emotional waterboarding you're in now.

Here are the self-calming abilities you wish you had but don't:

- A yoga routine that puts you into such a deep state of relaxation, you can practically float
- The money to build your own soundproof room, house, or estate with guards to keep your annoyer out
- A hypnotist who tricks you into finding all the annoying crap this person does to be Clooney-level charming
- The plans and means to execute the perfect murder

Among the wishes would-be nice guys express are:

- To feel like a good person, not a petty jerk
- To harbor no animosity
- To get through the day (or night) with less internal turmoil
- To make troubled relationships better or find a way to change them

Here are three examples:

I never liked my mother-in-law, but ever since I lost my job, we had to move in with her. She has an opinion about everything, and since it's her house, we've got to listen. She's not much help with our kids, and she expects my wife to cook for her. I hate coming home and thinking of her, sitting in the big chair, watching her shows with the volume blasting away because she's deaf, knowing there's nothing I can say, but oh so much she has to say about so many topics I couldn't give a shit about. If I complain to my wife, even though she's the one who bears the brunt of it, she defends her mother, which, while understandable, just makes me madder. My goal is to be less angry every time I come into this house that isn't my home.

My boss is a nice guy, but he was never cut out to be a boss. Because he'll do anything to avoid making a decision or taking a stand, he lets the worst jerks in the office walk all over him, and he gives much more to the squeaky wheels who complain to him than he does to people who shut up and work hard. In other words, he's a giant wuss who rewards dickheads, so no matter how nice he acts, I want to strangle him. I can't quit because the job pays too well and the benefits are too good, but the problem isn't so much that I hate him but that I hate hating him and my wife hates hearing about it. My goal is to go to work without having nasty thoughts all day.

Not long after I moved into my new apartment, I met one of my neighbors in the elevator, and thought we had just a pleasant, harmless conversation. Little did I know that I had just signed on to become the best friend/unlicensed therapist to a sixty-something guy with no boundaries, other friends, or ability to take a hint. He comes by at all times of the day and night to tell me about how nobody loves him, how he'll never find anyone as great as his late partner, what he saw that day on TV. . . . It's exhausting, and I work from home, so I can't escape. I've talked to other people in the building, and they say the only way to get him to leave you alone is to pretend to be dying or not speak English, but that seems so evil. My goal is to get this guy to leave me alone without having to do something hurtful (or move).

Irritating qualities are a lot like dog whistles; some qualities are universally perceived, and others strike a frequency only certain individuals hear; i.e., one person's idea of a maddeningly annoying laugh is another person's charming chuckle.

Once you tune into the frequency, however, it's nearly impossible to turn it off, and if you can accept that there's no resolution or way to tune it out, it's time to embrace your pain and develop a management plan.

The first step, of course, is not to blame yourself for murderous urges and snotty thoughts. Make a list of the statements or situations that really light your fire, and develop scripts for responding briefly and politely, such as "that's interesting" or "huh, weird" or "sorry I'm not responding, I've got to concentrate because I'm memorizing pi."

A loud mother-in-law who never gets out of the way is going to drive most sons-in-law crazy, even if she has a perfect right to sound off in her own home. It's important then to develop not just a series of scripts but some mental rules of necessary (dis)engagement. Find a hidey-hole (bathroom, car, Starbucks) to cut you off from having to hear or see your annoyeur or annoyeuse. Develop a script for using it; e.g., that ol' chestnut "gotta go." It's necessary to be polite, respond to medical emergencies, do your share of chores, and provide paid-for services, but this way you never, ever prolong contact because of guilty feelings or forceful demands.

A wussy boss will aggravate hardworking employees who resent the way their whiny, manipulative colleagues always come out ahead, but remember, it's only a job, and you're there to make a living, not make the workplace better or fairer. While some may work to please the boss, your goal is to meet your own standards for a good day's work while staying employed. List your own reasons for being there, then think of the never-ending irritation as a form of industrial pollutant that's worth putting up with, if the money is right.

Don't force yourself to be extra nice to the obnoxiously needy to prove you're not as mean as your urge to avoid him makes you feel. Maybe he can't help being obnoxious, needy, or lonely, but his problems are not your responsibility. If you don't limit your exposure—politely, and without evident guilt—your irritation will grow as you open yourself to his passive-aggressive home invasion. Your job is to take credit for politeness, ignore nasty feelings, and give yourself the right to spend time with people whose company you actually enjoy.

No matter who the source of your annoyance is, don't require validation from like-minded people before telling yourself you're not a bad person. Maybe you have a bad person inside, or everyone around you is nicer or just tuned out. You're basically nice if you don't let the nastiness out. If you overcompensate, or try too hard to find support, you'll only make things worse.

You can't change irritation or the irritating, but you can stop taking undue blame for being mean and start taking deserved praise for your restraint. You might not feel like a good person, but it's a much bigger achievement to act like a good person when the inner evil is ringing in your ears. Remember, very few people are naturally, effortlessly good; we leave that up to dogs.

Quick Diagnosis

Here's what you wish for and can't have:

- An ability to change others or get them to see why they should change themselves
- A life with better people or more options
- Escape from the tension
- A less touchy personality

Here's what you can aim for and actually achieve:

- Tolerate long periods of wishing you were with other people while going about your business
- Control your mouth even if you can't control your feelings
- Be proud of what you've accomplished even if you're irritated and unhappy most of the time
- Not let the lack of escape make you despair

Here's how you can do it:

- Remind yourself regularly of your reasons for putting up with unending annoyance
- Develop practical ways to block annoying people from your perception
- Develop your own rules for doing so and polite ways of defending those rules against objections
- Keep track of, and give yourself credit for, things left unsaid

Your Script

Here's what to tell someone/yourself when you're tempted to let an irritating person know exactly what's on your mind.

Dear [Self/Person Who Always Ruins My Day for Most of the Day]:

I've tried to [like/understand/ignore/accept] the things you do that drive me [insert synonym of "ape shit"] and have discovered it's not going to happen. Therefore, I want you to know I appreciate our good [working/living/unintentional] relationship. If I sometimes [leave the room/read the paper and refuse to look up/remain in the bathroom for an hour], don't feel insulted or ignored—I simply like my alone time. I look forward to many years of [collaboration/cohabitation/gritting my teeth, possibly to nubs].

Did You Know . . . How to Deal with a Crazy Person?

Being forced to spend time around people you can't stand is difficult, but being confronted by someone who's insane is downright scary. Your stereotypical crazy and confrontational person is some variation of that guy on the subway who always appears to be arguing with the ghost of a burrito (at least until someone accidentally and foolishly makes eye contact). Unfortunately, you don't need to go underground to find somebody that crazy;

you can share an office or even a bloodline with someone just as unstable.

In-laws, especially older ones, are frequently missing marbles, and there's always that one coworker who smells like socks dipped in milk and looks like he cuts his own hair with safety scissors. You can be trapped on a subway car with an angry, crazy person just as easily as you can be trapped at a Thanksgiving dinner, so it's important to know how to react if such an encounter presents itself.

Just as we're told to ease the task of public speaking by imagining the audience in their underwear, it helps to put the behavior of an aggressive crazy person into perspective by just imagining you're being attacked by a bear. That way, you won't find yourself tempted to reason with your attacker, or assume that kindness or friendly, calm words will tame the crazy beast; as with a charging grizzly, they do no more than catch his attention and make you a target.

Then, as you would with a bear, get as close as you can to playing dead, and, if need be, get help. Call a cop if you think someone is too crazy to stay out of trouble, or might attack someone, and meanwhile keep your distance, eyes down, and stay close to an exit. If your Good Samaritan instinct kicks in, remember, Good Samaritans are good bear food; you are not failing your fellow man, because your fellow man is not currently in control of his or her words and actions, and you have an obligation to protect yourself.

The basic rule of thumb when being threatened by a crazy person is to accept your lack of control; your best option, as with bears, is to make yourself invisible and survive so you can ride the subway/eat Thanksgiving turkey another day.

Facing Fear

A little bit of fear, in small, controlled doses, can be enjoyable; that's why people pay money to see scary movies and ride roller coasters instead of just screaming and puking at home for free. Then there's the opposite kind of fear—random, sometimes inexplicable, debilitating—which isn't enjoyable, and can cost you your peace of mind.

The unfun kind of fear is the common denominator of anxiety disorders, and those who suffer from them often share, and run into, the same bullshit attitude that depressives have; their emotions must be understandable, like normal anxiety and sadness, so if they just figure out what's bothering them, confront it, and move on, they'll be anxious no more.

In the same way most people confuse depression with passing sadness or sulking, anxiety is often mistaken for plain, old horror-movie-style fear. In reality, anxiety can get much worse and appear in many forms.

Some people feel anxious all the time and just can't shake it, even when they're wrapped in love and security. Other people experience sudden bursts of fear called panic attacks that can come out of nowhere, last hours, and drive strong, sane people into thinking they're dying, even when they know they aren't. And some people can't stop feeling jumpy and spooked long after they've experienced trauma, be it a car accident or time in combat.

Depression and anxiety are basically stepsiblings; one can cause or feed on the other in the same person, they sometimes respond to the same medications, and both can keep coming back, off and on, throughout a person's lifetime.

People expect to cure those disorders by getting to the root cause or undergoing some kind of corrective experience, from exposing themselves over and over to whatever scares them to finding religion to just willing their minds into health. As with all severe illnesses, mental or otherwise, there is no "cure" (see: cancer, the common cold, that clammy feeling you suffer through after eating a big steak). Therapy sometimes works to some extent, but generally, these syndromes tend to persist and even worsen during one's middle years, and treatment is no cure.

If you believe in the curability of anxiety (or depression), persistent symptoms just mean you haven't found the right treatment or done it properly, faced your fears, found Jebus, grown a pair, or let yourself be loved. The more things you try and the longer your symptoms last, the more your sense of failure grows.

What you should do instead, if you've made reasonable attempts to cure persistent fear to no avail, is accept that life has simply given you a burden you must learn how to bear. Many good people live with fear, and there's nothing wrong with having a powerful imagination, a scary past or future, or an anxious brain, other than the pain.

You're not immature, weak-willed, or lacking in courage; you're just stuck with a particular kind of chronic pain. You will never enjoy it (or a scary movie ever again), but you can learn to bear it, so no matter how much fear you're experiencing, you won't be afraid to face each day as it comes.

Here's how you'd like to fight fear, but can't:

- Remember the wise, calming words of your guru
- Breathe (which you're doing all the time, by the way)
- Take a nonaddictive pill that acts like Drano on fear and clears it right out
- Undergo a tribal initiation ceremony/boot camp/TSA screening so scary it leaves you with no fear of anything else

Among the wishes fear-ridden people express are:

- To grow up and stop being scared
- To find the deeper cause of their anxieties, which has so far eluded them
- To stop being afraid of things they simply shouldn't be afraid of
- To finally find treatment that works

Here are three examples:

I was violently mugged six months ago, and ever since, I get the jitters every time I'm out after dark. I've gotten therapy, learned meditation, taken meds, and I'm still on edge. Sometimes I catch myself avoiding plans and choosing to stay home because I just don't want to face that anxious feeling that comes with being on the streets alone at night. My goal is to stop living in fear.

I used to take my health for granted, but since I got diagnosed with multiple sclerosis last year I can't stop thinking about dying. My symptoms aren't that bad and they're pretty stable so far, but I feel like death is around the corner. I've gone to support groups and talked to counselors, and I've become a lot more serious about my health, dedicating a lot of time and energy to researching my disease and changing my diet and exercise, but the fear won't go away. I know there's no cure, and I can't get over feeling helpless, like I've got a terminal illness and it's only a matter of time. My goal is to stop being afraid of death.

Everyone else seems comfortable with the boss, but he gives me the willies. I don't think he likes me, and he's not the sort of person who pats you on the back or jokes with you, so I just don't know where I stand. I dread having a one-on-one meeting with him, partly because I'm afraid my fear shows, and partly because every time he wants to talk to me, I'm convinced I'm about to get fired. I need this job very much—I've put in quite a few years at this company, and I think I'm too old at this point to get hired for the same work anywhere else—so the thought of getting fired is terrifying. My goal is to figure out a way to get over it, be myself, and not let anyone terrify me.

If people who suffer from anxiety are guilty of anything, it's being born at the wrong time; there was a time when being hyperalert and quick to fear was the best way to keep from being eaten by a prehistoric megabear or stay prepared for an attack by a rival warlord.

Alas, in today's world, where megabears are long gone and rivals post all their moves in advance on Twitter, such hyperalertness is more of a burden than a gift. That said, it's not a burden that's impossible to bear (pun intended).

After all, the reason you have PTSD after being mugged and hate to walk alone on dark streets is that your brain is trying to protect you from ever, ever being in that situation again. It's the megabear reflex, not just because that's where its roots are, but because, like a megabear, it's incredibly powerful. More powerful than your efforts to persuade your brain that you need to go out and the street is safe.

While you may never be able to erase that reflex, there are many treatments to try. Check out cognitive treatments (e.g., talking about the details of the traumatic experience in a controlled, calm manner), biofeedback, and self-hypnosis. Given the fact that fear usually prompts helpless, negative, irrational thoughts—e.g., "this is going nowhere, I'm wasting my money, and I'm going downhill"—cognitive treatment that gets you to recognize and challenge these thoughts is of first importance.

There are nonaddictive medications that help all kinds of anxiety, as well as some addictive medications that pose very little risk if they aren't taken daily. Many people who suffer from anxiety attacks find that just carrying medication around and knowing it's there, just in case, provides some relief. It also helps to meet people with PTSD, or whatever anxiety syndrome you experience, who live full lives in spite of their symptoms.

If facing a life-threatening illness triggers obsessive ruminations about death, you may find yourself stuck with them for a long time, like with PTSD; once an external event triggers repeated symptoms, they tend to last. It's as if fear has worn a path in a brain that was a bit soggy to begin with.

Yes, it's tough to be terrified of dying and have people trying to comfort you by reminding you that we're all going to die, because they don't have the burden of knowing exactly how and feeling like they should be able to do something about it. That said, talking about your fear repeatedly and thinking about medical solutions will only make you worse.

So stop focusing on the importance of a clean or not-so-clean bill of health, and instead block behaviors that make fear stronger, like oversharing and giving up regular life activities that might otherwise distract you. Look at a fear of death as a bizarre brain symptom, not evidence that you're a deep admirer of Woody Allen and Ingmar Bergman.

It may help you to hang out with other people living with MS who share your fears and nevertheless live fully, much as it helps an alcoholic to spend time with those who are in recovery but still feel vulnerable. The need for reassurance, like the need for alcohol, however, is simply a drive for unhealthy behavior that you're not responsible for having, just for blocking.

If you get terrified in anticipation of a social or work situation or performance, your anxiety will get better, to some degree, if you do the same scary thing over and over, but it won't necessarily disappear. It's amplified by thoughts about being afraid "for no good reason" and wondering if fear will cause you to stutter, blush, fart, and thus embarrass yourself further. Fear is amazingly good at causing fear; it's the mind's best perpetual motion machine.

A cognitive technique that helps with fear of embarrassment is to spend time every day defining your own goal for pushing yourself into the danger zone. Keep reminding yourself that you're at work because you're there to make a living, and you have your own definition of a good presentation. Then define goals that derive from your own standards and needs, not the response of others, and applaud yourself for pursuing those goals in spite of persistent fears.

What's most important, assuming you accept the unfairness of having to live with fear, is respecting what you do every day to limit its reach. Challenge fear-driven thoughts about what you should have done to avoid anxiety, or about the horrible effect it will have on your life and relationships. Every time you stop yourself from seeking relief in avoidance, substances, or other behavior that interferes with your goals, give yourself a cheer.

Although relaxation may be good for your blood pressure, remember, it's that good ol' fear reflex that made your life possible, since it kept your ancestors alive long enough to have kids. Like your pelt-wearing forebears, you're never going to relax for very long, so take pride in what you do with your fear. If you can tolerate it without letting it take over your life entirely, use it for self-protection so you, too, can stay alive.

Quick Diagnosis

Here's what you wish for and can't have:

- A cure for attacks of irrational fear
- Total, quick control of fear without risk, side effects, or possible relapse
- Elimination of the stupid, irrational fear-inducing thoughts you get when you're afraid
- Freedom from urges to do unhealthy things when you're afraid

Here's what you can aim for and actually achieve:

- Develop an ability to assess realistic risk
- Form habits and procedures for doing what you intended to do, in spite of persistent symptoms
- Find treatments that provide partial relief some of the time
- Control fear-driven behaviors
- Respect what it requires to live with fear

Here's how you can do it:

- When common methods for fear relief fail, accept that you're fucked
- Learn how to tell when a negative thought is lying to you and how to challenge it
- Survey the many treatments for fear management and try out any that seem helpful
- Don't avoid treatments that carry risks if your risk of not doing them is greater
- Remember alcohol is a treatment with high risk and brief benefit that breeds dependency and could make you into an Asshole
- Learn to talk calmly and humorously about fearful things so that other people won't get spooked by your fear
- Respect yourself as a fear manager

Your Script

Here's what to say when you're fed up with being afraid.

> *Dear [Self/Quivering Wimp/Fragile Phobic],*
>
> *I hate living in [fear/dread/retreat], but so far I haven't been able to figure out [why I'm scared of nothing/can't get the help I need/have these weird moments where I'm fine one second and the next can't breathe and feel like my heart's going to explode]. Having failed to find happiness, I will now [give up the chase/learn meditation/get back to business] and ignore thoughts about getting relief from [insert illegal controlled substance here] or [avoiding people/discussing my anxiety constantly so that people avoid me/seeking a magic cure]. I will run my life as if I wasn't scared, no matter how much work it takes.*

Realistic Mantras to Try If You Feel an Anxiety Attack Coming On
This too shall pass, and shall pass quicker if I take the special pill I always carry in my pocket
Life is a journey, not a destination, and anxiety isn't fatal according to the Internet
Remember to breathe (although if breathing didn't come naturally, I'd be in deep trouble since I often don't remember where my keys are)
I can find my center and endure this day, or I can find my boss, tell him I have diarrhea, and deal with this at home
I am a leaf on the wind, watch how I soar, listening to anything but my brain

Healing Heartache

It's hard to discuss heartache without sounding sappy or using purple prose, but the fact is, if your heart gets attached to something or someone, and you take that something away, the heart responds to the loss of the loved person with pain.

If you want to know what depression feels like, or even what being an actual zombie feels like, have your heart broken; it's the same rare, poisonous cocktail of grief and sadness accompanied by hopelessness, anger, self-reproach, and an inability to experience pleasure or feel engaged in life. With grief, though, you know why you're sad, can expect an eventual full recovery, and don't crave brains.

In most cases, people recover by accepting support from friends, keeping busy with work and friendships, and taking good care of themselves. Like depression, however, the grief of heartbreak can be destructive, even fatally so.

If you believe that healing from loss is always possible—as do many therapists, most owners of scented candles, and all screenwriters—then you're sure to feel like a loser if your grieving doesn't end. It means you didn't succeed in moving on, letting go, getting help, facing your feelings, or whatever.

Unfortunately, some people don't recover from loss, even when they get lots of support and work hard to move on. It may be that loss triggers an innate vulnerability to depression, their personalities are unusually loss-sensitive, or they lack the ability to control destructive impulses. Again, it sounds sappy, but not every broken bone or heart is guaranteed to mend.

If you are living with a broken heart, your pain doesn't go away, and neither does your hopelessness about life's ever having meaning again or your anger at anyone whose behavior might have prevented the loss, including yourself.

If you recognize the sad truth that some people never stop hurting from a loss, then you're ready to find ways to live a meaningful life, even when grieving seems like it's never going away, and perhaps never will.

Since getting over loss is not always within our power, living with grief is a failure only if you let it prevent you from living a good, productive life. Living with a broken heart is hard, but it can never doom you to be a broken person.

Here are some heart-healing abilities you'd like to have but don't:

- The gift to weep so intensely that you purge yourself of grief even if you become dangerously dehydrated
- The kind of faith that allows you to believe that every loss, betrayal, and disappointment is part of God's/Xenu's/Satan's greater plan
- A surgery that removes the grief-affected part of your brain while leaving the part that knows song lyrics and how to walk
- An insight into persistent grieving that actually makes a difference, like "time heals all wounds," but helpful

Among the wishes people express are:

- To stop hurting and feel like living again
- To stop obsessing about why they weren't there and what they didn't do to help
- To get back to where they were before
- To find something to care about again

Here are three examples:

I loved my wife and family, so when she said it was over, I hadn't seen the divorce coming. She said I hadn't done anything wrong; she just stopped loving me. We've remained friendly and we co-parent well, but I felt like home was where we lived and now I'm in exile, getting a glimpse of the woman I loved as she's moved on to her next husband, who, of course, my son really likes. I can't stop pining for someone who is no longer attached to me. When I see her and we chat briefly every two weeks when I pick him up, my heart still breaks. My goal is to get over her.

My mother died after a long illness, so I'm glad she's no longer in pain and that I got so many wonderful years with her, but she was the best friend I had and I still miss her so much. Every day I miss talking to her on the phone, and every time I see a good movie or hear a funny joke, I can't enjoy it because I realize I can't tell her about it. There's almost nothing that doesn't remind me of her or something we used to talk about. It's been two years, and I can't seem to stop crying. She would never want me to be unhappy, but I can't help myself. My goal is to get over my grief.

After so many years of putting up with my wife's drinking and untreated depression, I'd had enough (and couldn't put the kids through any more), so I filed for divorce. As I feared, she went downhill after that and unfortunately never really recovered. A few months after the divorce was final, she started calling me when she was drunk and suicidal to tell me the divorce had killed her and there was no point in living. After I stopped answering her calls, she overdosed and was taken to the hospital. After that I got full custody of the kids, so I still hear from her regularly because of them, and she always sounds reproachful. My goal is to stop having to worry about her and feel tortured by guilt over this unending misery.

When grief seems to go on forever, you want to ask your friends, your cat, and your god why the suffering won't end. Instead, ask yourself (and maybe a therapist) whether you're doing something to prevent yourself from recovering.

When it comes to endless heartache, there's a good chance you're not doomed, just doing it wrong. Pain-driven behaviors, like drug using, stalking, or immersing yourself in the past, may all set you back.

If you're not doing anything wrong, however, the bad news is that persistent grieving is not under your control, recovery is not a sure thing, and your cat has no healing powers. The good news is that there are lots of ways to help yourself once you stop looking everywhere for a cure and start looking at how to live life under new, less-than-ideal circumstances.

Continuing to stay in contact with someone you've loved and actually lost, while necessary in a co-parenting or workplace situation, may be misused to prolong the pain of grief; the more you seek a connection, the more powerful it gets. You may even fool yourself into thinking there's nothing wrong with being friendly, chatting, and making lots of eye contact when you drop by your ex's for visitation. What you need to do to break the connection is avoid direct contact and instead communicate by any of the cold, twenty-first-century methods—email, text, emoji, whatever.

Like an alcoholic, you may think you don't need to stop reaching out until the pain's lessened enough that it no longer requires drowning, but in truth, the pain will stop only when you dry out. Test this assumption by breaking off face-to-face contact and see what happens; if you find yourself jonesing for some eye contact, you know you're on the right track. Then perhaps you'll find the strength to examine and control your grief-stalling behavior.

When sorrow doesn't stop and you're sure you've done nothing to hang on to the past and everything to live in the present, then get the kinds of treatment that help chronic depression, such as cognitive therapy, exercise, and medication. Get help from friends and therapists who can tolerate your pain, not be overly affected by it, and continue to give positive encouragement.

Don't tell yourself that time heals all wounds or that all things pass, because somebody has to be the exception to those truths, and alas, it's you. Instead, continue to look for positive meanings in your loss, using ideas you glean from books, religion, therapists, and friends. Avoid therapists who are interested in talking about your feelings of loss if you've already gone that route and it hasn't worked. Instead, look for a positive coach who honors your relationship with your late parent, regardless of how empty its loss has left you, and respects your efforts to keep moving in spite of feelings of emptiness.

Sometimes you can get as paralyzed by someone else's grief as by your own. If your ex can't get over you and tells you she'll die if you don't take her back, don't feel guilty until you've decided for yourself whether you tried hard to make the relationship work and whether you can ever, ever accept responsibility for the life of someone else who isn't a minor, a soldier in your platoon, or a patient on whom you're doing open-heart surgery.

Certain people are very vulnerable to rejection, and if you didn't know it before you got together, you sure know it now. You probably know that this isn't her first rejection, and if you don't, ten seconds of googling will make it clear.

Don't bend over backward and offer support, or you may find yourself intensifying contact that needs to stop. Get advice from a therapist or moral adviser for your right to end the relationship and do what will cause the least pain in the long run. Then declare your intentions without showing guilt or fear, keep your distance, and hope that your ex can find a way to survive.

Just because loss precedes a long period of misery doesn't mean that you or another person or pet have it in their power to stop the pain, and even when your behavior is part of the problem, you may not have the vision or strength to control it. What you can do in the face of endless grief is to accept that fact and respect whatever efforts you make to go on with life instead of waiting for heartache to end.

Quick Diagnosis

Here's what you wish for and can't have:

- An end to heartache, daily sadness, and negative thoughts
- An ability to control your heart
- A time machine
- Certainty that you'll feel better

Here's what you can aim for and actually achieve:

- Stop grief-prolonging behaviors
- Challenge despairing thoughts
- Don't link grief and responsibility without careful thought
- Live a meaningful life

Here's how you can do it:

- Don't hurt yourself to flee grief
- Seek ideas, friends, and advisers that fight despair
- Try treatments for symptoms
- Don't hold others responsible for your grief or accept responsibility for theirs
- Continue to do what's meaningful, regardless of how you feel

Your Script

Here's what to say about grief that doesn't heal.

Dear [Grieving Self/Frustrated Friend/Long-Aggrieved Other],

I don't know why I can't seem to get over this [loss/death/divorce/ playoff defeat] but I'm proud I've stopped [insert bad, health- endangering, money-losing habit] and have started [keeping busy/ working hard to think positively/compulsively checking Petfinder for a high-maintenance animal to adopt and take over my life]. I'm ready to accept that I may never feel [insert adjective for "not-shitty"], but that won't change my approach to life or my belief in what's important.

Accepting Enmity

There are people who seem to thrive on being hated, but besides assorted YouTube commenters, professional wrestlers, and one Donald Trump, most people in the world hate being hated, especially when the person who's angrily cut you off is somebody you were once close to.

Usually, the hate is not active and violent, but more silent and passive-aggressive. Still, it's hard to find inner peace when someone you care about is shunning you, as happens in families and small communities. It's harder still when there's nothing you can do about it, including apologizing, humbling yourself, accepting doctrine, or kissing the ring/something else.

If you're an introspective self-doubter, you keep wondering what you could have done differently to head off or mend trouble. You're not afraid of admitting you did something wrong; you either can't figure out what it was or what's wrong with your apology.

It doesn't help to be assertive, silver-tongued, or sorry. You can be a great defense lawyer who makes juries weep, and you've got no one to plead your case to. You get the feeling that, the louder your protests, the more satisfaction you may be giving to your enemies.

When you hear false rumors about your alleged wrongdoing, you can protest sincerely, but the more time you give it, the more attention it gets; it's often impossible to prove that you didn't do something negative. As was famously asserted at the 15th International Conference on Agile Software Development, "The amount of energy necessary to refute bullshit is an order of magnitude bigger than to produce it."

You may miss your shunner and want to reconcile, or you may be afraid of them and want to move behind a security fence. In any case, you never know, day to day, whether you're going to run into them and be reminded of enmity you just can't stop.

If you expect eventually to find a solution, you won't stop trying to find an effective answer, and everything you do will make things worse. If you accept the fact that life sometimes imposes indefinite enmity on you, then you're ready to learn how to endure it for as long as necessary without breaking, feeling you've failed, or becoming a heel/Trump and learning to love it too much.

Here are telltale signs that reconciliation is highly improbable:

- A call to ask what you did wrong leads you to discover that the number's been changed (as has their address, and legal name)
- An attempt to just talk it all out leads to an attempt on your life
- An apology bought you five weeks of peace (better than the last one, which only bought five days)
- The declaration that you don't want to pick sides has landed you outside, and the door is locked

Among the wishes people express are:

- To get their ex–best friend to see they did nothing wrong
- To get someone they love to listen
- To stop a personal war they have no interest in continuing
- To stop the pain of being hated by someone they love

Here are three examples:

When my brother stopped talking to me, it felt like I lost my best friend. His decision was unexpected and I think it was because his wife decided she hated me. I can't think of him without wanting to pick up the phone and find some way to resolve the problem, even if I don't know what I'd be apologizing for, and we can probably never be close friends again. I wish he'd just tell me what this is about, but he never explained and he won't answer my calls. My goal is to find a way to restore contact since I've got absolutely no hostility and every wish to get my brother back.

I know I had to divorce my husband because he was a mean drug addict, but that didn't stop the trouble. Periodically he tells the police I've violated our divorce agreement and sounds so convincing that I have to answer in court, and even though the cases get thrown out again and again, he won't stop trying. Every time I've just about stopped thinking about him, he does something to make me hate him again, which is the opposite of what I need. My goal is to get him to stop picking fights with me, because until he does, I can't get on with my life.

For ten years, I had a book club with a group of my closest friends from college, since we all ended up in the same city. I always looked forward to our meetings, which were basically just excuses to drink wine, gossip, and laugh. Then, a few months ago, I don't know what happened or who offended whom, but suddenly there were two groups who hated one another, and I had to take sides. I want war with no one—these women are all friends with me, even if some of them aren't friends with each other anymore—but the group won't allow neutrality. My goal is to stay at peace and not lose one or both groups of my closest friends.

Most people know that if you find out you're the object of someone's romantic interest, it's important to stop and consider whether the feelings of your newfound sweetie are worth taking seriously. After all, it's nice if somebody is into you, but not if they're really just interested in your car, tush, or bank account.

What fewer people realize, however, is that you have to stop and apply the same level of skepticism to angry overtures as you do to affectionate ones. Whether someone has the hots for you or has it out for you, an initial assessment is required.

So before you leap to react to somebody's grudge, judge your behavior by your own standards. Form your own opinion about whether you really did something wrong before you decide whether you deserve his anger, and what response he deserves in kind, whether it be a slew of apology bouquets or a silent shrug.

Then, regardless of what others say (or don't say, if they freeze you out), you know whether somebody's anger is something you can or should do anything about, without needing to argue, change a mind, or feel validated.

If you failed to live up to your values, make amends. If, however, you know you haven't done anything wrong, then make peace with the fact you're screwed; if somebody decides seemingly arbitrarily to dislike you, even if that person is your brother, then you just have to wait for them to arbitrarily decide not to dislike you anymore. In other words, if you had no direct influence on changing his mind in the first place, then don't expect to have any influence on changing it back.

Sure, your brother's silence may be due to pressure from his wife, but it also may be due to a head injury or his zodiac sign; what's important is that you know his decision isn't really personal or deserved, so accept his behavior and decide whether you wish to leave open the far distant possibility of a relationship. If so, keep texting him when your team wins, or forward him occasional funny emails, as long as there's no expectation of a reply, no mention of strong feelings, and no political humor emails, because that's asking for trouble.

If it's not him but his wife who hates you, and you're careful to stop addressing issues or expressing pain, distress, or anguish, he may be glad, eventually, to say hello at neutral gatherings. Sometime down the line, events and positive feelings will push you back into casual contact, but be aware that hatred could return just as randomly as it went away.

Then there are enemies, usually exes who are often into harmful substances, who feel they have very good reasons for punishing you and yearn to know how much their hatred hurts you, so they know you care. They don't want to get even with you so much as they want a response, because their new addiction is your strong emotion; if you fight back and let them have it with all guns blazing, they're getting what they need.

Before spending money on a therapist to help you deal with your rage or trying to have a heart-to-heart with your ex to resolve things, get a lawyer, preferably one who will tell you to get your head out of your ass (or get a restraining order). Once you change your perspective, then change your locks, and stop answering your phone.

Know what challenges you're legally obliged to respond to—e.g., about kids and alimony—and respond only when necessary, briefly, and politely, using both email and restraint when it comes to sharing anything but basic information. Then, if you have money left over, ask a therapist to help you develop scripted responses to your ex, so you can fulfill the basic requirements for communication but not his need to feed on your emotional blood.

If it's a group of friends who are freezing you out, you've got the bad luck to have friends who are part of a close, mutually connected group. Whether it's at a club or workplace, you're in big trouble if the politics go nuclear; nobody wants to hurt you, but everyone will cut you out (and hurt you) if you don't take their side for seemingly no reason.

That's when you find out who your true friends are (they're the ones who still speak to you, because the bar gets set pretty low). In any case, you need new friends, because unless you're living in a full-time, adult summer camp, this behavior is not okay.

Since neutrality is your only option—again, if you didn't directly cause the rift, you can't do anything to repair it—be prepared for your Swiss status to leave you isolated and unannexed as the war continues. However sad your loss is, it teaches you why it's good to move on from high school cliques, even if it takes a while, and make friends one at a time.

When you realize a relationship can't be repaired, don't torture yourself by trying to figure out why or finding a new approach. Make sure you're clear with your own conscience, and then learn to live with a broken bond.

Don't expect to end the pain of not being at peace with those who've become your enemies. If you can accept rejection, however, and wait for those who love you for the right reasons and don't hate you for the wrong ones, you can be at peace with yourself.

Quick Diagnosis

Here's what you wish for and can't have:

- A chance to communicate
- A good response from negotiation
- A way to reclaim your old relationship
- Relief from feeling dumped, shunned, or worse

Here's what you can aim for and actually achieve:

- A belief in your own conduct
- Behavior that doesn't make conflict worse
- Protection from additional damage
- A policy that allows reconciliation but doesn't beg for it

Here's how you can do it:

- Judge your behavior by your own standards
- Don't keep trying what clearly hasn't worked
- Accept enmity if you must and start to protect yourself
- Stop emotional communication but keep the door open if you decide it's worthwhile
- Remind yourself that rejection is never a punishment if you don't deserve it
- Respect the effort it takes to force yourself to move on

Your Script

Here's what to say about being unavoidably rejected.

Dear [Self/Remaining Friends/Rejecters (If They're Listening and Not Just Heckling What I Have to Say)],

I have tried to reconcile by [trying to understand/explaining/ groveling/keeping my temper/truly giving a damn] and it clearly hasn't worked. I will not make myself responsible for doing things I don't consider [wrong/harmful/in poor taste], regardless of whether they cause a permanent [insert synonym for "deep chasm"], I will accept a loss I can't help, and I will learn to protect myself by [not begging/ not sharing/not making significant eye or voice contact]. I will respect myself for retaining my self-respect in the face of rejection.

Did You Know . . . That There's a (Relatively) Nice Way to Cut Someone Out of Your Life?

While being shunned or spurned by someone you care about is always painful, there are ways to push someone out of your life that aren't dramatic or traumatic. It's like the difference between having an appendectomy in a hospital, and having someone cut your gut open with the neck of a malt liquor bottle in the garden shed; you can get the same result with a fraction of the suffering.

Besides, dramatic shunnings are usually mean and ill-intentioned; it's much easier to push someone out of your life, and find nice ways of doing it, if your reasons are well thought out and benign.

For example, you may decide a friend is too high maintenance, or discover that, as much as you like her, you can't trust her. Assuming you're wise enough to realize she's not going to change and that talking about the issue will do nothing but cause hurt, your only option is to back away while doing your best to be respectful.

So instead of planning a grand confrontation (or letting yourself get so irritated you have one by accident), do a slow fade and gradually make yourself less available, claiming it's due to pressing business, not a personal beef. Don't assume it's good to have a talk unless it's unavoidable; your goal is to painlessly downgrade your friendship without calling attention or causing hurt.

If confronted, be truthful but not emotional. You can tell her she's right, you've put other priorities higher, and as much as you wish you could give your relationship the same time as you used to, you can't, not because you're angry or hurt but because it's unavoidable.

Keep to yourself the fact that, in this case, events are also driven by a decision for which you take responsibility, because sharing your reasons will open up an impossible discussion and cause unnecessary hurt. Just because you've made a conscious decision doesn't mean that any one person is to blame; you're ending things because you believe it's best for you both. Eventually, your former friend will call and email less, and while she may harbor some resentment, you have no reason to fear running into her, or she you.

If you keep the separation impersonal, you're rejecting the friendship, not the friend. As far as cutting someone out of your life goes, it's the safest, most sterile technique, and it leaves the smallest scar.

As pleasant as serenity feels—if you ever have the good luck to experience it—don't seek it too hard. There are so many situations in which it's a false, unrealistic, impossible goal that will give you a headache and drive you to ever-more-strenuous and prolonged efforts to still your mind and improve your spirit. Once you accept your inability to feel serene, as well as the fears, stresses, and difficult relationships that you can't escape, you'll become more effective at dealing with them and proud of how well you do it. Better to give up on peace of mind and focus on the small piece of your mind that still works.

chapter six

fuck love

Love is supposed to be the antithesis of hate and the ultimate solution to all of life's problems, so it's natural to idealize it, market it, and make finding it your life's goal. Anything that's strange, conquers all, *and* is Jesus's idea of what you should do to your neighbor as you would to yourself must truly be, well, all you need.

In actuality, love and hate aren't that dissimilar; both evoke the kind of passionate, heated, needy feelings that create more problems than they solve.

Sure, love has the potential to make you very happy, as it does when you're in love, or being loved back, or getting a lucky chance to combine love and sex. That's why it can also distract you with new worries and generate lots of yearning, unhappiness, and anger whenever something gets in its way.

Love can also push you to do things that aren't good for you and are bound to turn out badly or make you act like a wuss, a schmuck, or both. It can cause you to forget your values and ignore realities about character, bad habits, and feelings you can't change. That's why love can be one of the ultimate obstacles to being a good person and finding lasting relationships.

Again and again, you have to face the fact that someone you love can't love you back, or you can't find someone to love when that's what you want and need. Failed love almost always feels like a personal failure, so if you're a good person who hasn't found someone or can't turn a loving attraction into a good partnership, you're probably ready to ask a magazine, psychic, or even a shrink what you've done wrong.

Almost always, your lack of love isn't because of anything you've done wrong. Life is unfair and the world around you stirs up intense needs while offering false satisfactions. If you're extra careful and selective about loving and being loved, you'll probably find yourself spending more time feeling lonely.

On the other hand, if you realize that love is a risky business and can accept pain, frustration, and hard lessons as unavoidable, you can survive and learn from your losses. You need never feel ashamed of wounds acquired for a good cause, and often your wounds will ultimately help you find loving relationships that are consistent with your values and are likely to last.

Remember, the true opposite of love isn't hate; it's indifference. If you care enough to find someone who's right for you, not someone who makes you feel right, you'll truly find what you need.

Finding Someone

Most creatures choose a mate based on two factors: the ability to procreate and the possession of a pulse. Humans are obviously a lot more complicated; we screw up by putting too much weight on appearance and spark.

In fact, if you value attractiveness when looking for a good partner, you'll go on too many dates for the wrong reasons. If you're not good at screening out the beauty- and lust-struck, you'll end up wasting a lot of time. Sure, you'll have hot dates and passionate encounters, but you'll be distracted from looking for the qualities that make a good partner.

Couples bound by mutual chemistry can be blind to the fact that the relationship lacks qualities necessary for a partnership and enables red-flag behaviors that no partnership can survive. So attractiveness and chemistry may be good for generating hot affairs and cool couples, but they're also good for driving up the divorce rate.

If you're looking for a partner, look beyond attraction, figure out what qualities of character and personality you require, and be ready to ignore strong attraction if those qualities aren't there. No matter how hot the package or interpersonal sizzle, remember what you've learned about what spoils a relationship, no matter how much you are tempted.

Since you've probably read a landfill's worth of magazine articles on how to be more attractive or get the other person to like you more, and they haven't improved your own garbagey love life, it's time for a new strategy.

Learn how to define what you're looking for, focus your appeal in a way that shows your strengths, and conduct an efficient search for a partner who won't wear you out or waste your time. If you want bliss and romance, this strategy won't work. If you want a partnership that's as solid as a swan's and won't end in divorce, we can help.

Here are assets you'd like to have before you start dating, but don't:

- A body that Photoshop couldn't touch
- Access to a bar that does not admit men who watch porn on their cell phones in public, women named Amber, and anyone with an orange spray tan
- The confidence you once felt (briefly) when you fixed that hot girl's phone after she started to cry
- A procedure that takes the shame away from flirting and transfers it to your unnecessary insecurities

Among the wishes people express are:

- To get better at putting themselves out there
- To find "the one," not the next
- To change an attractive person into a responsible person
- To find a boy- or girlfriend and stop being just a friend
- To figure out why two people who are attracted can't make it work

Here are three examples:

I don't know why I have trouble meeting people. I'm willing to hang out in bars, but as an average-looking shy person, I don't get approached by too many guys. If I do, then I don't know how to flirt, so the conversations tend to be short. I'm a smart girl, I have a good job that I love, and I've got good friends who say I have lots to offer, but meeting guys, let alone cool ones who find me interesting, feels impossible. Maybe I need a makeover. My goal is to find someone, not be everyone's friend.

My friends are getting married and I can't find anyone I can see myself being with for the rest of my life. I can find girls to date, and even had a serious girlfriend for a while, but no one I could really see myself growing old with. I never really had a problem being the unattached guy, but the older I get, the more I feel like I'm being left behind. My goal is to figure out why I never click with someone or how to change my luck and find someone I really want to marry.

I get along well with women and have no trouble meeting and dating some of the coolest, most interesting women you could imagine. We have great chemistry, lots of laughs, and amazing sex, but then it always unravels the same way; they become supersensitive, tell me I make them feel unloved and ignored, and then get into a breakup/makeup cycle that drives me crazy. My goal is to figure out why I'm always attracted to the wrong woman and whether it will ever change.

You've probably read that the first step toward the right partner is to change something about yourself, be it your attitude or your waistline.

But if you get caught up in thinking about yourself, and what you can alter and why you're doomed to die alone, you'll lose sight of your goal; namely, to take stock of your strengths—i.e., the things you know you shouldn't change—and figure out what you want someone for.

If you concentrate on what you want, not wanting to be wanted, you're more likely to find someone who meets your long-term needs, wants the same things out of life, and won't get on your nerves, at least not too much.

If you're shy and relatively nonverbal, and find it hard to meet people or get them to think of you as anything other than a quiet pal, you may try the well-established route of looking for common-interest clubs and activities that help people get to know one another without having to get personal or make a lot of early eye contact.

If activities are not your style, however, use Internet dating sites to widen the field. As with a good cover letter for a job search, use a coach if necessary to create a brief, one-paragraph description of what you have to offer, and avoid the sites and apps that are focused on image. People searching for a mate based solely on looks are not the kind of people you have much use for.

Yes, most people may not be interested in responding, but you're looking for that rare person who is on your wavelength and will know it, without your having to be sociable or charming in a way that you're not. The Internet gives you the opportunity to reach those people, wherever they are, without having to waste time feeling rejected by people who like playful banter. You can find someone who is impressed enough by your basic credentials, goals, and interests to try out a conversation, someone who is checking out the fit, not the fun.

If you find yourself dating (but not wanting to commit to) women after you've experienced companionship, beach walks, and close feelings, then you're looking for a dog, not a lifelong human commitment. Instead, ask yourself what you want out of living with a partner, given your experience of families, children, roommates, and close friends. Think about needing help in a crisis, building a family, and having financial security.

Put together a job description for the person you're looking for. Then, if you decide you want a life companion, it's because you're ready to commit to what you need and you know the kind of person who might be a good fit, whether or not they make you buzz and tingle.

If you have no trouble meeting and getting attached, but always to the wrong person, remember that love is blind and just as likely to link you to a jerk as to a nice person. Once you have a good description of the person you need, learn to ignore that exciting initial burst, because, as you've learned the hard way, it inevitably leads to an infuriating crash.

Limit your dating to the kind of person who will make a good, reliable partner, not a fun, hilarious anecdote, then spend more time with the person you like best. Aim for good-enough attractiveness in a good, stable partnership candidate, not sweep-you-off-your-feet love in someone with bad credentials and a sad relationship history that you haven't checked out. Romance is fun, but background checks and compatibility are what prevent divorce.

Don't jump into a search by trying to change yourself and your basic traits and responses. Instead, use your experience to shape a search-and-interview procedure based on what you're looking for in others. That is what a good matchmaker would do.

What you put into your search is what you get out of it. If you're looking for short-term fun and excitement, then your search can be fun and exciting, but if you're looking for something long-term and serious, it's time to brace yourself not for a big makeover but for the tough job ahead.

Quick Diagnosis

Here's what you wish for and can't (always) have:

- Amazing attractiveness
- An easy time falling in love with the right person, while singing

- Access to good candidates through bars, weddings, and mutual friends
- Being most attracted to the person who is best for you
- No weakness for getting sucked into relationships with toxic people

Here's what you can aim for and actually achieve:

- Compensate for your hard-to-match nature by casting a wider net
- Use business techniques to conduct a job search
- Don't let attraction trump common sense

Here's how you can do it:

- Use special techniques and consultants for headhunting hard-to-find candidates
- Create a list of necessary qualifications
- Gather information about reliability in past relationships, money management, and drug use
- Don't violate your scoring system
- Recruit the best match, not the most attractive

Your Script

Here's what to tell someone/yourself when you can't find the right someone.

Dear [Self/Person Who Feels Love Will Lead Me to the Partner of My Dreams]:

I've tried to [dress both up and down/wear musk/lose neck fat] and still I haven't found a [date/candidate to love/not-psycho]. Instead of relying on my [insert positive quality, and you definitely have at least one, even if it's "all my original fingers"] to find me someone, I will use modern search techniques to find candidates with good [credit ratings/relationship histories/criminal background checks] and invite those interested in

partnership to talk about a possible merger. I will not let feelings of
personal rejection slow my search, and won't give up until it's done.

Did You Know . . . That Being Good Looking Can Be a Bad Thing?

At one point in most of our lives, we encounter an issue—from getting a speeding ticket to not getting a promotion—where we're certain that none of this would be happening if we were just better looking than we are. The desire to be desirable goes beyond wanting to be wanted; good-looking people can get away with anything, let alone get anyone. To not-beautiful people, it always looks like the beautiful ones have it made.

The problem, of course, is that people crave beauty the way Gollum craved the ring, so if you do happen to be beautiful, it can be creepy and unpleasant to be viewed by the world as less of a person and more of a "preeccccciouss."

Being too attractive might seem more like a blessing than a curse, but it doesn't mean you have access to the best mates; if anything, it can mean the opposite. As a beautiful, shiny object, a good-looking person attracts more than their share of Gollums; i.e., impulsive people with wobbly values who just want to be seen with (and sleep with) an attractive person.

It's a pain to keep them at bay while trying to find someone who actually wants to get to know you instead of keeping you in their grasp. Your suitors may normally date people who are very different from you in style, goals, and values, but your attractiveness persuades them, temporarily, that they want you instead. Good looks generate interest, attention, and activity—and bad matches caused by beauty-induced blindness.

If you're unfortunate enough to be both attractive and sensitive to other people's needs, you'll sympathize with their longings and feelings of rejection—and then you'll really just want to be alone.

The attractive may get out of parking tickets and into better jobs, but they also must develop the ability to ignore the yearnings of others and become tough and selective about whom they choose to interview and hang out with. So don't assume that being better looking means having the best life, because the best life wouldn't include being a magnet for some of the worst people.

Getting to Commitment

Many weddings aim to be public, romantic, and often insanely expensive demonstrations of eternal commitment based on a grand, shared love. The greater the love, the more extravagant the wedding, the louder the band, and the taller the chocolate fountain at the dessert table.

The problem with this logic is that commitment is not just the result of mutual love; true commitment isn't to a person but a cause, be that revolution, saving the whales, or a marriage. For commitment to work, both parties should be united in dedication to their shared vision of a partnership and, yes, loving the partner they've found.

If you think commitment depends primarily on love, then you won't know what to look for, in yourself or another, other than love. And love might be the key factor in committing to a pair of shoes or pizza topping, but not another human being. You'll either get a messy breakup prepartnership or, worse, a bad partnership and later an even messier divorce.

The fact is, not everyone is built for commitment. Some very nice people prefer independence, don't like to share life decisions, or don't want or need the security or family life that commitment enables. More men than women fall into this category, leaving women in the unpleasant position of playing musical chairs for potential male commitment candidates, knowing that there are not enough for everyone who deserves them.

Then there are people who, no matter how much you love them, will drag you down if you're committed to them because they can't manage their lives; they shower risk and trouble on everyone close to them, which, of course, makes them sexy and more likely to find suckers who will keep trying to make a relationship work. They may want commitment, but you don't need a crystal ball to predict the future for them and their partners.

Either way, don't try to convince yourself or your partner that committing is the right thing to do until you've reviewed the facts and your values and goals and still think it's a good deal for both parties. If that doesn't persuade your partner to take the next step, you'll know you gave it your very best try, and that she maybe wasn't the best match for you in the first place. But if you both are committed to the vision you share and working together to make it come true, then blow way too much money on jewelry. You're ready to propose.

> Here's what you wish you could find to turn love into commitment, but can't:
>
> - A way to change your feelings about family and commitment from "meh" to "gimme!"
> - A brand of beer for your beloved that both tastes great and makes the drinker a responsible adult
> - The name of the person who wrote the actual Book of Love (and his/her address, so you can hire someone to take him/her out)

Among the wishes would-be committers express are:

- To move a relationship to the next step
- To find a way, at any cost, to avoid having to break up and start over
- To get someone they love to see that commitment would be great
- To get someone they love to stop their bad habits and settle down

Here are three examples:

My boyfriend and I have been living together for two years, but when I bring up the subject of marriage, he says he's not ready or just doesn't see the point. We get along well and I'm sure he loves me, but he says we're basically married already so why spoil what we've got with a new title? Also, he doesn't see himself as a father right now, or maybe ever.

I'd really like a family and thought he'd come around when he saw how well we get along and how easy I am to live with. My goal is to get him to commit himself to marriage and the good life we could have together.

I love my boyfriend but I'm not sure I want to settle down, or want kids, or want to live in this town forever. He wants to get married, and I feel I'm just twenty-eight and I'd like to see the world and have more experience, maybe even live in another county for once in my life. We've known each other forever, started dating five years ago, and have lived together for three years, and it's all been great and progressing along, but for some reason, taking the final step and making it permanent makes me very nervous. My goal is to deal with the pressure he's putting on me.

My partner and I have been together for a long time—over ten years, at our last count—but neither one of us cares much about convention or ever starting a family, so we're happy to just keep things the way they are. We know that neither one of us is going anywhere. Our families, on the other hand, and you can add society while you're at it, seem to feel otherwise. Neither my partner nor I have led particularly conventional lives, so you'd think they'd just take our decision in stride, but no; both his parents and mine are constantly pressuring us to "do the right thing," often adding, "before we die," just to rub it in. My goal is to get people to accept that my partner and I are fine with the union we have.

Commitment is often presented as a mental, military-style obstacle course; if you can just get over the wall of anxiety, survive the electrified mud pit of personal baggage, and leap through the ice pool of faith, then you'll be ready to serve out your loving, eternal bond.

On the other hand, if you or your partner has real reservations that are making you reluctant to commit, then, like the military, you're probably charging ahead into another endless conflict.

That's why, if commitment isn't happening, it's your job to accept

the possibility that there are good reasons for not going ahead, because the best way to win a battle is to avoid it in the first place.

If you love someone and can't get him to commit, reassess whether
he's avoiding commitment because he doesn't like it, or because he's
just plain incapable of it. Some people may hold back because they're
restless and can't stand the idea of being tied down, and others may
not want the kind of life or family their would-be partner desires.
There are also people who like their pleasures, don't care for work,
and don't want to make sacrifices for someone else's dream. Even
their mothers refer to them as "winners" with dripping sarcasm.

Your job, if commitment isn't happening, is to consult a list of possible disqualifications. Gather information about past commitments,
if any; unless your candidate is relatively young, you should be able
to uncover a past-commitment story. If the story doesn't feature the
other person's problems, or a problem that is under better control
now than it was before, then keep history from repeating itself and
move on.

Don't let love, a desire to please, or an urge to prove yourself get in
the way of your doing a good, businesslike, due-diligence evaluation
of whether partnership would be in your interest, as well as whether
your would-be partner is reliable and has the necessary qualities and
values. Because if you have to talk, trick, or push someone into commitment, then you're both committing to a world of misery.

If the mixed feelings about commitment are yours, and you feel
pressured by your partner to make up your mind, don't dwell on what
she wants and how you feel about it. Instead, ask yourself what *you*
want, and whether your life goals (aside from pleasing her) would be
advanced by a partnership. Seriously consider whether you actually
want a family, common assets, and a lifelong partnership. Then determine whether your goals and your partner's match up.

Remember how you've managed commitment possibilities in the
past; whether you've just avoided them, encountered possibilities
that were bound to fall through, or had something good going and
then ran away from it. Be as realistic as possible about any of your
own negative behaviors that might interfere with partnership, and

don't assume you can change unless you've decided to try and made some progress.

If you think partnership is not right for you, of course you stand to lose a close relationship, but it's better to disappoint now than later, and it will hurt less to end things before you've taken vows you know you can't keep. Don't fault yourself or your love and respect the fact that partnership is not for everyone.

If you and your partner both prefer to be nonpermanent partners, and it's others who tell you that partnership is the only decent goal for good people, then your task is easier. In order to best manage the constant criticism, ask yourself whether there's anything about this love relationship that is bad for either one of you, and that would be mended by settling down, sharing assets, and legally promising to stay.

Examine whether your current relationship puts one of you, or people who depend on you, at a disadvantage, either now or when one of you dies. Look at future worst-case scenarios to see if noncommitment could cause harm.

Once you've looked closely at the ethical and practical meaning of noncommitment and found nothing wrong with it, don't enter into discussion or debate with friends and relatives who want to push you into marriage. You've considered their concerns, you've thought about the bad things that could happen, and you've done what you think is right. You're comfortable making it clear that no further conversation on the topic is necessary.

Instead of thinking of the commitment as a battle, see it as a business; it has to make life better for both parties, in a way they both value, using practices they both approve of, and relying on qualities of discipline and reliability they both have. If those conditions are met, they'll still be talking to each other, caring about each other, and even loving each other after they've encountered life's shit together.

In the meantime, don't make the quest for partnership a test of your love; make it a test of your intelligence and experience, despite whatever love, lust, or insanity you might be feeling. Stick to the basics of what you need and what you think makes a good partner, and the feeling that you are in basic training will vanish.

Quick Diagnosis

Here's what you wish for and can't have:

- Love being all you need to keep you together
- Certainty that, if you overcome fear and take the plunge, everything will work out
- A love so strong it can change personality problems, personality differences, and maybe the weather
- Family that is always accepting of an unconventional relationship, lifestyle, haircut, etc.

Here's what you can aim for and actually achieve:

- Be in love, and nevertheless be able to do an objective assessment of your lover's suitability for partnership and whether partnership is good for you
- Become good at avoiding love relationships with nonpartnership material
- Not feel like a failure, because finding a good partner is difficult and takes a lot of work

Here's how you can do it:

- Assess yourself and decide whether partnership is really what you want versus something you're expected to want
- List qualifications that a candidate must have to make partnership worth your while
- Describe the responsibilities and activities of the job your partner would need to take on
- Settle for nothing less than a good match

Your Script

Here's what to tell someone/yourself when you're making a commitment decision.

> *Dear [Self/Person Who Loves Me but May or May Not Want*
> *Commitment/Total Loser I Am Trying to Will into a Decent Person]:*
>
> *There's no question that our love is [true/strong/the best love that*
> *ever was in the history of all love forever], so now is the time for me to*
> *think about whether a partnership would be good for me and whether*
> *you would be a good [insert synonym for "boo"]. I've thought about*
> *whether I want [kids/life in the city/life in the country/a shared toilet*
> *and kitchen/a share of your college loan debt] and have decided it*
> *would be [good/bad] for me and you to partner up. Please give our*
> *commitment the same level of consideration, besides how much you*
> *like my [face/tush/laugh/entertainment center] and get back to me.*

True and False Tests for Commitment

True	False
Travel together in a small vehicle with no budget, A/C, or way to turn off the religious AM station.	Take a luxe vacation where you're only required to swallow your own food (someone else chews it for you, then wipes your mouth).
Stay by your spouse's side as he deals with an ailing parent.	Meet your partner's parents once at a cousin's wedding while you're all dancing to "Shout."
Get food poisoning together that involves leaking from all holes.	Put together a food order online, but let your spouse hit "send."
Counsel and support your spouse as she loses a job or starts a new, almost all-consuming career.	Get involved with coworkers because you're trapped together all day and that exact atmosphere did wonders for Anne Frank's love life.
Decide to get married because you're looking forward to starting a life together, not to having a wedding.	Insist on getting married because you want to make sure you get down the aisle before that bitch Courtney and also so your accidental miracle isn't born a bastard.

Changing for Love

For some people—particularly women; particularly women who watch too many Lifetime movies; particularly women who watch so many Lifetime movies they do things that could easily end up being the subjects of Lifetime movies—the ultimate fantasy is finding a diamond in the rough and polishing him with love and devotion.

Changing and nurturing the one you love, *Beauty and the Beast*-style, is a double love high, adding a layer of redemptive ecstasy to the natural pleasure of romancing a wounded outlaw. It gives you a feeling of power and affirms your own goodness, which is also what makes this kind of relationship attractive to certain priests and therapists, not just drama-prone ladies. In this context, sex takes on healing powers, in addition to providing physical pleasure.

Unfortunately, as time goes by and your more everyday needs establish themselves, you depend on your partner's fragile ability to stay good, responsible, and sober to protect you from being hurt, humiliated, and dumped. Relying on your love to keep a damaged person whole and well-behaved is like expecting a trained bear to stay upright; eventually, after the music ends and the circus audience leaves, the beast comes down on all fours again. A trained bear is still a bear, and a loved person with impairments is still impaired.

If you love nurturing people (and many people in professions like nursing and social work fall into this category), changing someone for the better is a measure of success. If, however, you lower your boundaries and become overattached, and your nurturee's change doesn't last, your disappointment is likely to blossom into anger that feels as unacceptable as shaking a baby.

In addition, if you want someone to be motivated to change because he loves you, but then he doesn't change, it must mean he doesn't love you enough. You're not just disappointed, you're insulted, and left wondering whether the person you love would have changed permanently for someone else whom they loved more or who loved them better. In reality, the only person with the ability to facilitate that kind of change is a wizard or an exorcist.

So as tempting as it might be, don't think of love as an instrument of improvement or redemption. Don't measure love's strength by its ability to turn a bad boy into the dream man. Ask yourself whether you can accept someone the way they are. If you can, and still love them, then congratulations; your story is not going to be dramatized on basic cable, but it is what you need for a peaceful relationship that is likely to last.

Here are some changes you wish your love could (but it cannot) make:

- Get someone to stop their drugging, drinking, or cheating ways
- Help someone who's never been a talker to share their feelings as if you were a social worker
- Show a compulsive pleaser why it's important to say no
- Get someone not to love you too much or not enough

Among the wishes people express are:

- To get someone to stop destroying their relationship, health, or job
- To get someone to see what they could accomplish if they were only more motivated, disciplined, or ambitious
- To stop someone from being a compulsive giver
- To change someone's sexual feelings

Here are three examples:

I started dating my boyfriend in high school, when he was in trouble with the police and using drugs all the time, and I got him to take care of himself and take work seriously. Now we're living together, and he works regularly, but he doesn't have any ambition and sometimes, when he gets into a funk, he binges on drugs. He adores me and tells me he would have been on the street if I hadn't rescued him, but I don't see him taking his binging seriously, wanting to get help, or doing more at work than showing up when someone gives him a job. I feel guilty about pressuring him and damaging his self-esteem, but I don't see how we can raise kids unless he's more responsible. My goal is to get him to see why he needs to take sobriety and making money more seriously.

I always admired my husband's love for his son from his first marriage; it showed me what a kind, nurturing man he is. What I didn't realize before I married him, however, is that he has a hard time saying no. Whether it's something his nine-year-old wants, or his ex gets the idea that he needs completely new sports equipment, my husband drops everything to comply. Often, he can't afford the time or the money, so indirectly it impacts my budget and our time together. My goal is to get him to see that his ultra-responsiveness to his son and ex-wife isn't good for our marriage or his son.

My wife was my best friend and dream girl when we were dating, and our relationship was the envy of our friends. After we had a kid, she went through a bad postpartum depression and gained thirty pounds, and now she spends a lot of time telling me what to do because she's anxious about everything. This isn't what I bargained for. She's seeing a therapist, so don't tell me she needs help. My goal is to figure out how to get back the woman I fell in love with.

Love can only change how we act, not who we are. It can make us blind, crazy, and happy, as well as very, very attached, but it can't reliably alter our personalities, outlook, or sense of self.

If you acknowledge love's limitations, you're not belittling love, you're being realistic about the fact that some things about character and relationships are beyond anyone's power to change. That's why you must be careful, when you have a choice, to love only what you're prepared to accept and to accept only what is healthy.

The intensity of love may feel like a kind of authenticity that gives special meaning to both the relationship and to life itself. In actuality, that intensity can bind us to relationships that harm, belittle, and drain our commitment to what we value. That's one of the major issues when love doubles as a rescue mission.

Quick Diagnosis

Here's what you wish for and can't have:

- More strength for someone (who doesn't know why they need it, except to please you)
- Discipline for someone who wants pleasure, including the feeling of being loved by you
- Better behavior from someone who has never behaved well
- Self-motivation from someone who is motivated by impulse and reaction to your feelings

Here's what you can aim for and actually achieve:

- Search longer and more selectively until you find the qualities you know are necessary
- Change people with surgery or hair dye, not love
- Expect change if someone wants it for themselves, not for you, and shows results
- Accept people as they are, without necessarily being able to live with them

Here's how you can do it:

- Never mix loving and rescuing
- Know what you need from a good love and make sure it's part of your partner's original equipment
- Always present the need for change in terms of advantages, not disappointment
- Know what you need to do, other than blame or complain, if change is impossible

Your Script

Here's what to say about romantic changes that are necessary but un-likely to occur.

Dear [Unsatisfactory but Irresistible Friend or More Significant Other],

I will never understand why you can't make the few small changes to your [character/substance habits/relationships/pants size] that would allow us to stop [fighting/living apart/going out together without knowing where it's going] but I realize you love me and that no amount of [synonym for interaction, naked or otherwise] is going to change things. I will accept you the way you are and I will not pressure you to change. Our relationship will continue with [marriage/occasional visits/occasional messages via carrier pigeon].

Enjoying Healthy Sex

Given the pleasure we get from sex, particularly if we find a partner who shares the right sexual and personal chemistry, it's hard not to regard good sex as a legitimate goal in life.

It's also hard not to put a lot of value on sex considering that, in America at least, it's everywhere; if there's near nudity in a prime-time advertisement for fast food, there should definitely be some sexy full nudity in your own home.

Many therapists believe that accepting your sexual feelings is important to mental health, and argue that there's nothing wrong with sexual pleasure between consenting adults now that birth control can prevent unwanted pregnancy and disease. They believe that if the little head is not happy, the big head will suffer.

Unfortunately, there are many things that can go wrong with sex, at least potentially, and the first is that we have so little control over it. Like the adolescent boner itself, attraction, performance, and chemistry are all random, sometimes unwanted, and often embarrassing and regrettable.

Remember, sex has tremendous influence over your identity and morality, whether you like it or not. Sexual preference, be it wrongfully stigmatized, like homosexuality, or justifiably stigmatized, like pedophilia, can put you on the social margins (or in a morally impossible position).

Strong sexual urges are impersonal and push the horny to treat other people as objects—indeed, like fast food. A strong wave of lust can sweep away concerns about the damage that may be done even if partners consent and have equally strong desires. Even if you're eager and attractive and find lots of responsive partners, you can get hooked on a super-drug pleasure that causes endless breakups and betrayals and prevents relationships from lasting. You may be envied, but you're really fucked, and not in the way you think.

If you're horny and unattractive, you feel like a perpetual loser who is always being teased, excited, and then denied. When you aren't feeling defective and envious of those who are getting some, you're angry at those who turn you on by looking attractive and who rub your nose in your frustration, and that anger makes you uglier than any facial feature could be.

Even those lucky ones who find compatible sexual partners and stable relationships are almost certain to run into problems eventually when aging, hormones, or stress affect the intensity of their sex drives. Of course, it never occurs at the same time for both partners, which is why the test of a good marriage is not sexual compatibility but what you do with sexual incompatibility when it arrives.

So yes, sex is a major cause for sin if by sin we mean moral compromise, selfishness, and broken promises, and not just an abuse of social conventions from thousands of years ago. It's hard to have strong needs, particularly ones that so directly involve other people, and still act like a good person. Sexual feelings take tons of management, and that's not just a polite way of saying masturbation.

If you're sexually frustrated, don't assume it speaks ill of your character; you may be a good person managing a time of little sexual opportunity. Likewise, if you're sexually satisfied, don't assume you've got it made, since you may have compromised more than you should or have formed a relationship that will not work out well.

If you're looking for good sex, you're looking for the wrong thing in the wrong place; "good sex" is as absurd as the idea of using sex to sell burgers.

Look instead for as much sexual satisfaction as you can find while standing by your values and, when sexual satisfaction is not possible, in remembering what's more important than sex to your self-respect. Just because sex is awesome and everywhere doesn't mean that it's actually everything.

Here are tools that sex therapists should be able to give you for a happy sex life, but can't:

- A certain look that, regardless of how long you've been stewing in silence about your partner's neglect, criticism, and disrespect, will put both of you in the mood, smiling and ready to go
- The key to exciting your partner and triggering orgasm, gleaned from years of patient study and ancient Mayan secrets, that works regardless of fatigue, tension, and medical disability
- Special cataracts that prevent you or your partner from observing wrinkles, fat, or those moles that look like cancer
- Universal, unlimited, constant child care

Among the wishes people express are:

- To figure out where their own or their partner's mojo went and get it back
- To stop wanting some kind of sexual pleasure that is bad for them or figure out why they want it
- To figure out what they or their partner is doing to kill the mojo and keep it away
- To make a partner understand that they want sexual satisfaction— before they start seeking it elsewhere

Here are three examples:

After three children and fifteen years of marriage, my sex drive has plummeted. Even though my husband is slightly older than me and has a much more stressful job, he still has the libido of a varsity high school football player, so the discrepancy has become a problem. He tried to be sympathetic to my needs (or lack thereof), but I know he's frustrated, and I do feel guilty about not being able to satisfy him or maybe making him feel unattractive or undesirable. The bottom line, however, is that I'm not feeling it, for him or anyone else, period. My goal is to figure out how to get myself into the mood somehow or get my husband out of it.

I feel bad about the fact that I'm not nearly as attracted to the guy I'm going to marry as I was to my former boyfriend. He was a jerk and our relationship was a train wreck, but I couldn't get enough of him. My fiancé is a nice guy and I really respect him, but he's not as attractive and the sex is nothing special. I wonder if I should be marrying someone I'm not more attracted to, and whether it's fair to him. My goal is to feel more attracted or more sure about my choice of a partner.

I'm a nice guy. I take care of myself and make an effort to look good, and I'm polite to girls and try to treat them right. But I can't get any of the girls I meet, at school or at clubs, to give me the time of day. It pisses me off, because they always go home with total assholes, and won't even give me a chance because I'm not super tall or a male model or something. I just want to shake these bitches and ask what's wrong with them that they'll fuck losers but not nice guys like me. My goal is to get girls to see that I'm a good guy, or at least good enough to sleep with.

Since sex is seen as one of life's natural functions, like sleeping or shitting, people often think there's something wrong with them if they can't feel desirable or attract sex. If they can just find the right makeover, guru, or carb-based diet to make them realize how beautiful they are, they will swell with confidence and finally be desired.

The problem, of course, is that sex doesn't come as naturally to some people as those other natural functions do (not that sleeping and shitting come easily to everyone, either, or there'd be no such thing as laxative yogurt or the Ambien empire).

In real life, many people can't be helped by a makeover, nothing makes them feel attractive, and their sexual feelings don't jibe with the sexual opportunities they have. It shouldn't be too much for them to expect to have sex, let alone happy sex or consistent sex, but it's just not in the cards, and making a good sex life a goal just turns frustration into personal failure.

Over a long marriage, it's not unusual for one person's sex drive to fade far below a partner's, and treatment doesn't necessarily provide a remedy. It's certainly worthwhile to check out possibly curable medical ailments, like thyroid deficiency, and sex therapy can help you overcome the sexual inhibition and discouragement that often follow poor performance. Even after all that, however, a fundamental difference in levels of desire may still remain.

If that's the case after a reasonably thorough medical and mental health exam, don't look too hard for further explanations or solutions, or you'll exacerbate feelings of failure and frustration. Accept that such changes occur and answers don't always exist.

It doesn't mean your feelings for each other are less sincere or matter less or that your relationship is weaker. It just means that sex will require good-hearted negotiation and a willingness to do what seems best. It might not feel as great as it used to, but if marital peace is at stake, then lying back and thinking of England seems like a worthy sacrifice.

Discuss sex as a potentially positive force for maintaining a relationship, even when one person enjoys it more than the other. Seek agreement on the benefit of having sex, unless it's painful. If you're no longer interested, take credit in the giving of a gift. If you're in the mood and miss being able to excite your partner, take pride in the gift you've been given.

It's also not unusual to feel strong sexual feelings for someone who may not be good for you, and less than intense feelings for someone who definitely is. Obviously, if you put more emphasis on your sexual needs than your assessment of someone's character, strengths, and reliability, you're asking for trouble (and maybe orgasms, but mostly trouble).

Yes, there may be a guilty, accusatory voice in your head that wants hot sex and feels guilty for finding your nice-guy boyfriend not as hot as a bad boy. Remember, however, you're the one who decides on the qualifications you require from a partner, and some level of attractiveness is a necessity.

Don't compare him to Mr. Sexy. Measure him against all the qualifications *you* see as necessary. Then do what's best for you, because that's your job. The problem with the Mr. Sexys out there is that they rarely double as Mr. Decent Partner, or, sometimes, even as Mr. Decent Human Being. Congratulate yourself for choosing a gentleman over a jerk, even if you sacrifice a degree of sexual pleasure.

Sometimes frustrated sex is as dangerous as fulfilled sex, particularly for men who experience sex as a hunger that women have the power to excite and then refuse to satisfy. In reality, women are not responsible for your male sexual chemistry or frustration, so treating them as if they *are* responsible and *owe* you some satisfaction is a good way of turning yourself into an overbearing jerk in the grip of sexual road rage.

As noted in the beginning of this section, humans are not objects, so women are not food; you might feel hungry for them, but they did not necessarily sign up to be your meal. They can, in fact, make their own choices, and they don't owe you anything. To further explore the fast-food-for-sex metaphor, they are not Burger Kings; you cannot have it your way.

Your goal in such situations is not to get sexist or angry, let alone get laid, because that won't improve your attitude for very long, and it certainly won't improve your standing with the opposite sex. Your goal is to accept that sexual opportunity isn't something owed. It's like luck. It just happens, like the weather.

Unfortunately, sometimes your luck is bad, and sexual hunger is hard to bear. In that case, get a therapist or coach to help you keep the negative thoughts under control and respect yourself for doing it with dignity.

Whether or not you're happy with your sex life, sexual hunger and the need to feel attractive create endless moral dilemmas and the potential for fatefully wrong partnership choices. Never give priority to satisfying your sexual needs before thinking through what you actually control and what you believe is good for you.

Then, when you get laid, you'll feel comfortable with yourself and your choices the next morning (since you're also totally regular and had a great night's sleep).

Quick Diagnosis

Here's what you wish for and can't have:

- Reliably great, mutual, satisfying, earth-moving whatevers
- The secure knowledge that it is always as good for them as it is for you
- A consistent answer to the call of the wild that you can count on

Here's what you can aim for and actually achieve:

- An ability to turn down sex when you know it will hurt someone, including yourself
- An ability to think ahead and remember the past when there's nothing but sex on your mind
- Values that put little merit on attractiveness and sexual success
- Respect that is unaffected by sexual nonperformance or frustration

Here's how you can do it:

- Learn to spot real vulnerability (yours and/or hers) to possible damage caused by so-called casual hookups

- Avoid sex if it endangers your heart
- Draw on your past love/sex experience to list essential personal qualities and run-the-other-way red flags for candidates
- Make sure partners score a ten for character before you let their sex-appeal rating take over
- Take your time before jumping into bed, marriage, a nightmare, etc.
- List your standards of personal conduct and review whether you've lived up to them

Your Script

Here's what to say about sexual opportunity and desire.

Dear [Self/Possible Partner],

I feel more confident and alive when I have [eye contact/conversation/ sexy naked times] with someone [antonym for Next-Level-Disgusting] who's attracted to me, but unfortunately, when I get involved with such a person, my [brain turns off/clothes fly off/life goes off the rails]. I will prepare for this state of brainlessness by [studying sexual ethics/ avoiding STDs/conducting FBI-level background checks]. If I can't get sex, I get [irritable/suicidal/the shakes] but I will try to take [cold showers/many breaks to jerk off/an inventory of my life and find other things that are at least as important]. If I don't feel like sex, I feel [irritable/ugly/freakish], but I know I have the power to give sexual pleasure when it matters.

Hurtful vs. Harmless Ways to Tell Your Partner You'd Rather Not

Ouch	Okay
I have a headache. No, seriously.	I love you, too, but let's find another time when I'm not so tired.
Really? Didn't we just do this, like, in the current fiscal year?	I'm flattered that you're attracted, but I don't recover my sexual energy as quickly as you do.
Very funny. Get off me.	I wish I felt as interested in sex as you do right now. I just need some rest and a little more time.

Ouch	Okay
Maybe. If you showered first. And did something about your eyebrows.	Why don't we just shower together? If you let me wash the stink off you, I'll let you polish my boobs. But that's it; I'm exhausted.
Maybe you could just wait until I'm asleep so I won't notice?	Let's go ahead, but I enjoy it because I feel close to you, orgasm or no.

Salvaging Lost Love

When love fails after seeming to get off to a good start, you feel like you've entered an evil, alternate dimension, and if you could only get back to where you were before someone meddled with space and time, you could get your relationship back, or at least keep things from turning ugly.

Maybe most people have a less nerdy take on the situation, but the urge to reset a relationship gone wrong is universal.

After all, if you felt wonderful before, you should be able to feel great again. The two of you just need communication, understanding, and maybe some sessions with a couples therapist and a trip somewhere warm with massage tables. Unfortunately, there are reasons that later-stage love goes sour that you can't undo, even with a four-star resort or a time machine, and many of them are foreseeable from the beginning.

For example, love doesn't usually survive a poor work ethic unless the person doing more than their share is unusually needy or unable to recognize the value of their own contribution. Love doesn't tend to last when the lazy partner is an addict, self-involved, or unable to understand the needs of others.

If you have the chance to do a dirty job with someone before deciding to date—helping her move, nursing her through a flu, going with her on a trip to a no-star motel after twenty hours of driving—you might well spot this later-stage marriage land mine before triggering it. With simple detective work, you can also tell who is likely to fall out of love with you because that's what she's done with previous partners.

If it's too late now, and your love is doomed by something about your partner's character or values that isn't going to change, trying too hard to salvage it can make you forget your own strengths and what you stand for. Failing to accept broken love is what makes failure personal and interminable, rather than just a natural and painful mistake.

Do your best to hold on to love, but when you know you've done your best to save it and it's not working, do what's necessary and let go. Ask yourself whether the problem is bigger than you are, and whether solving it is within your power. If it isn't, the best way to restore love to your life is to clear the relationship and reset your schedule. Then figure out what went wrong, and apply your wisdom to doing better next time, but in Akron, not Acapulco.

Here's what you'd like to find to save your love, but can't:

- What you did wrong, so you can confess, repent, and never do it again
- Loving words, maybe from a song or poem, that will go well with flowers and begging
- A couples therapist who can get you to see the other person's point of view, and vice versa, without triggering the usual fight
- A love potion and a nonlove potion, to be taken as needed by whomever you prescribe it to, including yourself

Among the wishes people with breaking relationships express are:

- To find a way to feel the same, or make the other person feel the same, as before
- To figure out why they were so stupid
- To get the other person to see what they have and why it's worth saving
- To get the other person to see what they don't have and why it's worth walking away

Here are three examples:

I think my ex-girlfriend was sexually abused, and needed to know that she could trust me. I was very gentle with her, and I never loved anyone the way I loved her. What I can't understand is why we were very close one day, and the next day she stopped talking to me and said we needed to take a break. I spend all my time trying to figure her out, and how I can get her to see how much I love her. Obviously, she needs more reassurance, but I don't know how to do it. My goal is to understand how to make her feel loved and win her back.

I always had a good relationship with my husband, so it destroyed me when I found messages on his cell phone and discovered he was having an affair. He was very remorseful and says there was no issue, but that just makes me more mistrustful. I don't think I can trust him again until I know why he did it. My goal is for us to get to the root of the problem.

When I broke up with my ex-boyfriend three months ago after a year of dating, I tried to be very clear, but not unkind; we had a good time together, but I didn't see a future for us, so I wanted to move on. He was devastated and tried to convince me I was wrong for a few days, but I held firm, and he finally seemed to get it. The problem is that he now wants to "be friends," but it turns out his definition of being friends is a lot like dating. He calls me all the time, keeps trying to make plans, and as guilty as I feel about saying no, I feel guiltier about saying yes because I'm just leading him on. My goal is to get my ex to understand that it's over without having to really hurt him.

Because relationships can have a competitive element (e.g., who will win control of the TV, the right not to take out the garbage, custody of the kids, etc.), they're often compared to sports, particularly baseball. That might work when you're comparing sex to home base and rejection to striking out, but overall, the metaphor doesn't totally work.

That's because in baseball, when a team loses, there's always the next game, and when the season's over, there's always next year. Hope springs eternal in America's pastime.

On the other hand, when a relationship is in big trouble and not getting better—as in, all strategies have been tried and Hail Marys have failed—then there is no hope. You can't improve or have a re-match the next day; you can only accept things as they are and decide what to do.

Of course, it's human nature for you or your partner to keep try-ing, and propose one more talk, therapy session, or set of rules for ending hostilities or solving an issue that isn't going to go away. Yogi Berra would agree that it ain't over till it's over, but don't pretend it's not over when it is.

If you want a chance to get back into the game with this or another franchise, however, you owe it to yourself to stop the bleeding, figure out exactly what went wrong, and either accept the team you have or start over. Obsessing or ruminating over what you should have done is a waste of time; learn from your mistakes and move on.

Some people's love has a limited use-by date (see: borderlines side-bar on page 213) and when trust is gone, the relationship is over, even though, as far as you can see, you did nothing wrong.

When she first loves you, she's crazy about you because you're bet-ter than all those prior lovers who always let her down, but when she sees you're not the messiah, then she's crazy with disappointment, or just crazy, period. Any anger, incomprehension, or protest you ex-press is further proof you can't be trusted.

Look into your ex-partner's past, and you'll discover similar trust swings. The first swing may well have been triggered by actual sexual abuse, but later swings, you'll discover, involved lovers who were not abusive, but your partner experienced them as if they were. So you're fucked, but you're not alone.

While your heart is mending, learn to spot the warning signs so you won't make the same mistake twice: e.g., intense intimacy right off the bat, a feeling of being a savior, if not The Savior, super sex (no offense to the Savior), and a string of evil past lovers. As we've said before, if a relationship begins with sudden or near-baseless feelings of love, don't be shocked if it ends with sudden or near-baseless feel-ings of mistrust.

More complex is the problem caused by a partner—usually a guy—who loves you but is also impulsively responsive to exciting, shiny new relationships and endless sexts from someone-not-you. If you're a nice, humble person, you may wonder what you did wrong, or whether there was a problem that you failed to perceive.

You will wish, very strongly, that you or a therapist could fish out an issue from your partner's past or present involving hidden anger or unconscious needs that, once expressed and shouted or cried over, would never cause infidelity again. Unless your therapist is a genie, that wish will be in vain.

The good news is that your partner probably loves you as much as ever. The bad news is that the tendency toward infidelity, like one toward addiction, is not curable, and that's what a good therapist will tell you.

Decide for yourself whether you can accept your partner's having this kind of weakness and whether he recognizes having it and seems determined to do better at controlling it in the future. If he pleads and says it will never happen again, his thinking is as wishful/bullshitty as yours. If he says it's hard to resist, but he's going to join a twelve-step group to help him stay away from trouble, he might actually succeed.

What's most important is not to take the problem personally or try to solve it once and for all. Once the anger has started to fade, decide whether your partnership—which you now know is higher risk than you thought—is worth continuing. You can salvage it if you wish, but what you're salvaging is not what you thought you had in the first place.

Sometimes, of course, you're the one who falls out of love, which is particularly likely to happen as you get to know someone who is not nearly as good at doing his share as he first seemed. That's why the getting-to-know-you phase of a relationship is important and carries risks of heartbreak for both sides.

Your job isn't to feel guilty for dumping someone and then to stick around to feel her pain, particularly when you began a relationship honestly believing it could work out. Review your conduct to see if you did right, given how you felt at the time. If you were honest and had good intentions, the pain of a breakup can't be helped and shouldn't be your responsibility.

Don't try to "friend" your ex into feeling better, particularly when you see it prolongs their need to hold on to the old relationship. Say good-bye, putting your own judgment ahead of what your ex says is best and effectively putting her out of her misery. The difference in your perceptions is one of the main reasons you couldn't continue the relationship and decided to move on.

Don't try to salvage relationships if it doesn't seem possible or desirable. As much pain as it may cause you or your partner, accept what you've got and learn from it. Then you'll be much more likely to do better next time and find a love that doesn't need to be salvaged because it had a better foundation from the beginning. You might need a rebuilding year or two before you win it all, but it's the losing seasons that make victory possible.

Quick Diagnosis

Here's what you wish for and can't have:

- To avoid heartbreak for you or your partner
- To keep a good thing going or get it going again
- To not feel responsible for heartbreak
- To take all the responsibility for mending the break

Here's what you can aim for and actually achieve:

- Not be a schmuck, even though you're hurting and it's probably unfair
- Do all the right things to communicate, figure out if you did anything wrong, make amends, and improve what you can (until you can't)
- Accept it when you've run out of things you can try
- Decide what's best to do with the pieces
- Spot the flaws sooner next time (assuming they could have been seen in the first place)

Here's how you can do it:

- Shut up about your negative feelings and be patient, attentive, and understanding, even if you're hurt, angry, and misunderstood
- Ask for ideas from friends, family, and, last resort (as they're expensive), shrinks
- List what you can do to improve the relationship, then go down your list and force yourself to stop if your list is complete and things aren't better
- Be judgmental—i.e., judge whose weaknesses are responsible for the breakdown—not in order to blame, but to decide what you can do
- Ask yourself what you want to do about this relationship if it is what it is
- Look for some way to improve your selection process next time, even if it means being alone for a long time.

Your Script

Here's what to say when you're faced with a relationship that's ending.

Dear [Self/Unhappy-with-Relationship Partner],

I don't want to [give up on/destroy/endure another painful second of] our relationship, but I've tried [expressing my feelings/shutting up about my feelings/making all the effort] and things aren't changing. I will finally accept that we can't change this relationship [in five minutes/with all the therapy-speak that ever was/if we're arrested again] and decide whether we'll live [together/apart/with one of us in witness protection]. Even if it can't help me change this [synonym for shitshow], there may be a lesson here about what I need to make love work, and if there is, I will learn it.

Did You Know . . . What A "Borderline" Is?

"Borderline" might sound like a ye olde Madonna reference, but it's also shorthand for a psychiatric term, "borderline personality disorder." These are the people, usually women, who lonely, crazy-prone single guys often find irresistible.

The term was originated to identify people who seem to be at the borderline of psychosis. The condition is something of a first cousin to bipolar disorder in that both disorders entail wild mood fluctuations and intense feelings. While a bipolar's mood cycle can take weeks, however, a borderline's moods/feelings about you can move at the speed of light.

Borderline people quickly tear through friendships, careers, sex partners, and, more often than not, drinks and drugs. They see rejection everywhere, react before they can stop and think, and can't tell the difference between feeling hurt and actually being mistreated.

Their dates (and friends and family) are always walking on eggshells, which makes sense when you're dealing with someone who treats each thought and feeling as empirical truth; i.e., "I am attracted to that guy" quickly becomes "that guy is the best thing to ever happen to me and I must get his baby in me ASAP." She is incapable of doubting her instincts, but she makes up for it by constantly doubting the motives of everyone around her.

Borderlines always get dates because most men are biologically drawn to very emotional women, even when they're not being sexy. The initial excitement borderlines provide can be attractive, sure, but they cast a kind of spell—the intoxication of intense, mutual attraction—that makes you blind to the fact that the fun girl you met in the bar is not so fun anymore. You can't see how the girl who decided after ten minutes of chitchat to have sex with you in an alley is not actually just "fun," but somewhat *insane*, even as she tries to burn your house down because she *knows* you don't think she's as pretty as that girl at the drive-through at Taco Bell.

By the time you do finally figure it out, you may be so addicted to the excitement of starring as both hero and villain in her crazy drama that you ignore the warning signs in the next girl. Crazy becomes your new normal. Borderlines are addictively exciting, and it's hard to say no to a girl who'll jump your bones in a bathroom stall, or accept a dare to flash a cop, or drink you under the table. At least until she kills your dog.

So, men, if you're drawn to exciting women but can't understand why they always freak out on you, this is probably why. You might want to consider dating women who are more boring, or at least own some life insurance. In short, a borderline is many things, but she is most often known as the reason men think all women are nuts (aside from the ones that actually are).

Love and hate may feel like opposites, but they're equally huge challenges to your being a good person who makes smart choices. Love can push you to ignore your own needs, get attached to the wrong person for the wrong reason, and feel like a loser simply because you're loveless. Working hard at managing love doesn't mean becoming supremely unselfish and generous in a totally unconditional, nonjudgmental way; it means becoming very judgmental about what you can expect from people and yourself and putting conditions on whom you allow yourself to get close to, love be damned. You can manage love successfully, but it requires lots of learning from painful experience and a willingness to do without until both your heart and your head agree that the right thing has come along.

chapter seven

fuck communication

Even though it's incredibly easy to communicate almost anything to anyone—via text, bumper sticker, or middle finger—most people wish they could communicate better. Turns out it's much easier to tell someone via your shirt that you got naked in Miami Beach than to use words to explain why you're frustrated in your marriage.

Many people believe communication is the key to encouraging intimacy, straightening out misunderstandings, ending conflicts, and basically achieving everything short of cold fusion. They think that if you want a better relationship, job, or life, then you need to communicate better; that's why people go to college to major in it and see shrinks or business consultants when they feel they can't do it.

Unfortunately, however, many problems do not, in actuality, represent a failure to communicate. Rather, they arise from differences in character, culture, or values, and communicating these differences is a bad way to bridge gaps and a good way to cause disagreements. If you're doing a good job of being diplomatically persuasive and still find you're getting nowhere, then you may not need to become a better communicator; you may need to find something better to talk about.

If you can't get through to someone, take time to figure out why communication isn't working, because maybe it just can't and, more important, really shouldn't. Communicating may do more harm than good when what you're trying to communicate is perhaps best not shared in the first place. In the end, knowing that your communication abilities are limited is essential if you are to know when to shut up, leave things alone, and console yourself that you're not responsible for whatever happens next.

The potential for communication may seem infinite, but if you find yourself incapable of communicating something more complicated than what can be expressed via a text or tweet, then you may have to accept that sometimes, communication is not possible. Even then, it's not the end of the world, just the end of that particular conversation.

Nurturing Closeness

Any relationship guru worth his or her Internet certification will tell you that you cannot have love without communication. In some ways, that's true; opening up to a new partner is a big part of falling for them, and so much importance is attached to communicating the words "I love you" that you'd think somebody was getting royalties.

Communication may be a key part of a relationship, but that doesn't make it a cure-all. Sure, being shut out of someone's feelings or thoughts can feel like you're no longer close or important to them. That leads to trying to fix the situation by talking . . . about why you don't talk anymore. Which can often lead to yelling about how annoyed you both are.

Then you find yourself going to a couples therapist, so that one person can find out why the other person isn't close and at least feel closer by hearing her share with the therapist what she won't say otherwise. The problem is that most of that stuff went unsaid because it was unpleasant, mean, or unconstructive enough that it never should have been said out loud.

So while communication is important, you can have too much of it. Cheese is the main building block of pizza, but if you push the balance too far, you'll either ruin the pie or destroy your health.

If you try to fix a broken relationship with communication—stuff the crust with it, as it were—you may just do more damage, especially if you're in a relationship with someone who isn't much of a talker, is poor at describing his feelings, or has those fun feelings that are best left unexpressed.

Closeness also cannot be forced, particularly when people are familiar with one another. A couple may feel close without being able to talk to each other, or may never be able to feel close in spite of lots of talk, but short of cramming themselves into a small space, they can't will closeness into being.

So accept the fact that there's much about communication and closeness that you can't and don't control and don't rate the success of your relationship by how you're performing in those areas.

Then be proud of your ability to make the most of a relationship, and accept its limits, even when they prevent you from feeling close or sharing what you're thinking and feeling, whether it's love, hate, or anything in between.

Here are communication tools you wish could make your relationships closer, but don't:

- A translator you can hire to turn your words into the language of your listener, carrying your meaning but leaving out the irritated, insulting bits
- Charisma that makes someone trust you and want to talk with you, even after you've lived together and shared the same sink and toilet for five years
- An answer to the question "Why can't we just get along?"
- A human shock-collar that monitors what you're saying and shocks you whenever you should just be blandly agreeable or silent

Among the wishes people express are:

- To get through a wall of silence
- To open up oneself or others
- To find words for reducing loneliness or conflict
- To create trust and teamwork
- To say what will make others happy

Here are three examples:

My wife says I never talk to her, but I'm just not a big talker, period. I like to talk about sports and business, I guess, but they aren't her interests, and I don't know much about most of her interests, so when she talks about them, I don't have anything to say. She says I keep things in, and that I'm not interested in what she has to say about important things, like her friends and the kids. It leaves her feeling alone and resentful, so she never feels like having sex. My goal is to figure out a way to communicate better so she'll feel closer and our marriage, and sex life, will get back on track.

My son and I have always been close, particularly since he was four and his father divorced me and went to live in another city. He loved to tell me everything that was going on and spend time together, until suddenly, a few months ago, he clammed up. He's a good kid, still doing well in school, and I've got no problems with his friends, but he has stopped confiding in me; he answers every question with a one-syllable response and spends most of his time in his room. When pressed, he says there's nothing wrong and that I'm being too sensitive, but I think he's going through puberty and doesn't want to talk to me because I'm his mother. I know if I push him I'll make it worse, but I guess I just miss what we had. My goal is not to lose the wonderful closeness we've had as mother and son.

I think I'm a good boss and like to run a happy office, but the five people who work for me just don't seem to enjoy one another's company. They're all competent and hardworking and seem to like what they do here, and there's not a lot of conflict, but there's also very little team

spirit, which can create a really strange and unpleasant office environment. I'm thinking of hiring a psychologist who will put them through
a ropes course or something that gets them to loosen up and get to
know one another. My goal is to create some closeness and better communication.

Sharing thoughts and feelings with someone is always a delicate
business; you have to be comfortable enough with a person in order
to be honest and open, but you also have to know that person well
enough to judge when it's time to shut your mouth and listen instead.

For some couples, the perfect amount of communication is the occasional grunt or sigh in front of the TV, while others enjoy a full
monologue detailing the minutiae of an appetizer. Everybody's needs
are different, and as with hair color or sexual preference, one's ability
to share and tolerance for listening are solid parts of who we are.

If despite the complications, you can achieve that communicative
balance, it should feel good and satisfy your need for companionship
and contact. If you can't, or just can't anymore, it will feel like a problem in need of fixing, and trying to fix any problem that involves uncontrollable, quasi-genetic factors is like embarking on a conflict in
the Middle East: endless, bloody, and ultimately futile.

Regardless of how good it would feel to be able to communicate, or
how bad it feels not to, don't try to force communication until you've
assessed whether it's possible and if not, why not.

If someone wants you to open up and you're not a talker, don't assume that talking is the only way to express affection or commitment.
Lots of people—mainly men—express positive feelings by showing
up and fixing the sink or roof. For many men, their primary means of
communication is not their voice but their feet and power drill.

It's useless to start believing you should be more of a talker when
you're not, because you'll just get more depressed and irritable as you
feel increasingly responsible for your talk-deprived partner's unhappiness. Yes, you might benefit from good Mars/Venus advice from
a therapist, but at a certain point, if your quiet friendliness isn't

enough, you must ask yourself whether you're being a good enough partner, after your own fashion.

Your partner must have known you weren't a talker, given your history of near chatlessness, so if she thought she could change you, that's her problem, not yours. Instead of apologizing or getting defensive, remind her of the good things you bring to your relationship, other than chattiness. Tell her she can take it or leave it, but you hope she'll take it, and then don't worry about telling her too much else.

It can be even more frustrating to endure silence in a longstanding, close relationship with your child when you not only miss the intimacy but rely on it to feel you're doing a good job as a parent. When your child clams up, you have less information to tell you whether he is happy, in trouble, or doing the right thing. Of course, prying just makes the information blackout worse and induces enmity and defiance that may not have been there in the first place.

Instead of getting spooked by the loss of closeness, assume that it may be resulting from normal growth and development and a teenager's need for privacy. Now that easy communication no longer tells you how things are going, gather information from teachers and your own careful observations of schedules, homework, and friendships. With a little work, you'll determine whether things are still going well, or whether silence represents depression or school problems.

In any case, don't get discouraged by the loss of closeness or believe that you're a bad parent when your child gets quieter. Indeed, it takes a particularly good parent to stay on task and manage your child's growth while ignoring and hiding how sad you feel without the old intimacy.

You may not expect to have the same level of comfort and intimacy in the workplace that you have at home, but team spirit among employees also seems desirable and likely to improve morale and profit. In spite of what the business journals and consultants say, however, the problems with team building are often not remediable.

Some people do their job well but are not much fun to have on a team, and some bosses are Assholes (see chapter 9), but they're the boss and aren't going anywhere. If you like and enjoy the company of your coworkers, you're lucky; if you don't, cash your paycheck and make friends in a bowling league.

Before closing your office and blowing a bundle on a team-building retreat and spa weekend, ask yourself how people are likely to respond if they start saying what they really think. Don't accept reassurance from HR or a presiding psychologist—they don't have magical protective powers—just rely on your experience and common sense.

You may look like a great manager if your team whistles while they work, but you're an even greater manager if they're not whistlers and still show up on time and get the work done.

Although talking may help you get close, it isn't the only way to get close, and it can't be used to create intimacy that isn't already there. Before trying to improve communication, ask yourself whether more closeness is possible and whether talking will actually help.

Remember, good communication doesn't produce miracles of intimacy and good will; it respects limits, avoids trouble, and keeps a fragile peace.

Quick Diagnosis

Here's what you wish for and can't (always) have:

- Feel closer to someone you love
- Know better what someone is really thinking
- Hear the words you need to hear
- Feel free to speak your mind

Here's what you can aim for and actually achieve:

- Know the limits of speech and intimacy in any relationship
- Not force anyone to be more verbal than they are
- Shut up when silence is best
- Not put additional strain on a relationship characterized by limited communication

Here's how you can do it:

- Rate a person's ability to communicate feelings objectively, before you start taking it personally
- Expand your own ability to read and send out nonverbal messages
- Learn to measure commitment and achievement through actions, not words
- Assess your ability to tolerate silence without becoming negative
- Think about what happened the last time you expressed your feelings before you do it again

Your Script

Here's what to tell someone/yourself when you can't find words that will bring you closer.

> *Dear [Self/Person Whom I Can't Communicate With/Yes, You—Are You Even Listening to Me?],*
>
> *Given the need for us to [live/work/do homework/get naked/raise kids] together, I wish we could communicate better. I know, however, that you never talk about [feelings/relationships/sex/my friend Janet/ America's foreign policy], so there's no reason for me to think I'm doing something wrong. I have also noticed that forcing you to talk often causes [synonym for "not talking"]. I will accept whatever prevents us from talking and respect what we're able to accomplish anyway.*

Communication No-Nos, Explained

Never Say	Why Not?
"If you go through with this, you're a fucking idiot, you know that?"	He's only an idiot if he acts on his dumb impulse; you, on the other hand, are unconditionally an idiot for insulting and alienating someone you were trying to help. Never anchor an attempt to be helpful with hurtful words.

Never Say	Why Not?
"It's either me or your family, make your choice and make it final."	This would be true only if the not-chosen party was subsequently murdered; otherwise, you're making the choice to enter a world of sulking and resentment. Ultimatums work only on game shows.
"Okay, somebody's gotta say it, so here goes . . ."	Actually, it's very likely that nobody has to say "it," ever. Not unless that somebody is willing to burn his bridges and then salt the earth where they stood. "Somebody" should stay silent instead.
"If you don't talk about the pain, it will eat you up inside."	Her suffering might eat you up inside, but that doesn't mean talking about it is best for her. Offering support and urging confessions aren't exactly the same thing.
"You're right, that dress does make you look pregnant."	You can't even tell a pregnant woman she looks pregnant, so if you really want to tell someone how bad she looks in a dress, be prepared to hear how you look like a pullout sofa in that pantsuit.

Airing Trauma

Enduring the effects of trauma is extremely difficult, but it is almost as difficult to have to watch someone you care about suffering through trauma's aftermath. As he thrashes through nightmares, anxiously paces through his days, and struggles with negative thoughts, those close to him can only do their best and bear witness. The traumatized are haunted by past events, while in the present, their loved ones now feel as useless as ghosts.

Intuitively, one might feel that sharing fears and nightmares would provide some relief—expose the real ghosts to daylight and they should disappear—but the symptoms of trauma are often hard to soothe, and the memories that cause them don't vanish so easily.

Trauma probably has such lasting effects because our brains adapt to overwhelming stress by turning us into super-alert, always-on-guard soldiers, so that we won't be taken by surprise a second time. The symptoms are a torment, but they also save the lives of those who can't leave a dangerous war zone. Unfortunately, for many people, there's no off switch once the war is over.

That's why just sharing intense feelings does not necessarily purge them, no matter what movies and books tell you. Often, it leaves people feeling more shaken and helpless than before, even when friends or therapists are there to offer support. So don't push someone who has been traumatized to tell their story until you're sure they can do so without feeling overwhelmed and that it's more likely to do good than harm.

In the end, there may be no way to get certain kinds of trauma off your chest, be it by sharing, deep hypnosis, or textbook revenge scenarios. Certain treatments may help reduce symptoms and other treatments may help you live with them, but there is no literal or figurative sure-thing trauma eraser.

If you suffer from trauma and symptoms persist, never assume it's because you failed to open up or that you need to open up more. Credit your nervous system with having a very active emergency alarm while discounting the negative, dreadful warnings and dire predictions it puts in your mind. Respect your ability to disregard those warnings, predictions, and symptoms while you go about whatever business matters to you when you're not coping with emergencies.

You may never be able to turn the system off, either by sharing or coaxing someone else to share what the trauma feels like. You can learn, however, to listen to your own needs, interests, and priorities, either in spite of the anxiety you now have to experience or the pain you have to witness.

Here's what you wish you could find to stop feeling haunted by trauma:

- Earplugs, but for your thoughts
- A white noise machine that induces night-long comas
- A therapy that makes you feel so safe, it's like a mental airbag
- A visit from Mr. Rogers (though the fact that he's dead would make that traumatic)

Among the wishes trauma survivors express are:

- To sleep before insomnia drives them crazy
- To recover from pain an enemy has inflicted on them
- To feel better so they don't have to drink
- To not frighten their families with their unhappiness and silence

Here are three examples:

I've dealt with depression since junior high—I used to cut myself when I was a teenager, and had to be hospitalized for a while in college—but therapy and medication have helped me to live a relatively normal, happy life. My husband knows about my history, but until a couple of years ago, I didn't tell him that one major source of trauma was being molested by my stepfather when I was a kid. He was very supportive until a year ago, when I went through a bad six-months-long depression, and he started to nag me about how I obviously needed more, intensive therapy, because I clearly hadn't really faced my old demons. I needed to get over a nasty depression, is all, and I resented the idea that he was blaming me for avoiding issues and treatment. He won't let it go. My goal is to get him to accept that I don't need to talk it over with someone right now, or maybe ever again.

My husband hasn't been the same since he got back from his last tour of duty in Afghanistan, but he won't talk about it. He has nightmares, he's depressed, and he's very jumpy when we're around crowds. He says he knows he probably has PTSD, but he talks about it with a couple close friends he served with who go to therapy, and he thinks that helps probably as much as anything else since nothing really seems to work for the guys he knows. I just think he doesn't want to deal with the stigma, wait to see a shrink, or start taking a lot of drugs, which is how the VA seems to handle the problem. In the meantime, he's just suffering, and I know he'd feel better if he could talk about it. I try to get him to open up with me, especially during episodes, but he gets irritated when I push him and then completely shuts down. My goal is to see him talk things out with a professional and get some relief.

My teenage son has never found school easy, but he was a pretty happy kid until a year ago, when he started hanging out with some bad kids and coming home drunk and stoned. He's irritable and unhappy most of the time and gets really angry if my wife and I confront him or just ask if something's wrong. He's just not the same, but we can't get him to talk about what's bothering him or go see a shrink, so we feel helpless and say nothing until we're ready to explode, which we know will do no good. My goal is to figure out how to get him to talk about what's really bothering him, either with me or a shrink, so he can start to get better.

Don't trust the instinct that tells you that the worse the problem, the more talk it needs; sometimes talk is healing, but a lot of the time it has the opposite effect, picking scabs off psychic wounds that would've been best left untouched.

People recover from trauma in their own ways, and while talking may be the best way for you, it may leave the other person raw. Worse, it may leave them infected, so that their trauma now envelops and defines them, making normal life even more difficult.

Instead, use your experience and common sense to examine whether important issues have been talked out, if the effect was positive or negative, and if more words are really what's needed. Then you'll know when enough is enough, and further exploration of feelings is likely to be useless, costly, or actually make things worse. When you know you've done as much talking as will help, prepare yourself and your support team for the next step.

If you've suffered childhood trauma, there will always be people who can't believe you can overcome the problem until you've had a major cathartic experience, first in therapy and then in court, and transformed yourself from victim to avenger. In their fantasies, your empowerment should put an end to the helplessness of depression. In reality, it's not that simple.

Many abused people continue to experience depressions, which

aren't necessarily crippling, long, or resistant to symptomatic management, but also don't go away after a good talk with a great therapist or loving spouse. Their recurrent or persistent symptoms aren't
evidence of a failure to share or communicate, just of bad luck and a
bad illness.

You'll speak with great confidence if you don't try to persuade anyone other than yourself. Simply announce to your significant other
that you've benefited a lot from talking in treatment and from your
close, valuable relationship, but have come to accept the fact that,
like most people who experience severe depression, you'll have recur-
rences no matter what.

In the meantime, take good care of yourself to reduce the risk of
relapse, manage symptoms when they arise, and ignore them and go
about your business whenever possible. Then you can be proud of the
way you keep working, parenting, and seeing friends when you're not
feeling well.

Don't let anyone say differently without letting them know you
disagree. If they can accept that there's no "getting better," they'll be
better about accepting your illness.

If you're close to someone who suffers from PTSD, it's hard to bear
their pain and silence, particularly if you're sensitive and need a close
conversation. Then your willingness to listen makes their silence
seem stubborn and self-defeating. When you know that they've educated themselves about treatment and tried whatever they thought
would work, however, don't assume that persistent symptoms mean
they haven't shared enough.

Yes, your closeness and sensitivity force you to share in their pain
and maybe experience it more than they do, but that's part of the
marriage package. If you really can't bear to witness your spouse's illness, ask yourself whether the entire package is worth it.

If it is, learn to ignore your spouse's pain when there's nothing you
can do about it; if your relationship is then too silent, spend more
time on the phone or with the dog. Remind yourself repeatedly that
it's not personal, you have a right to feel lonely, and you're doing a
good job of putting up with it, even if your spouse isn't.

If you think that talk will help you figure out what's wrong with someone who has started drinking and drugging, your good intentions will be foiled by unrealistic expectations. Trauma may have started it, but once someone has developed bad habits and addiction, talking about the source of trauma doesn't make the addiction go away. The problem has morphed, and so must your approach.

That's because it's hard to stop bad habits for avoiding pain once they've started, regardless of how much insight someone has into why he's doing it and how much support he receives from people who love him. There's nothing wrong with trying to have a good talk, but be prepared to discover that talk is nothing but a distraction and excuse for delay until he decides to stop the bad ways of getting relief.

Talking about his trauma, and other therapies, will help after someone gets clean and sober, but they won't make sobriety happen. If his addiction stems from self-medication for trauma, he must decide whether he's ready to get sober in spite of the additional PTSD symptoms he may have to experience as a result. If he decides it's worthwhile, then he's ready to begin.

Don't accept the wishful thinking that symptoms of trauma can be cleared up with enough sharing; deep psychic damage is not as easy to get rid of as athlete's foot. If you or your loved one is well informed about treatment and you're sure that talk therapy and openness have been given a good try, accept the fact that, whatever their benefit, they're not a cure. Now it's time to learn how to live with and manage symptoms and curb addiction for an indefinite period so the wound can heal.

Quick Diagnosis

Here's what you wish for and can't have:

- Healing through sharing
- Confidence that the right words can help you control your symptoms
- To be able to feel close, regardless of symptoms

- Friends and partners who will always tolerate your symptoms as well as you do

Here's what you can aim for and actually achieve:

- Know your own response to sharing feelings, both when you're symptomatic and not
- Communicate what you think is necessary and helpful, only when you think it will do some good
- Accept that some symptoms are permanent and impersonal

Here's how you can do it:

- Try different talk therapies, including those that encourage you to share how you feel and those that encourage you to stay calm while you review what happened and evaluate your actual options
- Watch what happens when you share too much
- Work and engage with friends and family despite all but the most severe symptoms
- Let people know your silence doesn't mean you're angry or disapproving, just having some symptoms
- Select friends who can tolerate your symptoms and their effect on your ability to talk and have fun

Your Script

Here's what to tell someone/yourself when you're unable to talk because of trauma symptoms.

Dear [Self/Person Who Can't Stand It When I Get Grim and Silent],

I often wonder what I did wrong when I find myself getting [shaky/ scared/completely disconnected from the world around me] for no reason and remember the horrible [event/person/Middle Eastern conflict] that spooked me in the first place. Since then, however,

I've become expert at [meditation/self-hypnosis/exposure therapy/ skydiving] while still maintaining my [business/family of six/bluegrass band], so I haven't let my symptoms stop me, even if I had to grit my teeth and [synonym for "nearly soil myself"]. That's what I'm proud of.

Did You Know . . . How to Communicate in Asperger-ese?

Of all the natural obstacles that get in the way of basic communication—differences in age, culture, gender, etc.—one of the toughest (and increasingly common) to both overcome and understand is the autistic mind. Asperger's syndrome may no longer be in the *DSM*, but it's still a shorthand label for someone who functions at a very high level, often with above-average intellectual skills, but who is socially impaired, mostly due to below-average abilities to recognize and respond to emotions and thus engage in the most basic "hi, how are you"–style conversation.

That doesn't mean a person with Asperger's is robotic and Spock-like—he can have lots of feelings and can be strongly attached to other people—but at any given moment he may have more intense feelings about finishing whatever task it is he's doing, or not being forced to change his habits or routines.

So you may think he doesn't care about you because he's too busy solving a problem or watching TV to look up, smile, and remember you were supposed to go out to dinner. In reality, he may care a lot, but his brain won't let go of what it's doing and will snarl if you pull it away. Then, if you talk about your hurt feelings, his brain is truly in turmoil and communication is over.

If you look for it, you'll find evidence of personal caring, but if you need to talk and break his superfocus, you'll feel hurt, insulted, and disregarded. In other words, it's easy to speak Asperger if you don't have immediate emotional needs or are very good at delaying them while gentling someone out of an obsessive preoccupation.

A good introduction to conversational Asperger-ese is to talk about what he's interested in (e.g., the program or bridge he's building, the game he's playing, etc.) and the frustration that goes with having to stop and eat, sleep, or pee. If you have a more complicated topic in mind (e.g., how his day went or if he wants to see a movie tomorrow), try to schedule it for a time he's less occupied, like right before bed, over dinner, or while he's peeing. If you can wait for his attention, he will be happy to give it.

As long as you share some genuine interests, respect each other's space, and stay away from gossip, emotional confrontation, and discussions about how hurt he's (inadvertently) made you feel, there's much to talk about and genuine friendship to be formed. You just have to remember the key elements of the language to get the conversation started.

Venting Anger

We often talk about anger as if it's a volatile chemical that must be vented from the human body, lest the angry individual combust like a tanker full of gas, a water balloon, or a Spinal Tap drummer. We convince ourselves it's either talk or explode, when in reality, they're often the same thing.

Talk often just triggers an explosion, or vice versa; after a verbal burst, we end up looking for better words and/or the services of a therapist, referee, or diplomat who can keep the destructiveness in check while the anger gets talked out.

Meanwhile, we assume that it's unhealthy to stay angry and advise couples to talk out their problems before they go to sleep, which often means they fight even more because they're tired and cranky, fall asleep exhausted, and wake up even more irritable.

Unfortunately, there's no resolution to many of the problems that make people angry, like having a temper, or an unavoidable relationship with an Asshole (see chapter 9), or a spouse who has a disgusting way of sipping her soup.

Frequently, the only thing we're able to vent, in all honesty, is that we want someone to change in a way she can't and won't, which is a good, reliable way to trigger an explosion. So being angry and looking for a way to communicate may be a bad idea.

Before venting, ask yourself whether there is, indeed, any hope that communication can be helpful. Then be prepared for the possibility that the answer will be negative, and sharing feelings will do nothing but stir up a shit storm.

If you're angry and need to keep your mouth shut, don't despair. Once you stop thinking about what you want to say, you can invent easier ways to bear your burden, while also saving money on therapists and mediators.

Don't think of noncommunication as failure. Remember, no matter what the common wisdom on venting is, nobody's ever died from bottling up their anger, but plenty people have died, usually violently, from letting their anger out.

Here is what communicating your anger should provide, but won't:

- Instant persuasion of the target of your anger to reform, followed by a parade in your honor
- Insight into the other person's point of view so you don't hate or want to punch him so very much
- A deep sense of relief and Zen-like calm after each tantrum, like an anger orgasm, with no repercussions

Among the wishes people express are:

- To be able to express criticism and unhappiness without triggering a fight
- To feel less hate for someone they have to live or work with
- To have their feelings respected or validated
- To get something off their chest

Here are three examples:

I've got to say something to my father before I explode. I've been angry at him for years for the way he abused my mother and me when I was growing up. He's been pretty well-behaved since he got sober ten years ago, so I've respected my mother's wishes to be civil, put the past behind us, and keep the family together. Even if I'm keeping my mouth shut, however, I still can't stand being around him, and I don't want to be in a family that includes that asshole. I know that he deserves to hear what I have to say, and I deserve some relief before I go nuts and just leap up and kill him. My goal is to let him know how I feel, so I don't have to keep that anger in all the time.

My husband and I have been bickering a lot lately, over a lot of issues, like I want him to spend more time at home and he wants me to criticize him less. It seems like the fights never get resolved, and maybe there are bigger problems that aren't being addressed because we can't sit down and figure out what they are. I want him to come with me to see a family therapist so we can have it out in front of a referee, get to the bottom of things, and put our fighting behind us, but he says the therapist will just take my side. My goal is to find a way that we can let out our anger safely, and then maybe we can get along better.

For my first five years at this company, I put up with my racist boss because I needed the job, was young, and didn't want to be "the angry negro," which would have ruined my career. Time passed, I worked hard and got promoted to another division despite him, and now I have a family and a job I love. When I look at my daughter, however, I regret that I didn't take a stand; I get mad at myself for being a bad role model for her and not making her world a better place. I don't think it's right to let injustice like that slide, nor do I think it's healthy to let someone make you angry, day after day, and not let it out. My goal is to be brave and let my old boss know how I feel before rage and regret eat me up inside.

Fear might be unpleasant and often unnecessary, but not every impulse it inspires should automatically be ignored; that Y2K bunker was probably a bad idea, but the concern that convinces you to keep your anger bottled up is usually justified. So before you decide to be courageous or foolish, ask yourself what's likely to happen before letting someone have it with what you really think.

Instead of assuming you've got to make yourself understood or air your feelings, determine whether it's possible to do so without creating a nasty scene and adding to grievances all around. Consult friends if necessary.

If the person you can't stop hating is a flawed parent, ask yourself what you want from him, given his failures. You usually won't get an apology and you can't change the past.

In most cases, he'll respond with blame, evasion, or blank denial, which will just make you angrier while magnifying your vulnerable bond to someone whose influence on your life you'd like to diminish. Unfortunately, true Assholes can't help themselves, and there's nothing to stop them from having sex and kids.

Don't bother to forgive your Asshole parent, because it's pointless to forgive someone who never had a choice. Accepting an Asshole is part of accepting what's unfair about life and the baggage of your own personality, including a piece of it that may share your parent's temper.

So instead of trying to get a nasty parent to see what he did wrong, start thinking about the good things that you and your other parent did to help you survive. Take pride in your ability to keep your mouth shut for the sake of family stability. Use your adult authority and experience to exercise your right to keep conversations politely short and exit them at will. Like venting, any extra attention given to an Asshole parent is a waste of your time.

If the anger you wish to ease is the kind that fuels low-grade marital bickering, it may not help to focus on what you're *really* angry at or to get your spouse to see how annoying he is. As we've said many times on the F*ck Feelings website, the sort of venting that goes on in couples therapy is a lot like the venting of intestinal gas; it provides immediate relief for the venter, but soon poisons the air for everyone in the fallout zone.

If bickering just causes more bickering, try shutting up instead. Then talk to a therapist on your own, identify what you want, and see if there are positive ways to negotiate. Yes, there are things your spouse says and does that will always drive you crazy and aren't going to change, so talking about them will always lead to frustration and ugliness.

Assuming, however, that there are things about your life together that you like and wish to expand, good negotiation requires positive speech, which means keeping your anger to yourself while showing your spouse the valuable things you wish to prevent both of you from losing. So don't just bottle up your anger; bottle it up tighter while describing simple, doable changes that can lead to a better life for both of you.

If your anger is rooted in being the victim of a social wrong, such as racism, attacking bad guys may just strengthen your connection to them, particularly if their attitude isn't going to change. Remember, you don't need to prove your courage; you've already done so by going to work every day, knowing you risk humiliation because you need money for your family.

Fight racism when you think there's a chance to win; otherwise, keep your mouth shut and move away as soon as you can. Racist-killing superheroes aren't just good at standing up to evil; they are also good at choosing their battles and the time for fighting. Don't let anger control your decision about whether and when to fight, especially since most civil rights battles have been won by peacefully letting the racists shame themselves.

Instead of using angry, alienating language with those you most wish to persuade, describe the facts of racist behavior and their destructive impact with regret. No, you don't have to keep your anger a secret, but restraint does demonstrate objectivity and self-control, which can help win people over to your cause.

If you decide that silence is better than self-expression, it's not because you're a coward; it's because you have goals more worthwhile than venting the inner rage-volcano, like keeping a family together, getting the best out of a relationship, and preserving your power to negotiate. If you've got a killer temper, hate injustice, and get hurt easily, then you'll be most tempted to let loose against evildoers, and most heroic when you don't.

Quick Diagnosis

Here's what you wish for and can't have:

- Relief from hateful feelings
- Self-approval that comes with liking everyone and wishing them well
- Freedom from the temptation to open your mouth and say something nasty
- Freedom from the temptation to open your mouth and say something reasonable and righteous that will nevertheless cause a fight

Here's what you can aim for and actually achieve:

- Know when expressing negative feelings will lead to more negative feelings
- Develop the ability to keep negative feelings to yourself while working on broader goals
- Develop skills for negotiating when irritated
- Develop skills for waging war effectively when enraged

Here's how you can do it:

- Develop a procedure for recognizing and accepting anger stalemates
- Look for all realistic, worthwhile goals other than expressing anger or changing unchangeable provocations
- Protect yourself from unnecessary exposure to harm, insult, and provocation
- Learn to negotiate while fuming
- Learn the art of the necessary but silent war

Your Script

Here's what to say about angry feelings you know better than to express.

> *Dear Asshole, aka My [Colleague/Relative/Mighty Potentate],*
>
> *I wish I could tell you how [mean/abusive/insanely horrible] you are, but I won't. We have [many/some/just one] good reason(s) for [working/living/sharing a planet] together, and I am always interested in [some German word that means "allowing and sometimes acknowledging the existence of"] suggestions for improving our relationship. Otherwise, if I occasionally seem abrupt in ending a conversation, it's simply because I [gotta go/have to take a call from the president/hate your guts]. As always, I wish you well and to go [in peace/to hell].*

Life-Changing Conversation

If you see someone about to jump off life's proverbial ledge by making what you're sure is a terrible decision, it's hard not to resist talking her out of her dumb choice and into some common sense. When we know we're right, we want to do good.

Unlike those trained hostage negotiators or crisis counselors, an average person's negotiation skills are mediocre at best; when blunt commonsense talk doesn't work, we usually say the same thing, but louder, and then maybe louder still with an overcurrent of fury.

That might be the right way to grab attention, get someone to think twice, and maybe even scare someone straight, but it's not a great way to get someone to change her mind (especially the mind of an adolescent, for which loud opposition affirms whatever their dumb idea was in the first place).

If volume and bluster don't work, our second instinct is to use the language of selling to persuade someone she'll feel better, sexier, richer, more powerful, and less anxious if she takes our advice. How-ever, even if we're a genius at sales, and offer to throw in free ship-ping, there are many people who can avoid this pitch as easily as that of any infomercial.

What's toughest to accept is that, even when we're good persuad-ers talking about something in which we believe completely, our words may well fall on deaf ears. At that point, not getting through can feel like a terrible failure that makes us partly responsible for whatever ensues.

Instead of trying to be a better communicator when you can't get through, try to honestly assess whether you've put your argument as well as possible. If you have, then you yourself need to step away from the ledge and not take responsibility for anything more.

Have faith that life will eventually confirm your argument. At that time, if noncommunication hasn't made you bitter, angry, and un-able to say anything but "I told you so," you will be heard and have a chance to make good things happen.

In the meantime, approach every crisis negotiation hoping to do your best. If someone ignores your pleading and chooses to make what you know is a mistake, let her, knowing you tried everything you could to protect her, and that if she survives the fall, you'll be there to help pick her up.

Here is what you'd like to have (but don't have) when you can't get through to someone:

- A Vegas magician's skill at creating illusion (and, if necessary, making someone disappear)
- A constantly updating PowerPoint that will confirm the truth of everything you've been saying
- The Oprahesque ability to bring anyone to the light, either by making them cry or giving them a car

Among the wishes people express are:

- To get someone to realize what she's doing to herself and stop
- To get someone to see what harm she's causing others and stop
- To get someone to see they're just trying to help
- To get someone to see that they're the good guys here

Here are three examples:

I need to get through to my sister about how self-destructive it is for her to keep going back to her alcoholic, abusive husband. It seems like every month or so he goes on a really bad bender and slaps her around, and then she comes to my house with her kids, crying, saying this is the last time. But then he eventually calls her in tears, or comes by to apologize with flowers and fast food. He promises to change or just makes her feel guilty for tearing their family apart, and she buys it, over and over again. My goal is to find the words to get her to see what a useless piece of shit he is and how she needs to break the cycle before it's too late.

I thought things would get better at work after corporate ordered a 360 degree review and my boss got feedback from all of his employees. It was a great opportunity for all of us to let him know, anonymously, how we all thought he can be a bully and a poor communicator. Unfortunately, he now says he wants us to sit down and explain what we mean; he says it'll be a constructive exercise, but we're all certain that he really just wants to know precisely who said what, exact punishment, and make this office unbearable. My goal is to find a less confrontational, civil way to get him to see how unfair he's being so that he'll take the review seriously, mend his ways, and not ruin this job.

I wish I could get my husband to see that he needs to lose weight and get a physical. He just won't take time to see a doctor, even though he's overweight, eats all the wrong things, and doesn't make any effort to exercise. You don't need to be an MD to know that he's putting himself at risk for a heart attack and diabetes, but if I try to encourage him to eat better or go for a walk, he says I'm a jerk for calling him fat. If I explain that I want him to do something about his weight because we all depend on him and that I'm scared of what will happen to him, he says I'm a drama queen. I just can't seem to get through. My goal is to find words that will get him to see how important it is for him to get help.

When you can't persuade someone to take what you feel are life-saving measures, you have to be careful not to push so hard that you end up persuading him to avoid your angry, scary self altogether.

Instead, accept your lack of influence—including an ability to save and protect—and then present your reasoning with respect and patience instead of rage and hysteria.

If you're trying to talk someone out of an abusive relationship that might become fatal, don't attack the abuser who, after all, is someone she loves desperately. Respect her love and her hope to rescue the relationship, which she may think is the only thing she has, no matter how toxic you know it is.

Instead of telling her that her husband is human garbage, advise her that certain very unfortunate people—often they've been abused as kids—can't stand the pressures of loving and needing someone without becoming overwhelmingly angry. While she might initially think that *her* love will be so solid and secure that it will ease his pain and douse his anger, what she will find is that there's something wrong with his personality that can't be helped. No matter how solid her love is, any loving relationship stirs up his pain and rage; some people are just allergic to love, and instead of getting hives, they get scary.

Urge the abused to respect her love while assessing its risk for exposing her and her family to harm. Assure her that she has much to offer and that her relationship would be happy if she'd had the good luck to find someone who didn't have her partner's terrible problem. Assuming it can't work, she will help herself and, in the long run, her partner, by moving on and finding someone who can respond positively to her love.

If you're called on to provide constructive criticism to someone who doesn't normally take it well, assess your risks before trying to address his weaknesses. Even if he sincerely desires input, his allergy may not be to love but to criticism, so he may not be able to stop himself from retaliating, no matter how pure your intentions.

Don't then let your desire for a better relationship or workplace lure you into saying things that will get you into trouble. You know the limits of your diplomatic abilities, as well as the weakness of the person whose faults are being addressed. You also have a responsibility to protect yourself from backlash when you know it's inevitable.

If you know that your constructive criticism has a better chance of getting you fired than getting through to your boss, then keep it to yourself; if you let your desire to fix things take over, you probably won't be able to keep your job.

Persuading someone to change bad health habits, particularly when you need him to stay healthy, is a pushy proposition to begin with; given how ingrained such habits usually are, you have to do a lot of nagging and reminding to try to change anything, and then accept that all your nudging probably won't succeed. In the end, he'll claim you're making his health habits worse by making him feel criticized and helpless.

Instead of criticizing bad habits, use whatever control you have over money and together time to encourage better habits. Don't presume to punish and don't expect to change him; simply use your power, when you think it's legitimate, to advance an important value. For instance, if you're the one who shops, you can refuse to buy unhealthy food and lock up whatever snacks you take home. You can reward regular exercise by providing more snacks.

You can't take responsibility for someone else's bad habits, but you can experiment creatively with incentivizing healthier behavior without overreacting when your efforts are defeated. Either way, don't stop acting according to your values, and whether or not your partner ever comes around, you'll know you've done your best to provide him with opportunities to better his health.

To be most effective at persuasion, you have to accept what we call "Rogers's Condensed Principle"; you have to know when to hold 'em, fold 'em, walk away, and run. In other words, if the person you wish to persuade may not be ready, you have to be ready to limit your sense of responsibility and let it go.

Instead of blaming him for being stubborn, stupid, or self-destructive, praise the side of his personality that wants to do better and respect the fact that he can't listen, at least not yet. Remember, the less you push, the more you pull him to your point of view.

Quick Diagnosis

Here's what you wish for and can't have:

- The ability to persuade when truth is on your side
- Personal credibility and respect, so people will believe you without your having to plead, reason, or bargain
- Mind control to make people do what they need to do when they disregard your warnings

Here's what you can aim for and actually achieve:

- To realize that, since you lack persuasive superpowers, you're not responsible for how other people respond to your arguments
- To put together good arguments (even if they fall on deaf ears)
- Maintain your other priorities knowing that, persuasive or not, you've done your job
- Know you're not responsible for harm that could have been prevented if people had listened

Here's how you can do it:

- Assume that obstacles to understanding are not willful or ill-intended but rather driven by wishes and needs people can't resist
- Ignore willful, ill-intended attacks
- Ask people to consider their values and what they think will result from their actions, rather than paying attention to pain, feelings, and wishes

- If you have the opportunity, turn ensuing crises into teaching opportunities
- Know that your effectiveness depends on urging people to do what their wiser side wants them to do, not what *you* want them to do
- As usual, give yourself credit for effort, not results

Your Script

Here's what to say to people who desperately need your advice but, for whatever reason, won't take it.

Dear [Friend/Family Member/Colleague/Self-Destructive Imbecile Who Needs a "Come to Jesus" Talk but Will Listen Only If Jesus Delivers It],

I feel like you're about to get yourself [screwed/addicted/played/in deep shit/killed] but I know you've been [antonym for "encouraged"] and can't stop yourself because you're too [ADD/in love/doomed by poor decision-making genes]. Instead of trying to [convince/bully/ bribe/smack] you, I'm going to ask you what matters to you and whether your current behavior will take you where you want to go or to the [ER/police station/morgue]. Then, if you want, I'll share [methods/ written rules/the number of a good shrink] for improving your self-control, or, if you prefer, I'll leave you alone.

The Best and Worst Means for Communicating Specific Messages

Message	Best	Worst
You want to tell someone she's making a mistake.	In person, in private, and in supportive language that doesn't condemn her choice but encourages her to explore alternatives.	Via text, especially involving angry-faced or turd-based emoji.

Message	Best	Worst
You want to support someone through a painful experience.	Taking that someone out to lunch is nice, but a phone call is acceptable, as is a nice card if you don't know him that well.	Through a public Facebook post that says, "Sorry about your [very private, traumatic event]! I've got your back, kid! YOLO!"
You want to warn someone that her actions are bad for her health.	This can really only be done in person, and in an indirect way—i.e., if the person is overeating, don't stage a cupcake intervention, just invite her for a hike followed by a shot of something juiced.	Via any direct confrontation, even if you just go through her Instagram for photos of food and make obtuse comments about diabetes on all of them.
You want to end a relationship.	Either in person in an easily escapable location or on the phone in a quiet, private space.	Via almost any other medium, up to and including paying to have "We're Over" put between "happy birthday" announcements and ads for local steak houses on the Jumbotron at a Miami Marlins game.

If you view communication as a means to problem solving and not the magic cure to all disagreements, your abilities will certainly improve, especially if you can control your wish to control others, regardless of how benign your intentions. Keeping negative opinions to yourself while finding ways to help people see their own choices is a common ideal for mediators, parents, and therapists. No matter how skilled a communicator you are, however, there are always limits to the ability of communication to solve problems; sooner or later, we all encounter our version of the Middle East, and at that point, you need to know you've done your best and respect your efforts while shutting up and letting it go. Sometimes, the best response is no communication at all.

chapter eight

fuck parenthood

Depending on the day, the child, and where the bail is set, parenthood can either feel like the most worthwhile thing we do or the worst mistake of our lives. Either way, it's certainly not guaranteed to make us happy or give us good results for year after year of hard work. It isn't just about the circle of life, but also the fundamental *suck* of life—that it's relentlessly unfair—and the best efforts at parenting can still result in a baby that grows up to be an illiterate toilet goblin.

It doesn't help that the major causes of horribly difficult kids, from genes to brain wiring, are due to parents but also completely out of their hands. The only way parents can control the traits they pass down to their kids is by using birth control, but after that, all bets are off.

That means parents always feel that their kid's issues are their fault, even when there's nothing they can do. If you want to have a child in order to have a beautiful, permanent experience, just get a tattoo of a dolphin riding a unicorn over a manatee. It will always be with you, stay exactly the way you made it, and bring you and the world joy without ever crashing your car or getting a stupid tattoo of its own.

So before you freak out about your parenting mistakes and make things worse by trying to figure out and solve problems that can't actually be solved, stop and ask yourself how much control you really have. Your goal, as a parent, isn't to solve your problem with a child; it's to figure out what's solvable, so neither you nor your child has to go crazy.

The way to figure out what you can solve as a parent, of course, is to try everything and see what succeeds. Then, instead of trying again and again, accept your helplessness, keep up morale, and hope it's just a stage and not the birth of Hitler II.

Respect the parent who solves problems, but reserve your highest honors for the parent whose kids *are* problems but finds the courage to keep going and accept them anyway. And remember, being a good parent doesn't mean you should worship parenthood; it's worthwhile, but it's frequently an affliction, as you will often tell your children during their lives, that's not fair.

Not Ruining Your Baby

People like to say that childbirth is a miracle, but to paraphrase the late comedian Bill Hicks, having a baby is as much of a miracle as eating food and then passing a turd. It's a basic biological function, not the parting of a raging sea with a wooden staff.

Perhaps it's that kind of "miraculous" thinking that puts an insane amount of pressure on so many new parents during their child's early years. They obsess over every decision involving their personal baby Jesus, from what preschool waiting list to get on to whether or not they'll expose their child to the evils of TV to the precise plan for how they're going to bring their miraculous creation into the world (in a bathtub/yurt, with no drugs/extra pain, with a midwife/chorus of handmaidens, etc.).

There's obviously a good side to getting obsessed about the healthy development of babies and children; fetuses and newborns are vulnerable, and the first few years of development have a big impact on a child's life. Parents who worry more about doing things right are probably going to have healthier children who develop a wider range of skills. Parents who worry too much, however, are going to make themselves and their miracle crazy.

That's because, in spite of modern medicine and new knowledge about child development, neither parents nor doctors nor the world's most in-demand holistic midwives have that much control over the strengths, weaknesses, and many potential illnesses that a child brings into the world with its genes.

The fact that we feel increasingly responsible does not mean that we have correspondingly greater powers over the outcome, just a few more tricks for heading off certain disasters. So whether you're responding to instinct or culture, don't let yourself feel totally responsible for what happens to your baby.

Instead of operating in panic mode, do smart research. Read all the books that you think will help (namely the ones with practical advice that are written by experts, not celebrities who happen to be fertile), talk to all the parents you respect, and reflect on what you think did and didn't work for you as a kid.

Parents have to make lots of decisions that may impact their kids, from minor (whether to name their kid Aiden, Jayden, or Kayden) to major (how to proceed if your child gets sick and the treatment can't be provided in gummy form). If you can calmly assess each choice's risk versus benefit, instead of immediately freaking out because the wrong decision could turn your child into a sea monster, you'll make your job as a parent, as well as your kid's life, much easier and even enjoyable.

If you've got the resources, go ahead and buy the best stroller, the finest dairy cow to ensure the most organic milk, the fluffiest sleep sack that will give your little one the sweetest dreams. Just remind yourself periodically that conception and early development are particularly susceptible to bad luck, and that your power to prevent it, no matter what stroller you wasted thousands of dollars on, is limited.

Give yourself credit not for producing a healthy baby but for doing your best to promote health in a chaotic world, and give yourself extra credit when things don't go well in spite of your best efforts. Childbirth may not be a miracle, but successfully raising a healthy child, despite what the universe throws at you, always is.

Here is what parents wish they had to ensure healthy development, but don't:

- A molecular condom that could protect your infant from all genetic disasters
- A giant, plastic bubble that ensures the world's safest, risk-free pregnancy
- A spouse who's also a Zen master
- A technique for delivering a child in the time it takes and with the risk required to eat a Cinnabon

Among the wishes people express are:

- To make sure fetuses are healthy
- To make delivery a positive, safe, and sublime experience
- To make sure breastfeeding goes well
- To develop a positive bond with a baby right away
- To ensure normal development

Here are three examples:

There's nothing I take more seriously than my baby's health, and I know how important it is to breastfeed, but for reasons neither my doctor nor I can seem to explain or remedy, my breast milk just will not come in properly. I spent two agonizing weeks trying, during which time I was in pain and my daughter was continually wailing for food, but eventually I had to give in and start feeding her formula. I know I'm doing what's necessary, but I can't stop worrying about the harm I'm doing her immune system (and maybe her brain, who knows?) by not giving her the breast milk she needs. It doesn't help that all the other moms I know react to my decision with barely concealed disgust, as if I were a war criminal or something. I can't escape feeling like I've failed as a parent before I've even started. My goal is not to feel like the worst mother in the world every time I think of what I've exposed her to.

I love my husband and we both really want kids, but I can't stop thinking about the problems I may be creating by having waited until I'm thirty-five, and then choosing a nerdy, fifty-year-old academic researcher to be the father. The risk, of course, is that between our ages and careers (we're both PhDs), the chances are very high that any child we have will be somewhere on the autism spectrum. I'd like to think I'd be able to rise to the challenge of having a kid with special needs, but I'd feel horribly guilty for purposely bringing a kid into the world who'd have to suffer through a difficult life. My goal is to stop being paralyzed about having kids (and what issues they may have) and decide what to do.

Right after my son was born, we discovered that he has cerebral palsy that affects his right leg. So far there have been no signs of mental impairment, but I see how much harder he has to work on crawling and walking than his big sister ever did. I wonder if I somehow did something to give him this handicap and I promise myself I will do everything in my power to make sure he never feels different and gets all the help he needs. He's starting kindergarten, so we moved to a school district that has more resources for special needs students, even though we can't really afford the taxes, and the teachers know I'm ready to march in with an advocate and lawyer if I feel he's not accommodated properly. My wife says I'm ignoring my other kid and making my son feel worse, but she's missing the point. My goal is to make sure this problem will never, ever hold him back.

It's hard to describe to people what most mental illnesses feel like, but if you want to understand how severe anxiety feels, become responsible for an infant.

Not only are these creatures completely dependent on you for every basic need, but they also demand constant attention and will prevent you from taking care of your own basic needs. They might grow, but your sense of duty does not shrink proportionately.

Unfortunately, most major problems threatening a child's safety and development can't be prevented or corrected, even by the most attentive parent in the world. Holding yourself responsible will potentially exhaust you, put an unbearable strain on your marriage, and turn you into the thing you fear most, a bad parent.

That's why parenting is the ultimate walk-a-fine-line job, requiring you to knock yourself out only for the big-deal threats and truly curable problems, while ignoring the multitude of terrible things you can do nothing about. That way, you can go out, make a living, and not actually go nuts for real.

From the moment you start thinking about pregnancy, you enter a world of worries and magical ideas about controlling the creation and production of a perfect, safe baby. Of course, it's the supreme importance of that task, together with its impossibility, that drives everyone into a frenzy of fear and guilt.

Yes, breastfeeding helps, as does good nutrition, avoiding alcohol, and delivering within close range of good medical care. However, the scientifically proven benefits of these behaviors help a little some of the time, rather than guaranteeing a good result all of the time. Besides, there are always ways to salvage benefit and reduce risk when the solution you most desire is not possible. Indeed, making adjustments and compromises is what parenting is about.

Instead of seeing yourself as a soldier protecting your baby from pain and pathogens at any cost, be a manager who has to assess the relative benefit, risk, and affordability of many different options. You never have enough time and money to do everything, so get used to feeling as if you're making compromises you're not entirely confident about while other people seem to be doing it better.

And by the way, there will always be other people, mostly mothers, with strong opinions. Due to their evangelical nature, it's best to view them as the kind of religious solicitors that go door to door; when they start to preach breastfeeding and brimstone, just be polite, keep them at a distance, and lock the door behind them.

Assuming you've thought through your options and done your best with what you've got, stand by your choices, particularly when something goes wrong, as it sometimes does. Never judge yourself by how well your baby is doing, but rather by how well you're able to manage when your resources aren't what you want them to be.

Don't get scared by possible genetic risks until you've assessed them carefully. Newspapers always simplify cause and effect by taking a complicated study and turning it into a headline designed to scare the shit out of everyone over thirty-five. Read on, and consult experts to find out whether the risk is raised by 2 percent or 100 percent.

Remember, there are benefits to being older, geekier parents; the fact that you are old, smart, and have lots in common can make you better parents and partners. Your intellectual genes are more likely to give you a smart kid than they are to cause autism, and a smart kid is valuable, not just to you but to the universe. Instead of letting fear get you to think of nothing but worst-case scenarios, remember that parenthood requires us all to accept bad-gene risks while hoping that good-gene benefits will prevail.

If something does go wrong, like cerebral palsy, parental dedication can make a huge difference—for good, bad, or both. Stories about total parental obsession triumphing over ignorance, nay-saying, and bad advice always make for good TV movies and segments on newsmagazine shows.

Unfortunately, this kind of obsession makes for bad experiences for your spouse, other kids, and anyone who might be trying to help. If you are absolutely determined to completely normalize the life of a disabled child, you will exhaust your family's material and emotional resources without achieving your goal.

Learn as much as you can about your child's disability and decide for yourself what treatments and remedial programs are worth pursuing. If they don't work, however, or if they cost too much for the likely benefit, don't get obsessed or hold yourself responsible for finding an answer. Accepting your limits and conserving resources for future needs is part of being a good parent. It won't give you a good feeling, but tough decisions rarely do. Instead, it will allow you to focus on other stuff, like just having fun with your kid.

A good parent is vigilant, ready to work hard, and willing to make sacrifices for his or her baby's health. A great parent, however, can bear the anxiety of choosing between various sacrifices, knowing that bad outcomes can result from good choices, and that kids are vulnerable to many bad outcomes that no parent controls. If you choose acceptance over anxiety, both you and your child will have a better chance of survival.

Quick Diagnosis

Here's what you wish for and can't (always) have:

- A trouble-free pregnancy and delivery
- A perfect, happy baby
- Good genetic luck
- Sufficient resources

Here's what you can aim for and actually achieve:

- Avoid pregnancy until you have the resources you feel you need
- Reduce the risk of problem pregnancies and deliveries to a level you can accept
- Make sacrifices when you believe they're worthwhile and cost-effective
- Negotiate management differences between spouses

Here's how you can do it:

- Assess the resources (money, time, partnership) you'll need to raise kids before having them
- Avoid having kids if you don't have those resources, and plan for ways to obtain them

- Educate yourself about possible health and development problems and the benefits and costs of methods for managing them
- Don't expect to find answers that don't have costs and risks
- Learn to make compromises and don't expect to feel good about them
- Give yourself credit for making tough choices, regardless of how they turn out

Your Script

Here's what to tell yourself/your spouse about pregnancy, delivery, and child development.

Dear [Self/Person Who Should Be Doing More or Hasn't Been Doing Enough or Is Probably Judging Me for Not Doing the Right Thing]:

I feel like I can't possibly do enough to compensate for [our bad genes/ stress-induced fetal damage/my baby turning into a serial killer], but I know I've got a good partner and we've put together a good team with reasonable plans for [pregnancy/delivery/schooling/long-term psychotherapy]. I think we've got a good chance of [synonym for "not fucking up"], given horrible uncertainties.

Good Parent vs. Overprotective Parent vs. Bad Parent

Good	Overprotective	Bad
Helps with homework.	Has hired separate tutors for every subject, but still does homework herself to make sure the teacher isn't pushing too hard.	Doesn't know what grade he's in. Or where.
Whenever possible, attends his kid's games, recitals, and plays.	Makes it possible for his kid to shine (but shine safely) by coaching the team, producing the concert, and directing and co-starring in the play.	Whenever possible, invites the kid to join her to watch Ultimate Fighting or *The Bachelor*.

Good	Overprotective	Bad
If the kid wants to go out with friends, makes sure to meet those friends and have any necessary contact info.	If the kid wants to go out with friends, she needs their social security numbers and space in the car because she's coming with.	If the kid wants to go out with friends, then they should meet at this bar because Daddy needs someone to drive him home.

Stopping Constant Parent/Child Conflict

Misunderstandings with strangers—be they fellow drivers just trying to survive a lane closing, supermarket patrons struggling to find one stupid open register, or even coworkers who just want to know who's stealing their Lean Cuisines out of the fridge—are annoying yet understandable. After all, it's easy to miscommunicate or misunderstand someone you've never met whose intentions you have no reason to trust.

That's why, when you find yourself in perpetual conflict with your own child, it's both baffling and heartbreaking. Your kid isn't a jerk in an SUV trying to cut you off but a human you cocreated whom you've known since she was preborn.

You feel like your connection to your child, and the effort you put into parenting your child, should make such rifts impossible. If parents can't resolve conflict with a child, they assume there's something they've failed to do as parents, whether it's to communicate, instill the proper values, or express enough approval or disapproval.

Unfortunately, however, we often don't know why certain kids are in constant conflict with their parents; frequently, parents who are obviously competent and who get along well with their other kids have lots of trouble with one. Some kids are more irritable by nature, or experience mood disorders. Other kids just see the world differently and can't be the kind of person their parents want.

If you're caught in a prolonged conflict with your child, get professional advice and ask yourself whether there's anything you can do better as a parent. In many cases, however, there's nothing wrong with your parenting; there's just something about your child that is hard to accept and understand, and impossible to change.

If that's the case, you may still have a great kid, but not necessarily one you can talk to easily, spontaneously, and without anger and inner reservations. After all the good work you've done as a parent, that's hardly fair, but that's life.

Good parenting can't necessarily solve or prevent conflict, but a good parent can manage it for the sake of a long-term relationship, so he can keep the child in his life, whether or not they sometimes feel like incompatible strangers to each other.

Here are solutions to parent-child conflicts that you'd like but can't have:

- A kid who always says just what you were about to say
- A temperament that isn't a little too much like your kid's (but yours is better, of course)
- A spouse who is better at finding an answer than a source of blame, especially since it's usually you
- A way of addressing your child's grievances that doesn't create further grievances to bicker over

Among the wishes parents express about their conflicts with kids are:

- To find a sweeter carrot or a bigger stick
- To reach a common understanding of right and wrong behavior
- To agree on priorities and loyalties
- To not put one another on edge

Here are three examples:

Back before her puberty, my daughter was a cheerful kid who got along well with everyone in the family and didn't hate to be in my presence. The second the hormones hit, however, she became unhappy, superficial, and perpetually antagonistic. Her grades are failing, she's obsessed with boys, and she responds to even the most polite question or suggestion with a truckful of attitude and the need to start an argument. I'm completely losing my mind. I don't know if this is my fault or if it's just a phase, but if we can't stop battling soon, neither one of us is going to survive to see her graduate high school. My goal is to stop the perpetual fighting.

I'm not too happy with the direction my sixteen-year-old son is going in, and I have no choice but to let him know it. He avoids studying, doesn't care about homework, spends all his time working on his horrible car, and says he really doesn't want to go to college. I expect more from him and have let him know it—I hate to see him make so many foolish choices that he's going to live to regret—but all it seems to do is lead to bickering and resentment with him and worry and sadness with my wife. My goal is to point my son in a better direction while not arguing with him all the time.

I never had a moment of conflict with my son until he married his wife a year ago, and since then, we agree on nothing. His wife is impossible, doesn't like to spend time with my husband and me, and tells our son we've been a bad influence on him somehow. He doesn't necessarily agree with her, but he doesn't stand up to her and tends to go along with what she wants. The things she's said about us are awful, but he won't ask her to apologize, so we avoid her, but then we seldom see him. When we do see him, he tries to get us to be nicer to her, but we honestly don't know how since she's the one who goes after us. My goal is stop the bickering and restore the good relationship we once had with my son.

Once you've tried to do everything in your power to get along better with your kid—attempts at being more understanding; good cop/ bad cop with your spouse; advice from shrinks, friends, and books (why, hello!); attempts at being less understanding—it's time to concede that you are actually powerless and figure out how you're going to deal with it.

If a hormonal shift has turned your little girl into a giant terror, check to make sure your child isn't dangerously depressed, because, for teens especially, anger is depression's most obvious symptom. There are many depression questionnaires online, but they're all based on asking straightforward, commonsense questions (about mood, negative thoughts, suicidal impulses, etc.) and not about being subjected to secret pressures, losses, or trauma.

If, regardless of her answers to you or questionnaires, you think she might be depressed, get her evaluated by a mental health professional. If you don't believe her answers, or get none, the big question changes from whether she's depressed to whether she's suicidal. Take her to an emergency room, regardless of her objections, if you have any doubts about her safety.

Keep in mind that parents are in the best position, potentially, to investigate and sort out the causes of an outburst of irritability or possible depression because you have the best insider access and knowledge. Unless your kid is much more likely to talk to a nice shrink than to you, the shrink has much less to work with than you do.

If there's no issue for the child to talk about (either with you or a shrink), no hormone to be treated by a pediatrician (thyroid or otherwise), and no depression to be addressed with a psychiatrist, then the diagnosis is adolescence, for which the only possible cure is time.

Then all you can do is grit your teeth, set limits on really bad behavior, and mourn the loss of the nice kid you used to know, hoping that she'll return someday, and if she doesn't, hope she finds a spouse who is totally immune to moodiness and willing to take her off your hands. Meanwhile, respect yourself for being patient and tolerant when you have your own sorrow (and bratty door slamming) to deal with.

If you are sad about the kind of person your child is turning out to be, try to be objective about their strengths and not to confuse the chasm between who they are and your expectations with potential weaknesses or faults. Nonacademic children growing up in an intellectual family, for example, will tend to feel like failures, even if they're talented at sports or art. That's why it's important to find a way to value your kids for who they are, even if they're nothing like you.

Yes, it's worthwhile looking for learning disabilities and ways of using a child's strengths to overcome obstacles. Kids who are good with cars, for instance, often have superior visual-spatial skills that may not be reflected in their ability with words or numbers. If good tutoring, including whatever you and other adults in the family can provide, doesn't work, however, your bigger goal is acceptance, not academic performance.

Don't downplay the value of learning, but encourage your child by reminding him that many people learn more effectively after they leave school because their brains learn better by doing, not by sitting and reading. As long as he's found something he's good at and loves to do (and that thing is legal, nonaddictive, and can lead to a paycheck), then there's no reason to torture your family by trying to talk him out of it.

Meanwhile, keep your disappointment to yourself. If you want to bring out the best in your child, you don't have to force yourself to love him for who he is, but you do have to act as if you do, and stay positive. If you want to prevent conflict from dragging you both down, then it's time to give up whatever plan for him you had in mind.

If conflict arises from competing loyalties and commitments, asserting your right as family leader to determine priorities will probably backfire. You may be right, for instance, to resent the mean, unjustified, disruptive influence of a child's spouse. The cliché is that mothers-in-law are evil, but many begin their reign of terror by being a pain to their husband's parents (and maybe also their parents, as well as any human in earshot).

Once you've done your best to eliminate misunderstanding and establish a better relationship with this spouse, however, you have to face the fact, if strife continues, that it's beyond your control, your expectations must change, and expressing your real feelings is bound to push your son away from you and into his wife's insane arms.

Instead of trying to win your child back to your side, or protesting the loss of trust, stop expecting the usual easy communication and happy participation in family life you always hoped for. Instead, accept your loss and prevent it from getting worse by treating criticism and boycotts diplomatically, as differences that you're always willing to tolerate, even if you often disagree.

The more outrageous the criticism you receive, the less reason to take it to heart. Yes, it hurts to hear it from your child's lips, but that's the nature of his or her marriage, not the nature of your relationship or a reflection on your job as a parent. A good parent can have a child who chooses a crappy spouse, a decision over which you have no control.

If you're too quick to express yourself with your kids when you're hurt or angry, and your openness makes you a welcome addition to any poker game, learn how to keep your mouth shut and assess the reasons for conflict with your child. Sometimes you'll find a solution, but more often you'll find the causes of friction are due to outside forces that require the skills of a good lawyer, hostage negotiator, or magician, but not a good parent. At that point, it's time to accept that conflict, along with the need to manage and endure it, is now just a part of the family.

Quick Diagnosis

Here's what you wish for and can't have:

- The kid you used to know
- Your old authority, trust, and shared values
- Freedom to speak spontaneously without stirring up misunderstanding
- Spontaneous friendliness rather than careful feeling management

Here's what you can aim for and actually achieve:

- Learn not to respond to small provocations
- Set limits when necessary, while smiling
- Blame no one for the undeserved painfulness of your relationship

Here's how you can do it:

- Try everything you and others have thought about to ease conflict and reduce misunderstanding
- Accept unavoidable conflict, even if you have to live with it for years
- Set limits when necessary, without letting legitimate disappointment and moral disapproval make them negative or pessimistic
- Find strengths in disappointing differences
- Don't attack differences in values or loyalties that you can't change
- Respect rather than lament the extra effort this parenting requires

Your Script

Here's what to tell your child/yourself when you're unable to talk freely without quarreling.

Dear [Self/Dearest, Impossible Child],

I can't listen to your [sweet voice/provocative arguments/dumb excuses] without wondering whether you're [thinking this through/brought up by someone else/part of an elaborate prank], but I know you process information in your own [flawed/deranged/unique] way, and that a degree of [misunderstanding/conflict/loathing] is unavoidable. I will work hard to avoid [nasty statements/bitter regrets/the temptation to abandon you in a Walmart parking lot] and stay positive while we get through this difficult [antonym for "love fest"] together.

Raising a Jerk

When you see a toddler having an epic tantrum in the airport, or a teenage girl on the street with her tush hanging out of her shorts, or even a college guy outside of a bar having a tantrum that would rival the toddler's, it's tempting to wonder what kind of parents would let humans turn out this way.

The irony, of course, is that they might be the good kind of parents.

They just have the wrong (or just young, stupid, or drunk) kind of kid.

Logic may dictate that good work yields good results, but in the world of parenting, the logic of cause and effect is often nonexistent. Being truly deserving of a "World's Best Mommy" mug doesn't guarantee that you'll wind up with a respectful, friendly relationship with good kids, just a new vessel for your coffee.

Of course, if your kid is turning out badly, there's much that can be done to attempt to reverse course. You have power to limit some bad behaviors and reward good ones, provide incentives to keep busy, and give him or her good coaching. These methods are often helpful at getting a kid back on track or, at the very least, keeping him out of jail.

When good interventions don't work, however, don't assume that either your parenting or your kid's will is to blame. It may seem like your child chooses to be bad or make "bad decisions," but more likely, there's something wrong inside of him, and you, the school, and the therapists, from the bleeding hearts to the tough-love types, just don't have the answer.

Maybe time, hard knocks, and neurodevelopment will help in the end, but for the time being, the situation, like your kid, is out of your control and unpleasant to be around.

There's a certain freedom in knowing that, despite the lack of results, you've done your best. At that point, you don't have to repeat treatments that haven't worked, protective sacrifices that aren't effective, or efforts that expose your family to harm for no good reason. Now you can use your helplessness to be more helpful, knowing you're managing any parent's worst nightmare while feeling secure that you're not the nightmare parent behind it all.

Here's what should be shaping your kid's character, but isn't:

- Your own good example, perfect religious school attendance, and residency in a neighborhood with impeccable lawns
- All those vegetables, vitamins, and SAT books you made him consume
- A shit-your-pants scared-straight experience that involves not just prisoners but angry bears and hypnosis

Among the wishes people express are:

- To understand what went wrong
- To figure out how to improve their parenting in order to improve their child
- To change a child's choices
- To get help, treatment, a rescue (as if there was help that was likely to be helpful)
- To reach, inspire, and motivate with better ideals

Here are three examples:

I've lost all confidence in my sixteen-year-old son and none of the teachers or counselors at his school has been able to get through to him or get him off the path of flunking out. He steals anything in this house he can get his hands on so he can get money to buy drugs, and then insists he didn't do it. If the drugs weren't dangerous enough, he once passed out while making mac and cheese and almost burned the house down. He also took out the car without permission and crashed it into a tree in our driveway. We don't have the money to send him to a therapeutic boarding school, and insurance sure won't cover it, so we're helpless to watch him suffer and we suffer along with him. My goal is to figure out how to help him before he really hurts himself or, God forbid, someone else.

After the fifth time my teen daughter was caught stealing from the same store, they decided to press charges, and I can't blame them. No matter how hard my wife and I try to get through to her about her shoplifting—lectures, punishment, rage—nothing seems to work. We sent her to therapy, but that was also useless. She just insists that she can't help herself. Now her stealing has gotten her a court date, but I know she's not going to show up unless my wife and I force her into the car and take her there, which is time I have to take off work, which is time I need since I have no idea how we're going to pay for a lawyer. My goal is to help her avoid getting convicted and having a record, then figure out how to get her to stop stealing ever again.

From the time my son was little, he's always had anger problems, and he's been in therapy off and on since he was five. He can be a charming, loving guy, but when something goes wrong, his eyes just go dark and he rages like he's possessed. Afterward, he's very sorry and ashamed, but he still really sees his anger as the fault of whoever upset him. He's gotten arrested a couple of times for bar fights, but our lawyer was able to get the charges down to a fine and probation. We were relieved when he got married last year because it seemed like he'd finally grown up and calmed down, but now his wife is beginning to look scared and I've spotted a couple bruises. My goal is for my wife and me to figure out how to help him control himself before he really hurts her or anyone else and ruins his life.

When you know or care for someone who's falling into bad habits (addiction, uncontrolled anger, an intense new fitness routine), getting them help is never easy. When that troubled someone is your child, figuring out how to help him becomes nearly impossible, or about as hard as he'll find getting clean, calm, or away from CrossFit.

That's because even though you feel that you're ultimately responsible for this person and their well-being, your actual power to help has limits. Meanwhile, you'll feel a limitless amount of pain if you can't get your child the right help and he ends up shuffled off to jail, into foster care, or off this mortal coil.

Then your pain is compounded by the fact that the person you feel totally responsible for saving is acting like a petulant, selfish, combative garbage monster from hell; aka, the human you want to help the least. If nothing works, however, good parents must sometimes accept the possibility that, despite worthy attempts, bad behavior and rotten character aren't going to change any time soon.

At that point, you must acknowledge your inability to protect your child from the consequences of his actions and do what you can to protect yourself and others without giving up any values, love, and willingness to help when new opportunities arise. Unfortunately, the simplest and easiest conclusion is also the hardest to come to terms with.

If a kid's behavior threatens a family's safety, and intensive treatments, like hospitalization and moderate-risk medication, haven't made a difference, parents may do more harm than good by seeking better treatment and not giving first priority to protecting their family. Parents often say they'd take a bullet for their kids, but you shouldn't be willing to take one *from* them.

Spell out what you consider dangerous, unacceptable behavior that may, at least temporarily, force you to withdraw your welcome. Find out what your child's residential options are, given his or her age and the availability of public resources controlled by schools, courts, child protective services, state mental health services, and homeless shelters. Get advice and, hopefully, cooperation from local police.

Make a plan without letting guilt, fear, or a global sense of responsibility force you to compromise or blaming yourself, your child, or others for what he's doing and what he's become. If you can't protect your child from bad behaviors, limit the damage.

If a parent's prior attempts to defend, intervene, and treat a child's repeated criminal behavior have been unable to protect that child from doing something to get a record as an adult, a good parent may decide it's better to let the full weight of the law fall where it may.

While you might feel like such a parent would have to be heartless, the fact is, good parents don't always have good options, especially when all the best ones haven't worked. When you can't help your kid and she won't help herself, letting life do its own cruel teaching is all you have left. There's no better way to let your child know that responsibility for managing bad behavior—if it can be managed—belongs with her than to make clear it doesn't rest with you or other helpers.

Be sympathetic as you talk about how hard it is to control bad habits, and how hard jail might be. If your child blames you for abandonment, reassure her that you'll never stop caring or trying to help. The most important thing right now, however, is not to avoid fears of abandonment but to stop being a thief who can't stay out of trouble.

A violent adult kid is your worst-case scenario, and can happen in spite of many years of therapy, medication trials, and legal interventions. It's a parent's job not just to get their child access to any and every possible treatment but to be realistic and not cling to false hope about the therapeutic potential of interventions that have already proven ineffective. Instead of searching for more help or a deeper sharing, accept the risk of violence as unavoidable and decide how it should be managed.

If you feel threatened, avoid confrontation, refuse contact, and request help from the police as necessary. If you think the risk of violence is escalating, either against you or anyone else, ask yourself whether a brief stay in a hospital will restore calm or whether jail would be better.

Refuse to listen to your child's pain if it's used to justify violent behavior, and don't talk about what will make him feel better. His feelings are not all that important compared to what will happen if violence gets out of control; if your son is acting like a monster, you can't put protecting the monster ahead of protecting everyone around him who's now in danger.

Regardless of good parenting and all the help in the world, some kids can't stop acting like bad people and doing bad things that are dangerous to themselves, their families, and others. Parents who understand and accept when treatment and good loving can't help are better able to protect their families and the out-of-control child, even when the threat is from the out-of-control child. Your responsibility to save your child may feel endless, but in reality, it ends when your options do.

Quick Diagnosis

Here's what you wish for and can't have:

- An explanation of what went wrong and why
- An assurance that treatment, if done right, will help
- A technique that will allow you to control your child's dangerous behavior
- A safety net for your child that doesn't require you to create one for yourself

- A way to keep your child's record clean without sullying the lives of others

Here's what you can aim for and actually achieve:

- Learn enough about helpful interventions to know when there's nothing else left to try
- Fight undeserved feelings of blame and responsibility
- Balance your responsibility to keep your family safe against your responsibility to rescue a child
- Accept helplessness now without ever giving up hope for the future

Here's how you can do it:

- Find out everything you can about treatments, interventions, and sources of funding
- With your partner, decide how much risk you can tolerate at home, including harm to your child, family, and others
- Take desperate measures if necessary, weighing the risk of treatment against what will happen otherwise
- Without sounding helpless, declare yourself helpless when you see no new intervention that will help
- Limit your responsibility for managing unsafe situations while trying to pass responsibility to those with the resources

Your Script

Here's what to say about your child's persistently dangerous behavior.

Dear Child [you can show this to your friends/therapist/probation officer],

I can't help feeling that you could stop [drugging/lying/stealing my jewelry] while dragging your family into endless debt to [bail bondsmen/therapists/lawyers/injured victims] but I've watched you

respond to [come-to-Jesus/come-to-Krishna/go to hell/thirty days of
twelve-step/prayer/hexes] and nothing is working. I know we've done
our best and I believe you have also, but you can't stay home if you
[steal/sell drugs/punch]. I can't provide you with another place to stay,
but I'll try to help you find alternatives, like [list places; e.g., "not this
house"]. In the long run, I hope you'll become a strong, honest person
and that's what matters most. Good luck.

Stages of Child Development: When Your Child Is Likely to Be a Huge Asshole to You

Ages	Stage	Asshole Behavior
2–4	Toddler	Stubborn, self-righteous, and prone to tantrums, especially when it pertains to the right to shit his own pants.
12–18	Teen	Obnoxious, moody, and so antagonistic that you can't tell who's more terrible: her for how she's acting, or you for trying to plan the perfect murder.
22–26	Pre-Adult	Broke, self-important, and confident in his independence and self-worth, even though he's still on your phone plan and has eight roommates.
30–45	Midlife	Mopey, resentful, and maybe still broke. And exhausted because she's potty training your grandchild and the turd doesn't fall far from the tree.
Your age is 65–death	Your Ghost of Christmas Past	Now that you're deaf, senile, and easily breakable, he's not thrilled to be around you. But with everything you put up with while raising him, you've earned it.

Living with a Learning Disability

When kids respond to a difficult request by insisting they can't do what's being asked of them, the common response from teachers, parents, the saleswoman at Gymboree who's just about to lose her patience is something like "Can't, or won't?" It's a painless way to nudge kids into seeing that they might be giving up too soon, before they actually give something their best shot (or get down off the rack of Easter dresses).

The can't/won't question can get tricky, however, when it's posited to kids who won't do their homework, focus in class, or generally apply themselves in school. Not every kid with learning problems has a disability, but the ones who really do can't do the work as easily as everyone else, as much as both they and their parents wish it weren't so.

You can't blame parents for trying to push harder when kids don't learn; it's their job to see that their kids survive and flourish, and don't end up spending the next thirty years living in the basement. When it looks like learning won't happen but basement life will, parents get desperate, and pushing is the first instinct, starting with themselves and their kids before moving on to the teachers, principals, and therapists.

Unfortunately, however, there are many obstacles to learning that can't be overcome by any of these people, even if they're working their hardest. A child's lack of inner resources may block progress and require understanding, while external resources may be limited in ways that parents and school systems can't help. Even if treatment is readily accessible, it may have only limited benefit.

When you, your child, and education and treatment professionals are doing their best and you still push harder, things get worse. Kids hate school and lie about what they're (not) doing. Teachers know you think they're failing and find faults of yours to blame. Your sense of failure will envelop the entire team. That's okay if it's your fantasy football team, but not so hot for a team that includes your real child and isn't easily fixed with imaginary trades and call-ups.

So don't overfocus on any single obstacle to learning or, like federal politicians, assume that results will always improve if good teachers just do their work. Instead, assess what can and can't be changed, without letting fear shape your expectations. Be aware that there are many different ways for a child to learn, many opportunities to discover what works best, and many experiments you can do yourself, so that you're not dependent on experts.

Encourage hard work and develop methods for giving kids focus, priorities, and incentives, but be prepared to look for problems that hard work, good parenting, and good teaching can't necessarily overcome. Knowing what you can do is as important as knowing what your kid truly can't, because then you can appreciate the good efforts people are making in a way that can and will make a difference.

Here is what you'd like to have (but don't have) when your child is not learning:

- Bottomless funds for private schools, tutoring, and homework coaching
- A method for motivating your child without yelling, nagging, or tears
- Penalties for nonperformance that don't wear you down more than they motivate your child
- "Teacher Whisperer" skills that engage educators and soothe them before they become defensive

Among the wishes people express are:

- To figure out what's really bothering a child and preventing learning
- To get better teaching/general help
- To amp up the pressure on a child and the school to get better results
- To improve a child's attitude toward work and self-discipline

Here are three examples:

For as long as my kid has gotten homework assignments, she's been an absolute pill about doing them. Otherwise, she's very sweet and reasonable, but when dinner's over and she knows it's homework time, she starts avoiding it like her life depends on it. She tries to play video games, starts torturing her brothers, and has a tantrum if we tell her that enough is enough and it has to get done. I was hoping she'd grow out of it, but she's eleven now and the tantrums are just getting worse. We're sick of fighting, but she'll go nowhere without an education, and we're starting to wonder if this is part of her personality or part of a bigger issue. My goal is to get her to learn with less pain.

Since we discovered our son had learning disabilities two years ago, it's been a huge struggle to figure out what kind of help he needs, let alone get him any real kind of assistance. I try talking to his teachers, but the ones who do respond seem to just get defensive or apathetic. I know that if we could afford private school or even live in a better school district, this wouldn't be a problem, but that's just not financially possible for us right now. I also can't become a full-time advocate for him since I already have two jobs and three other kids. My goal is to get the help I need to get him the help he needs.

My son has severe learning disabilities, and while we've tried a handful of tutors, schools, and therapeutic approaches, none has really worked. His current school has had the most success, but at a recent parent/teacher meeting, they told us that they felt strongly that our son needs ADHD medication, which is the last thing my wife and I want to expose him to. Every parent knows that schools push those pills onto kids just to turn the students into quiet, addicted zombies and line big pharma's pockets. My goal is to figure out how to help him learn while protecting him from having to take that poison.

Learning disability, like autism and erectile dysfunction, seems like a disorder that was invented in the last twenty years, is suddenly omnipresent, and is thus greeted with a great deal of skepticism.

In reality, the disorders were always there, but the diagnoses weren't. Autism used to be lumped in with retardation, erectile dysfunction was considered an acceptable step on the march to the grave, and kids with learning disabilities were labeled willful, lazy, and just plain stupid. It might seem like there are more ADHD kids than ever before, but there are also more ways to help them.

For parents, finding out their kid has a learning disability is a mixed bag; on the one hand, you now know that your kid isn't being a pain in the ass on purpose, but on the other, you have to face the reality of having a kid who's sick, or at least not *normal*, and may require treatment that can be difficult, expensive, and iffy.

Once the diagnosis is handed down, however, you have to swallow your disappointment and panic and make some concrete, adult choices. Before you can do that, of course, you have to know what your choices are.

If a child fights homework with avoidance and tantrums, you don't need an official diagnosis before taking steps to improve the problem. Start by doing your own homework to bone up on behavior management. When homework time arrives, don't overexplain. Link meaningful consequences to easily observable behaviors, and enforce them without negative emotion.

If that doesn't work, review what you know about the way your child learns. Look for distractibility and problems following directions, remembering stories, or being able to understand their meaning. Ask teachers what subjects are easier to teach and what techniques seem to work. Finally, if the answers you're getting point in one likely direction, get testing for learning disabilities.

In the meantime, don't assume your child doesn't want to learn and never doubt the value of your own efforts as long as you're able to keep your frustration from becoming personal and negative.

If a learning disability is diagnosed but the school has little to offer, find out if advocacy will get you more. Hire a good tutor if you can, for at least a few hours, and observe carefully to see what works. Then see whether you can use those techniques yourself or find someone at school or a nonprofit who is responsive and willing to help.

Even though you have reason to feel angry at being underserved, making the teachers feel appreciated will get you a lot further than making them feel guilty and defensive. Get a lawyer willing to take on a worthy cause pro bono and fight for more services if you think it will help, but don't let teachers feel you don't value their efforts, even if you don't. Your goal is to motivate them positively, regardless of whether you like them or respect their work.

Try not to blame yourself or the school system for lacking resources, because those issues are outside your control. Instead, keep looking for ideas you can borrow, respect yourself for persisting, and stay hopeful that a maturing nervous system will allow your child to do better next year.

If lowest risk—nonmedical—interventions don't work, never feel obliged to try any medical treatment that you, as a parent, regard as too dangerous. On the other hand, it's your job to examine risk carefully and objectively before you decide, and not let fear or rumor affect your decision.

Learning problems don't automatically condemn kids to low self-esteem and low-paying jobs, but they carry that possibility, and parents are best able to assess that likelihood for their own kids. If you think your child is losing confidence and picking up bad friends and behaviors, despite attempts at nonmedical treatments, then that's the risk of not doing anything. If you think that probability is high, then it's worth intervening in ways that are not perfectly safe, but carry less danger than doing nothing at all.

Stimulant medication is riskier than nonmedical interventions for learning problems, but it's not hard for parents to check out that chance, which is very low, and to stop the medications quickly if they think they're harmful or ineffective. Don't pay too much attention to recommendations or rumors; no one knows in advance whether stimulants will help your child, and you won't know 100 percent how effective they are unless you try them out.

In the end, you're the best judge of how badly your child needs a trial of stimulant, how risky that treatment is, and after a couple days of watching what it does, of whether it works well enough to continue. Parents always tell their kids to do things that are necessary, no matter how scary or difficult they seem, and this is an opportunity to set an example.

Learning problems often make kids, parents, and teachers feel helpless and disrespected, but there's a certain hope in knowing that these issues arise from diagnosable problems, not the kids themselves, and that we now search for beneficial therapies instead of writing kids off or trying to redeem their wicked ways.

Good parenting and teaching may not always be effective at

overcoming learning problems, but they're a start, and if you can keep trying without blaming yourself or others, then learning problems won't stop you and your kid from having a normal relationship.

Quick Diagnosis

Here's what you wish for and can't have:

- The ability to pick your child's teacher, school, coach, future, etc.
- Obedience from your child, teacher, school, etc.
- Confidence in your child's truthfulness regarding their schoolwork
- A total lack of anger and bitterness when your child lies and breaks promises about schoolwork

Here's what you can aim for and actually achieve:

- Define your approach to learning problems in terms of trying hard and staying positive, not necessarily getting good results
- Not let your desire for better learning performance get in the way of a positive, accepting relationship with your child
- Not let a failure to learn imply that you, your child, or your relationship is a failure
- Keep looking for the things your child can't do, or is weak at doing, so as to find new tools for getting stronger (other than just willpower and obedience)

Here's how you can do it:

- Develop good measures for daily work performance and incentivize them with limits on bad behavior that don't exhaust or punish you more than your child
- Provide assistance with homework, scheduling, and good habit building
- If structure and limits aren't enough, keep looking for other causes

of learning problems, such as subtle cognitive impairments, depression, anxiety, and relationship issues
- Read up on learning disabilities, review what you know from helping with homework, and draw up your own list of strengths and weaknesses while looking for patterns
- Pick teachers' brains while helping them to feel less ineffective
- Focus on what you value about your child, aside from his/her ability to perform at school

Your Script

Here's what to say to yourself, your child, and other concerned educators and relatives about his/her inability to learn.

Dear [Child/Spouse/Entire Team of Teachers, Tutors, Therapists, and Advice-Giving In-Laws],

I often feel that [you/my child/the bane of my existence] doesn't want to [learn/do homework/do anything other than fuck up with other fuckups], but I know that your [disorder/attention span/brain, which you inherited from my jailed brother] makes it hard. I truly believe it's worth trying to keep you [in school and learning/busy and out of trouble/focused and off the pole], and that we have assembled a great team of [teachers/therapists/drill sergeants] who are eager to help you when you aren't doing [synonym for "everything but what you're supposed to do"]. We won't give up on trying to help, but we will also try to accept you the way you are.

Quick Diagnostic: Is Your Kid ADHD, Bad, or Just Lazy?

Issue	ADHD	Bad	Lazy
Learning	Not learnin' a lick, not appearin' to give a shit	Diligently learning . . . how to steal credit card numbers	Learning how to have a great time, brah!
Playing Sports	Surprisingly skilled as an athlete	Surprisingly deft as a bookie	Not surprisingly, no interest
Lying	Lies instantly without thinking (and gets caught, just as quickly)	Lies carefully, so as to get other people caught and seem totally innocent	Lies enough to make everyone feel good, but not if it means making an effort
Interrupting	Constantly, because he's not listening	Sometimes, when he has a scheme	Occasionally, with a loud snore, because he fell asleep while you were talking
Doing Homework	Loses it, forgets it, will do it after playing some Xbox, etc., etc.	Steals it from smart kids	Did it, if doing it means answering some questions and drawing boobs on others

Rebuilding Divorce-Damaged Parenting

It's part of our parenting instinct to create harmony in the families we're responsible for, no matter what the sacrifice, be it gritting our teeth through tasks we don't enjoy, doing things the other guy's way, and attending get-togethers with people we don't like and who don't like us but with whom we happen to share DNA.

All the while, we're working hard to keep sarcastic, negative thoughts inside, where they won't cause hurt or start a feud that future generations will inherit. A good parent develops lots of diplomatic skills and takes pride in maintaining the *pax parentis*.

Part of what divorce does, unfortunately, is directly disrupt not just these parental instincts but your child's expectations. By not keeping the family together, you're potentially disappointing everyone, and violating some credo in Latin.

It's natural then that divorced parents, particularly the nice ones who aren't bitter and nasty, feel responsible for conflict, enmity, divided loyalties, and lingering resentment. However, they can't control the bitterness of an ex, the resentment of hurt children with divided loyalties, and the impact of conflict on their pocketbooks, legal status, and new relationships. As much as you want to give peace a chance, everybody else just wants to give you a piece of their mind.

That's why the most important thing to do postdivorce, aside from getting a new haircut and blowtorching the ring off your finger, is to accept the fact that your parenting role may be changed and damaged in ways that are not your fault or responsibility, even though, again and again, there's someone to tell you the opposite and blame you for ruining the marriage, their lives, the known universe, etc.

If you try too hard to meet your expectations of normal parenting after a divorce, you're more likely to withdraw, feel defeated, or overreact when it turns out to be impossible. As a result, you say something nasty or try so hard to be nice that you become a total pushover and wind up weakening your ability to be a good parent.

If you're willing to accept bitter estrangement without taking it personally or feeling obliged to make it right, there are many more ways to avoid mistakes and build a new, solid foundation. Your old plan for peace may no longer be applicable, but with new boundaries come new opportunities for negotiation; just ask any teenagers who share a bedroom.

You may not be able to parent as effectively as you'd wish, but you can still offer good parenting that you can be proud of under conditions that you believe are good for your child and new partnership. Even if you don't know when your new family will stop trying to punish you and one another, you can lead them toward peace with the same amount of compromise and discomfort that any family would have.

> Here is what you'd like to have (but don't have) to neutralize the poison of postdivorce relationships:
>
> - A reset button that comes with your divorce agreement and wipes out memories of insults and injuries
> - The perfect words to break through the wall of suspicion and mistrust and get people to work together again
> - A powerful court-mandated moderator who stops people from acting badly
> - A guarantee that, no matter what you and your ex decide, your children will love you and not be scarred for life

Among the wishes people express are:

- To stop their spouse from making unfair claims and allegations
- To get their child to see they had good reasons to leave
- To stop their child from acting like a jerk with them or their new partner
- To get their partner to stop leaning over backward for her kids

Here are three examples:

My new wife is good with kids, and she's not particularly negative about my ten-year-old son from my first marriage, but he loathed her before he even met her, and being around her just made him even more hateful. I think it's partly because he blames her for the divorce (even though I didn't even meet her until long after the divorce was final) and the fact that I'll never get back together with his mother. In the meantime, he's unbelievably rude to her and says he doesn't want to visit me when she's around. My goal is to make their relationship work so it doesn't interfere with my being his father.

My wife and I weren't getting along for a long time, so when she told me it was over and I had to move out, I just did what she said because

I didn't want to fight her anymore. Unfortunately, she must have assumed I would come back, because after I left, she became even angrier and began blaming me for everything, which is why my kids now hate me. They used to have a great relationship with me, but now they blame me for the divorce and ruining their mother's life. They're rude and act like I'm their jailer when I have custody; everything I do annoys them and they're counting the seconds until they can go home, even though I bend over backward until my head scrapes the ground. My goal is to get back a positive relationship, but I don't know how.

I love my husband, but I didn't realize until we married that he can't say no to his bratty kids from his first marriage. I never expected them to like me (and they're out of the house, so thankfully, they don't have to), but I was determined to be patient and get to know them. What bothers me is that he's so totally responsive to their needs, whether they want him to cancel lots of plans, arbitrarily change the date of a visit, or give them extra money (outside of the generous divorce agreement), so that it negatively affects our life together. I get mad at them, but I know it's really his fault for letting them walk all over him. My goal is to get him to stop being such a wuss about his kids before it destroys our marriage.

If a team is only as strong as its weakest member, then a divorced team is only as amicable as its angriest ex. One partner can do her best to tolerate the kids' multiple loyalties and create stability in a new home, but if a former spouse or kids are bad-mouthing her, the settlement, or the new partner, then working for the best will lose out to the person acting the worst.

That's when divorce-surviving parents must accept chronic anger and potentially nasty behavior as part of the package, at least in the short term, if they are to retain their confidence and manage their new family successfully. If at least one person involved can't hold their shit together, then the family won't hold together, either.

Most kids like their parents' new spouses as much as they like shots, liver, and standardized tests, so if you can't stop your child from hating your new partner, don't be surprised, don't take it personally, and don't get too defensive, even if your new partner has no reason to like your child, and it shows. You can offer your sympathy, but any decent stepparent understands that it's a difficult adjustment for everyone involved.

Certainly, you can try to hear your kid out and give him a chance to talk about his resentment with a shrink if you think it will be constructive and not just a chance to bitch and fuel hatred. If treatment, mediation, and understanding don't work, however, accept the fact that their relationship is both terrible and out of your control. You can have them both in your life, but only if you create rules for good behavior, enforce them with your child, and encourage them with your new spouse. Buy yourself a striped shirt, because you're going to be a ref.

Create simple rules for respectful behavior, similar to what would apply in school if child and teacher didn't like each other but had to work together, and spell out your penalties. Rules include answering questions politely, not being rude, and not refusing reasonable requests. Enforce them without negative feeling. Buy a whistle if necessary.

You can't make the nastiness stop, but you can be confident in your belief that, the more they both avoid negative feelings and treat each other decently, the sooner they will be happier in their new home. Besides, if they both bristle under your authority, then they'll at least have something to build common ground on.

If you're the target of your child's divorce rage and the usual interventions aren't working, don't bend over backward or get defensive. Presumably you had good reasons to divorce and you made a settlement with your ex that you believe is fair. Trying too hard to appease or defend yourself makes you seem guilty for doing something wrong (like staying married to someone who hates you).

Your interest in your child hasn't changed and your insistence on visitation is not to control your child's loyalty but to do your job as a parent. So again, spell out a positive moral vision. It's right for you to share the job of caring for and guiding your child, even if your child doesn't like you (and even if you don't like your child). You can make life better, provide a good place to live, and do good things together.

While it's hard to live and work with family when you're not getting along, it's important in life to learn how to move forward when feelings are negative. In the long run, negative feelings often fade if you're working well together and feel like you're growing and getting somewhere. Just having confidence that things can get better is enough to create actual improvement.

Share your justified disappointment and anger with friends or a shrink, but not with your child; any obvious negative feelings toward your kid will just justify his negative feelings toward you. Parenting includes many thankless tasks, even when the parents aren't divorced, and providing reasonable parenting under tense conditions is one of them.

If the fallout of divorce isn't just persistent anger but also the way a parent's pushover tendencies can leave his new partner out in the cold, then there's no solution for you, the new partner, unless the pushover parent sees the problem.

Yes, you should ask a shrink or some other respected, neutral party to confirm your impression and validate your needs. Then, together, you can deliver a positively toned warning to the bad-boundaried parent and ask him whether he sees any reason to change.

As the new partner, don't spend too much time talking about your anger or apologize for feeling needy if you think your needs are reasonable and unmet. Otherwise, your overly reactive spouse will try to make you feel better by giving you a little more attention and love, perpetuating the problem instead of admitting that there's a problem in the first place. Instead, urge your spouse to learn to say no, not just to make you happy, but to become a stronger parent.

Make specific suggestions about limits that need to be set and positive ways for announcing them, describing the benefits in terms of less-spoiled kids and a happier partnership. Then sit back and assess progress by what happens, not by what's promised in order to soothe your worries away.

Parenting is always a team sport, even if the marriage ends, but divorce can cause problems that neither you nor your teammates may ever be able to resolve. If, however, you're careful to take responsibility for nothing more than offering good parenting, and you're willing to tolerate persistent conflict and hostility, you can be proud of the job you're doing as a parent, even if it seems like a losing game.

Quick Diagnosis

Here's what you wish for and can't have:

- The ability to get your postdivorce family to act reasonably
- An end to being held responsible for major family unhappiness
- Kids who don't feel they have a right and obligation to punish you and/or your new spouse

Here's what you can aim for and actually achieve:

- To offer and provide good parenting, regardless of nastiness
- To put limits on bad behavior after figuring out what it's really about and trying to be understanding
- To be a good parent of a kid who claims to be a political prisoner in your home
- To find time to build a new partnership despite demanding, needy kids

Here's how you can do it:

- Accept and learn how to live with grievances after all the usual attempts to address them (patience, sympathy, understanding, shrink visits) haven't worked
- Don't take grievances personally or let them influence your management decisions
- Envision a positive goal for your parenting, even if your relationship with your child can't feel positive
- Set limits on bad behavior, as distinct from bad feelings

- Respect the challenge you're facing and your achievement in persisting

Your Script

Here's what to say to kids and current and ex–family members who can't stop fighting with you or one another after a divorce.

> *Dear [Child/Ex/New Partner/Innocent Bystanders/Busy Lawyers and Therapists],*
>
> *I can understand how divorce sparked a [conflict/blood feud/personal hatred], but at this point I don't think continued [talk/mediation/ airing of grievances] will improve the [synonym for "shit show"]. I'm going to see my [kids/new partner/ex-dog] within whatever agreement the court authorizes, and I will be patient and avoid [small battles/ pissing contests/smashing windshields], both with my kids and my ex. I will not, however, let any major bad behavior happen without trying to prevent it from [happening/erupting/getting the neighbor to call the cops] again. I believe I can provide a good, secure home and be a good parent in spite of anger and unhappiness.*

There are many positive ways to manage parenting problems, but most require you to keep your cool, which is almost impossible if you feel totally responsible, which, for the first twentyish years, you legally are. Dedicate the same amount of time to developing your child's skills and potential as you do to meditating on the things that you and your child can't accomplish and shouldn't feel responsible for. Then teach your child how to do the same. Whether or not you can raise a kid you can be proud of, take pride in tolerating what you can't change and doing the best with what you've both got.

chapter nine

fuck assholes

Contrary to everything you've heard from preachers, alcohol counselors, and characters in angel-themed TV programs, certain bad people can't stop themselves from being bad. Sure, in an ideal world, everyone is endowed with the ability to make moral choices. In this world, however, these guys aren't. They're the source of many problems that drive people to seek treatment, which is why they get a chapter all to themselves.

We call them Assholes with a capital *A* (and on our website, we jokingly add a ™, but it turns out you can't do that in a book, because lawyers take ™s seriously). It's not an insult, but a technical term emphasizing the fact that they are who they are; there's no changing them and their attacks aren't personal, even though they mean them personally, because, not surprisingly, anyone who gets close to an Asshole will eventually get shit on. There's every good reason to give them a wide berth, for they are as the lord made them, just like rattlesnakes, tsunamis, and acne.

You could also call them psychopaths or say they have bad, borderline, or narcissistic personality disorders, or other fancy, multisyllabic
names, but those words imply more, take longer to spit out, and say
less. Simply put, an Asshole is someone who behaves like a jerk and
doesn't see it. These aren't people you call Assholes because you're
angry; they're Assholes because of the specific way they behave.
Where you see moral choices and harmful consequences, Assholes see
disrespect, intense needs, and the right to defend themselves against
injury and injustice every time those needs are frustrated.

If you're forced to live or deal with an Asshole every day, you'll
probably have strong feelings about them. This may prompt you to
seek help from the appropriate professional. If that professional isn't
a hit man, you will be tempted to find a way to help said Asshole or,
even better, get *him* help from a shrink.

While many seem to believe that shrinks have a special technique
for taming Assholes and getting them to see the light—Asshole whis-
perers, as it were—no one has such powers. Most people attempt to
be Asshole screamers, which is even worse. The sooner you learn that
all attempts to change Assholes are futile (at any volume), the sooner
you'll be able to live with Assholes in your day-to-day life.

After all, those who do have Assholes in their lives know from experience that no matter how many times you try, nothing helpful you or
anyone else has said or done has made a bit of difference (except possibly a negative one). In actuality, Assholes never come to see shrinks
except to complain about being traumatized and mistreated, often
by their prior (equally powerless) shrinks. Shrinks take consolation,
however, in the huge business generated from an Asshole's friends,
neighbors, family, lovers, contractors, ex-therapists, etc. Aside from
therapists, Assholes are also owed a huge debt of gratitude from lawyers, the communications industry, and the casting directors for any
number of shows on Bravo and MTV.

You might think that nobody would get close to an Asshole on purpose, but the problem is, Assholes are often attractive (just ask any
dog, har har). Intense emotions are attractive, even when they're ugly,
and Assholes, like crazy people (and "crazy women"—see chapter 6),

convey so much raw emotion that (a) it's like living in your own personal telenovela, and (b) they seem like tragic victims. When they turn to us non-Assholes for help and shower us with praise, one can't help but be sucked in.

Assholes offer us a chance to step into their drama and play a role—hero, victim, unjustly accused, you name it—without the need for talent or a ticket. In addition, they're naturally less inhibited by doubts and second thoughts than the rest of us so they speak with more confidence and conviction. Unfortunately, after initially being your best friend/indebted admirer, Assholes tend to graduate you to their enemies list (or at least force you to listen to their enemies list, the length of which should serve as a huge red flag).

If you're asking yourself whether you're an Asshole, don't; Assholes don't ask themselves whether they're Assholes. They know the problem is other people. Most of us act like assholes (no capital) sometimes, but try not to. This is part of being human and a good reason for getting help from shrinks, church, spin class, or whatever works for you. Many of us are possessed by instincts that sometimes turn us into assholes, but we work all our lives to keep those urges in check. Exorcism only works in the movies, but therapies of various kinds can make us stronger at keeping the inner demons from coming out, one day at a time.

Accepting the fact that you're dealing with an Asshole means giving up the hope that you can change their bad behavior with love, reason, therapy, or a talking-to of either the "come to Jesus" or "go to hell" variety. It also means accepting whatever pain and lack of control goes with that bad behavior. Once you do so, however, you will be able to stop useless conflicts and rescue attempts. You'll improve your ability to manage their bad behavior as effectively as possible. Assholes can't be saved, but your sanity can.

Fucked by Your Nearest and Dearest Asshole

It's hard to describe how violating it can feel to be fucked by an Asshole—first of all, it seems both disgusting and biologically impossible, and second, it often involves hearty helpings of betrayal, drama, lies, and everything that makes for great daytime soaps and terrible real-life situations. Most of the Assholes you encounter in life aren't the cold-fish Dexters or Madoffs whom you might slowly grow to trust after initially being very skeptical; in real life, Assholes' selfishness is stealthy and covered by deceiving warmth.

That means, in addition to dealing with the actual legal or practical impact of the bad things Assholes say and do when the relationship inevitably goes south, you suffer severe loss, begin to mistrust yourself, and cling to the belief that you should be able to straighten things out—if you could only find the right words to recover your old relationship.

It's hard to describe the experience because it seems so unbelievable, but when it happens to you, it's very real, and all too painful. Both Assholes and their wrath, like snowflakes and actual tuchuses, come in all shapes and sizes, but the steps to recovering from a run-in are comfortingly similar.

Here's how you can tell your trusted best friend is really an Asshole:

- All your reasonable efforts to swallow your anger and pride and reestablish communication after a disagreement have failed, or made things worse
- You realize all those bad people who hurt and betrayed your friend before she met you might not actually be so bad
- Her understanding of current events is all about what you did wrong, and not necessarily accurate or self-referential
- She's prepared to say and do things that will harm her as well as you in order to get "justice," usually of the biblical variety (wrath, hellfire, etc.)

Among the wishes people express when they write to us or come for post-Asshole treatment are:

- To understand how a former best friend could become so mean and impossible to talk to

- To get back the relationship they once had
- To get through to someone who was once so close
- To get her to stop

Here are some examples:

My business partner turned out to be a total asshole. At the beginning, we clicked perfectly. We had the same approach and he seemed highly motivated and receptive to my business plan. As long as we were doing well, we were a really great team and close friends. When the recession hit, he kept on taking money out of the business and denying it. When I confronted him with the evidence, he said I was doing the same thing and that he deserved a bonus for working harder than I did, both of which were untrue and which I can prove. Since then, he's bad-mouthed me to our associates and even accused me of stealing, which ruins our joint business, as well as my reputation. My goal is to get him to stop before his nasty lies destroy everything.

My mother died when I was a baby, but her brother and my cousins were good to my sisters and me. We all seemed to get along. After my maternal grandmother was hit by a city bus, however, everything changed; my uncle became hell-bent on suing everyone involved in the accident right down to the manufacturer of the steering wheel, and said that he was entitled to most of my grandmother's (meager) inheritance because we were "our dad's kids" and he had a closer bond. It's insane. He's dragging my sisters and me into a handful of lawsuits that none of us can afford and breaking the family relationships we came to rely on. My goal is to get him to stop being a money-crazed monster.

When I first met my girlfriend six months ago, she was recovering from an abusive relationship and was almost broke, but we really connected and I didn't hesitate to help her out. She told me I was the best thing that happened to her. I was really in love and felt it was the closest relationship I've ever had in my life. So I couldn't understand why she stopped talking to me about a month ago. Then, after weeks of my begging her to tell me what was going on, she said I tried to dominate her with money and sex and that she felt much more comfortable with a guy she met at her yoga class. I'm blown away and can't understand what I did wrong. My goal is to get her to remember what a wonderful thing we had going and try to get it back.

It's hard to believe that you can't spot a greedy, lying, unprincipled Asshole, particularly when you've known someone well for years. But sometimes you don't get to see a person's dark side until stress reveals it. That's another good reason God created hard times—so we can find out who the Assholes are.

We tend to like people who make us feel good and we take pride in our ability to make quick decisions and trust our guts. Given what our guts produce, however, and what orifice that product is excreted from, we should know better.

So it's not hard for smart, experienced people to be fooled by a good listener who makes an emotional connection. At any rate, after the end of a relationship with someone you would have trusted with your life (who then declares that you are *his* mortal enemy), you will have a new respect for due diligence and the value of trusting facts over feelings.

It's no fun to discover that someone's a bad person; what's harder still is hearing him tell you and everyone else who will listen that you've done horrible things you wouldn't think of doing. Efforts to communicate your honest feelings can be dangerous. Remember, you're talking to a suicide bomber wearing a vest full of explosive allegations. The first rule is to keep your negative feelings and thoughts to yourself.

Quick Diagnosis

Here's what you wish for and can't have:

- Your old relationship back
- An immediate end to the avalanche of bullshit

- Relief for your hurt and anger
- "Closure," which is an emotional unicorn
- Any sort of control over what he will do or say next

Here's what you can aim for and actually achieve:

- Understand and accept the nature of your new, broken relationship, giving up on logic and reconciliation
- Stop adding dramatic, emotional, damaging fuel to the fire
- Stop letting hurt feelings and anger control your decisions
- Use time to diffuse the emotion and drain energy from the drama
- Use what influence you have to protect yourself

Here's how you can do it:

- Let a lawyer be your primary therapist in terms of telling you what to expect, when to shut up, and what to document (remembering that sharing feelings with your legal representative solves nothing, could cost a lot, and isn't remotely covered by health insurance)
- Protect your assets from petty vindictiveness
- Communicate only what's positive and necessary, so as not to add fuel or show weakness (it helps to write out a statement in advance)
- Be prepared for the worst so that you don't respond with outrage or any visible emotion other than confidence and determination
- Be prepared for the worst-case scenario

Your Script

Here's what to say to the offending Asshole that will keep you on track regardless of how you really feel or how said annular friend responds.

Dear [Asshole Former Associate/Greedy Sibling/Ex-Girlfriend with New Yoga Boyfriend],

Although it's true that we're now having unfortunate differences, we used to [have fun/text each other with some frequency/share an HBO GO password] as friends and partners for so many years, and I'm sure we can address our differences in a positive way. In spite of our good efforts to overcome misunderstanding and reach an agreement, it's been impossible, so it's become necessary to figure out how to go forward from here. I propose we [keep our assets separate/agree to disagree/do a bunch of stuff a lawyer told me to do although I'll never tell you I have a lawyer]. I believe this is fair and will be good for both of us, but it's best for us not to speak further about this directly until all is worked out. Nevertheless, I wish you [the best/good health/a bountiful harvest] and hope this gets resolved soon.

My Parent, the Asshole

There's nothing to stop Assholes from having kids. Indeed, if self-centered jerks weren't reliably irresistible love magnets, shrinks would have trouble putting food on their tables. There are lots of kids who have to deal with Asshole parents. The problems these off-spring usually run into include lots of anger at having been ignored (if they're lucky), humiliated, and/or viciously attacked. At the same time, they often feel guilty and responsible for their parent's unhappiness and bad habits because, by definition, an Asshole parent is always sure that others are to blame. The kids are often touchy, nervous, and guilty, unless they're actively straightening out the world by being bullies, cops, or superheroes. Or therapists.

We want to honor and love our parents. That is hard to do and may be self-destructive when your parent is an Asshole. If you react to an Asshole parent without a clear sense of right and wrong, however, you can become dangerously reactive to negative feelings and the bad things they push you to do. What helps is to honor the *ideal* of a parent, accepting that, even if your parent is the anti-ideal, the ideal is well worth respecting and trying to live up to.

Here's how you can tell if your parent is really an Asshole:

- He constantly reminds you how you've ruined his life, at which point you wish you could
- He is always entitled to share his feelings about your faults because it's "honest" (which is a nice code word for "cruel")
- Apologies are never enough, so you're always trying to earn his love back
- He burns bridges in all his relationships (if he has any relationships left)

Among the wishes people express when they write us or come for post-Asshole-parent treatment are:

- To stop the nastiness and be a real family
- To get over an unhappy childhood
- To stop letting an Asshole upbringing cause them to be irresistibly drawn to dating Assholes
- To understand why they still feel helpless and enraged after their parent does the same old nasty routine for the millionth time

Here are some examples:

My mother is a drama queen who tries to control everyone in the family, and believes she's doing it for our own good. She can get verbally nasty, and when we were kids, she'd hit us. At seventy-nine years old, she still has a horrible temper, and when her fits are over, she either forgets her bad behavior or it's the other guy's fault. I avoided conflict with her until a year ago, when she was mean to my kids, and then I got terribly angry and literally told her off and cut off all ties. Since then I have suffered from terrible guilt and wondered whether I'm just like her. I know she sees herself as an abandoned, mistreated victim. I don't want to be mean to her and I don't want the insults to start again. My goal is to figure out what to do with her.

My father can't stop bad-mouthing my wife and refuses to talk to her at family events. He was always a difficult man—I don't know how my mother put up with him—but he was nice to me as his only son until I got married. Now it hurts when he doesn't return my calls, and I'm sorry he has no contact with my kids, but I don't know how to get through to him. My wife is fine not having him around since he's so mean to her, but I still feel like it's wrong to not have my father in my life, and in my kids' lives. My goal is to figure out how to do right by both him and my wife.

My father-in-law has always been difficult and had a drinking problem, but he's my husband's only surviving parent and our kid's only grand-parent, so I've found ways to put up with his visits over the years. The problem is that he's decided to move closer to our family, to see his grandkid, and it's turning into a nightmare. I'm a stay-at-home mom because my son's too young for school, and he shows up at all hours, unannounced, sometimes tipsy, just wanting me to amuse him and listen to him complain about how unfair his life has been and how unloving my husband is as a son. He also promises to do things with my son all the time, like go fishing or just to the store, and then breaks his promise at the last minute, or just forgets, because he drinks. My husband doesn't know what to do, but he's terrified to say anything because he thinks it'll break his dad's heart and he might harm him-self. My goal is find a way to get my husband to see how horrible his father is, and that we need a change.

If life were fair, you could get these parents to see that their bad behavior is ruining an important family connection you're doing your best to preserve. Assuming that you don't hold a grudge and aren't interested in confrontation or compensation, you'd like nothing bet-ter than for these grandparents to be able to control themselves and enjoy quality time with their grandchildren, their kids, and really any-one with a pulse.

In that fair world, they'd listen, apologize, and attend Assholes Anonymous (as if an Asshole would ever settle for anonymity), plus butter would be good for you, and we'd get more episodes of *The Wire* and *Firefly*.

If you pursued your wishes instead of accepting reality in our unfair *Firefly*-free universe, you'd tell these jerks what they did wrong, insist that they get help, and refuse to talk to them until they did. Well . . . they'd get help, all right. They'd join a group of Parents Abused by Their Adult Children, whine themselves to sleep, and leave multiple tirades on your voice mail. Then you'd agonize over your guilt with friends, therapists, deep-dish pizzas, etc.

It's hard to give up your wish to get through to an Asshole parent because their scary, irrational blame looms so large in a child's life, seeming to fill and control the world. You have to remember that, as an adult, you have your own values and experiences. Whether or not his anger can still cause you pain, it doesn't change your choices or your judgment of yourself. Don't try to get through to him when you know that it's never worked before. Accepting his nature as an Asshole helps you avoid conflict, minimizes his opportunities to do his Asshole thing, and gives him just enough contact and caring to fulfill your familial obligation/guilt.

Above all, don't take responsibility for an Asshole parent's guilt and unhappiness and don't show it if you feel it. You can't make him happy. You can't change your own feelings. You *can* become a competent Asshole-parent wrangler by setting the rules, looking confident, optimistic, and guilt free, and making the most of your allotted time with Assholes you love.

Quick Diagnosis

Here's what you wish for and can't have:

- Freedom from a feeling of impending doom whenever the Asshole is around
- The ability to make an Asshole parent happy (her happiness is way beyond anyone's control, including hers)

- The option to bring your parent into the bosom of your family if and when she needs it
- A way to protect your family from nastiness
- Peace, justice, fairness, and a good relationship

Here's what you can aim for and actually achieve:

- The strength to do what you think is right, regardless of an Asshole parent's anger, or your reaction to it
- A way to protect your own positive view of your family without referencing your parent's negative views
- Limits on the Asshole's opportunity to vent during brief, managed encounters
- Positive things the two of you can share and honor

Here's how you can do it:

- Determine whether there are any good things you can actually accomplish with and for an Asshole parent (like improving her health, security, and relationships) that are likely to do some good and not be defeated by her being an Asshole
- Given your limited resources and the above realities, figure out your own responsibilities, if any, for making this happen
- Use a variety of techniques (avoiding one-to-one encounters, meeting in public places or places you can leave, sending messages by mail rather than telephone or face-to-face) to keep emotions from escalating
- Respect yourself for what you're doing regardless of the negative response you'll probably get and the angry, helpless feelings you'll have to endure

Your Script

Here's what to say to an Asshole parent who is asking you for more
than you are prepared to give and charging you with crimes you didn't
commit.

> Dear [Asshole Parent],
>
> I appreciate all the good things you've done for me and I've listened
> carefully to what you have to say. I'm impressed with how [hard you
> work/well you get through crises/much you claim I put you through]. I
> don't agree with your thoughts about [my terrible parenting/
> ungrateful attitude/haircut], so I will stick with my plans to [cut short
> unpleasant phone calls /let a real babysitter who's sober watch the
> kids/skip that month-long family vacation to a one-room cabin in
> Alaska] because I think they represent the best compromise for
> everyone. Now that we've talked it over, this subject is closed. I'll be in
> touch in a couple of days, and we can discuss [what good coupons you
> have this week/that disgusting movie they talked about on the news
> that you thought I'd like /anything else].

Did You Know . . . Some Assholes Are Saintly?

Now that we've established that Assholes aren't intentionally bad (just dangerously disabled), it's also worth noting that some Assholes are actually
saintly, generous human beings who aren't so big into wrath. They're likable,
eager to help, and willing to make commitments until they're distracted by
someone who needs rescuing. Once that happens, all other kind words and
commitments to you are null and void.

What makes them Assholes is not just their unreliability but the fact that
if you're unhappy with their blown promises, it's your problem for being
overly sensitive and selfish. They're just doing what they think is right, and
you're the asshole.

Meanwhile, their friends and kids wonder if they have to act sick, injured, or obnoxious to get said Asshole's attention. Sadly, even if they do and it works, it's only for a brief moment until someone else more wounded shows up at the watering hole.

So while many Assholes are angry crusaders, saintly Assholes are kindly victims; they actually want you to be happy, even while they're fucking you over for reasons that, to them, are unavoidable. They're less likely to sue you and more likely to make you feel guilty for wanting to sue them, but they require the same amount of distance if you want to avoid being disappointed, angry, and (gently) screwed.

Rising Up from an Asshole Takedown

Given the Asshole's tunnel-vision, friend-or-enemy, black-or-white worldview, she has no choice but to turn everyone against you if she feels you've wounded her, even inadvertently. You may feel like she's using a next-level version of the playground strategy "I'm rubber and you're glue," where she tells everyone that *you're* the Asshole who did her wrong, letting the blame slide off her and stick to you. In fact, the gesture is deeper, more sincere, and a lot more desperate and dangerous.

Assholes share their feelings with your kids, friends, child-abuse hotlines, judges, the local news affiliate, the entire Internet. Since their feelings tell them what really happened, they never doubt themselves. Therefore, what they say carries the ring of truth. You're lucky if you can just leave town and start over under another name.

If, by any chance, being falsely accused of vicious, predatory behavior makes you angry enough to express your indignation and prove your innocence, you're in even deeper shit. You can never win a sincere outrage contest with an Asshole. Your anger just makes you look even guiltier.

In the long run, Assholes' lies often become obvious because they're not clever and calculating about covering up facts. Gathering and examining facts takes time; however, those who are skeptical and look for them will discover the truth. Meanwhile, you may find yourself answering embarrassing questions from people who don't believe you, losing the faith and confidence of your kids, family, and community, and facing restraining orders and mounting legal costs.

Instead of wasting time thinking about how this Asshole could ruin your reputation, motivate yourself to think strategically and keep your mouth shut. No matter how much you want to protest the sheer insanity of what's happening, do not give her that satisfaction.

Among the wishes people express when they write us or come for Asshole takedown treatment are:

When to fear social annihilation by an Asshole:

- You come home to the place where you've faithfully paid rent and your keys won't open the door
- The stern policeman at the door wants to speak to you about the paper in his hand
- You accidentally learn your closest friends had a party and didn't invite you
- Your kids stop calling, or treat you like a stranger
- You want to say you're not a bad person but you know no one will believe you

- To get people to see the truth and clear their name
- To make the investigation end already
- To be allowed to get their tools out of the garage and keep their ex from burning them
- To find a way to see the kids and explain their side
- To stop having to go to court to defend themselves against false accusations

Here are some examples:

My marriage has been falling apart for several years, but I've got two nice kids and the more my wife yelled at us, the more I felt they needed me to stick around and protect them. I didn't see it coming, though, when she had me served with a restraining order claiming

I had bruised her. I've never touched her in my life, but I couldn't get the cops or the judge to believe me and they just told me to calm down, as if I was explosive. Then I got a call from a social worker who says someone, she won't say who, has reported me for sexually abusing my daughter. Meanwhile, I can't see my kids. So finally I got a lawyer, whom I can't really afford, while I sleep on my mother's couch and borrow money from friends. My goal is to stop my life from falling apart.

My ex-husband was a smooth-talking jerk who never did much with the kids, work, or me. Mainly, he loved drinking and spending time and much of his paycheck with his bar buddies, who think he's a great guy, as do our kids. Meanwhile, I've become mean and cranky while earning the money he didn't bring home and doing all the parenting while he was out. I hid that from the kids, and he always acts like there was nothing wrong with his behavior and that our divorce was just me being mean to an innocent guy. The kids blame me and give my new boyfriend a very hard time, though he's a great guy who will almost certainly become their stepdad. I don't want to bad-mouth my ex to the kids but my boyfriend doesn't deserve this shit and neither do I. My goal is to get the kids to see their father for who he is and stop punishing me and my boyfriend.

My husband and I moved to a new town for his job a few years ago. I thought I found a nice group of friends here, though I never liked the way one of them bosses the rest of us around. I never made an issue of it because I assumed it's just her way of being overly possessive, but when I refused to accept her advice about how I should renovate my kitchen, she suddenly stopped speaking to me. I thought it would pass, but then our mutual friends stopped answering my calls and I realized I'm no longer welcome in our social circle. It's just like high school, except worse, and it's affected my kids, who know their kids. I feel terrible and can't stop crying. My goal is to find out what is being said about me and try to straighten things out.

Whether lies force you out of your home, get you targeted for investigation, or just alienate family and friends, they hurt like hell and the possible consequences can terrify you. Fortunately, in most cases, these consequences never end up happening to anyone who isn't in an old Steven Bochco cop drama.

When you're in the thick of it, though, it's hard to remember that damage can eventually be limited, friends who believe shit about you are not your friends, and time will probably restore your credibility with the people who matter most—particularly your kids. Patience and persistence *do* win out, but in the meantime, they require you to know that, regardless of what happens, you believe the truth about yourself. Do not take your misfortune as a personal failure. Do not feel obliged to control what people think about you when it's clearly impossible.

As wolves, *Survivor* contestants, and politicians have discovered, attacking your attacker may damage him or her without helping you. It can also stir up a nasty counterattack. Remember, an Asshole can always beat you hands down in a competition of angry sincerity, and again, the more you protest, the guiltier you look. It's only later, when you have had an opportunity to document facts about who said what and how the money got spent that you will have the advantage.

Instead of attacking or defending, take time to form your own judgment of the allegations against you, even if you don't know exactly what they are. Putting aside your feelings, ask yourself and those you trust why a good person would find serious fault with your conduct, paying particular attention to your own standards for being a good partner, parent, and friend. Hold yourself to any legal or fiscal standards your lawyer tells you to be aware of. Then judge for yourself whether you've done wrong, much as you would judge a friend. For the purposes of this exercise, you're not supposed to be perfect, just good enough.

Of course, you should also ask yourself whether these lies are truly coming from an Asshole by reviewing what you know about the person who made them up—specifically by assessing how nasty and black-and-white their thinking becomes when they feel threatened or unhappy.

When you're confident that the problem isn't you, remind yourself that, though you're in the eye of a shit storm, your only crime was to have a relationship with an Asshole. Even if you chose that relationship, it's not a criminal mistake.

Don't fight back unless it's in a court, you feel it's necessary, and you're likely to win; then get yourself the right help and assemble the tools you'll need for the long haul. You may never completely undo the social or legal damage, but you can strengthen your ability to believe in your own judgment, fight effectively when you must, and become a far better person than you thought possible; certainly better than the Asshole will ever be.

Quick Diagnosis

Here's what you wish for and can't have:

- To get people to see through the Asshole's lies
- To force the Asshole to acknowledge said lies, and any additional Assholery
- To get quick justice, or be certain of getting any justice at all
- To know when the shit will stop so at least you can be sure of the nightmare's end date
- To figure out how to recover from the feelings of helplessness ASAP

Here's what you can aim for and actually achieve:

- Learn how to assess and approve your own actions and use that certainty to weather the storm
- Prevent your anguish over damaged relationships from damaging them further or destroying your hope of ever having a healthy relationship again
- Learn techniques for winning a slander war (mainly through silence)
- Find better relationships, using what you learned during wartime

Here's how you can do it:

- Get legal advice on how to defend yourself and your assets (and forget about your good name, at least for a while)
- Stop yourself from saying and doing the things you'd most like to say and do, because your instincts, like Assholes in general, are wrong
- Use a coach, like a lawyer, shrink, or close friend, to help you respond carefully, positively, and in writing (without any profanity)
- Create a paper trail—email, bank records, or credit cards—to document your defense
- Respect yourself for what you're doing, regardless (and because) of the negative response you'll probably get and the angry, helpless feelings you'll have to endure
- Refuse to be drawn into meaningful talks about feelings that always end badly (see sidebar below)

Your Script

Here's what to say to an Asshole who is saying bad things about you.

Dear [Asshole Slanderer],

I am writing because I've always valued our relationship—it's always been [pleasant/well-catered/so much better than cancer]. I've heard, however, that you feel [hurt/violated/ready to murder my face]. My standards regarding the alleged [child abuse/marital infidelity/ disrespect to your homies] are, I believe, the same as yours, so I've reviewed my actions closely, looking for ways I might have failed to meet those standards. In the end, I disagree with your opinion, and can only hope that time and more evidence will eventually change your mind. Meanwhile, I will not let disagreement interfere with our ability to work together on [raising the kids/church bake sales/supporting the New England Patriots] and will not bring it up again. Feel free to contact me by email whenever necessary.

Grammar for Asshole Wrangling

Don't Say	Do Say
I honestly feel . . .	Great weather, am I right?
Why can't I get you to see the trouble you're causing?	I love spending time with you, but if we can't change the subject I'm going to have to cut this short.
If you can't change, I'm afraid there's no point in continuing this conversation.	Get some rest, and then maybe when you feel better, we should grab some lunch.
I want to clear the air . . .	Isn't this sweater crazy soft?
I didn't try to hurt your feelings and I didn't tell you to leave until after you started yelling.	Past, shmast—let's focus on the present. I think 3-D movies are stupid. Discuss.
You need to change your behavior.	You are great at finding good restaurants!

Saving Assholes from Their Shit

Although we address the twin evils of helpfulness and saintliness in chapter 4, the wish to save Assholes from themselves is worth special attention. This instinct is on a whole new level of damage and futility, like trying to help put out a fire by filling a hose with gasoline.

What's truly dangerous about trying to save Assholes from themselves—given your love for their charisma, your affection for some niceness you see trapped in there, and your pity for the suffering they bring on themselves—is that the main trigger to their awfulness is close relationships. The act of helping them isn't merciful; it's like poking an angry tiger with a cattle prod.

Yes, Assholes are often victims and deserve kindness in any case; if, as we argue, they can't help the harm they do, they still don't deserve blame. You have a duty to protect yourself, however, particularly when you know they're dangerous and that previous efforts to help have ended badly. There's no excuse for sentimental kindness when it pushes a knowing adult to take stupid risks.

The worst danger is not that you'll get hurt—after all, getting hurt is how you learn—but that your involvement will cause permanent harm and compromise other commitments. Here are some cautionary warnings about the risks of being a kind do-gooder when you're tempted to make an Asshole, aka, a do-badder, the object of your kindness.

How to know when you're doing too much for an Asshole:

- They tell you that you're the only person they trust, frequently during long, urgent, and ill-timed phone calls
- The confidences the Asshole shares remind you of, but are more interesting than, the golden years of *Days of Our Lives*
- Your other friends and family complain that you're unavailable (as you now double as an Asshole hotline)
- Other people are more worried about you and your level of involvement than you are about yourself

---

Among the wishes people express when they write us or come for treatment are:

- To save an Asshole from the past and present abusers who have driven them to your (temporarily) safe harbor
- To stop the abusers themselves as if you were the Asshole's personal Superman
- To free an Asshole from an addiction/bad habit by giving him unconditional support that will surely allow him to wean off heroin or alcohol or sex
- To show an Asshole there is someone he can really, finally trust. Yikes.

Here are some examples:

I'm trying to help an unusually gifted student whom I've mentored since he graduated from my high school English class five years ago.

He first came to me for support because he felt the guidance counselor was prejudiced against him, then stayed in close touch, and I like
to think my support sustained him through severe depression and a
bout of opiate abuse. Recently, he's been in crisis and is in danger of
dropping out of graduate school, so he's been calling me every night
and talking for an hour. I can't figure out why, but he hints that he's
using drugs again and having flashbacks to being physically abused
by his parents. I remember meeting his parents, and they didn't seem
like abusers, but the main thing I believe he needs from me is solid,
unconditional acceptance, so I don't want to say anything that he'll
interpret as critical or unsupportive. My goal is to figure out how to
win his trust.

My sister is her own worst enemy when it comes to relationships, and
I wish I could help her control herself. When she's in a good mood, no
one is more charismatic and friendly, but when her mood turns sour,
which can happen at any time, she tears people apart and drives them
away. She won't talk to our parents and stopped talking to our brother,
who used to be her best friend. Her only remaining friends live too
far away to be around when she gets mean, which is why they're still
friends. For some reason, she turned to me for comfort after she felt
the rest of the family had betrayed her. She's so tortured, it breaks my
heart. My goal is to figure out how to use the trust she gives me to get
her to see what she's doing.

My boyfriend is struggling to make some money and move out of his
parents' home, but the economy is terrible and I understand that it's
been hard for him to get a real job. Also, no one will hire him because
he has a conviction for possession when he was eighteen and it shows
up whenever an employer does a security check. So it's hard for me
to say no when he asks me to help him carry drugs, because no one
would suspect me and the cops are always watching him. All he needs
is a little more money, and then he can start his own business and we
can build a life together. I don't mind helping him because it's really a
way of helping both of us, but my mother says I'm going to get into big

trouble, and I've got a child to take care of. My goal is to figure out how to help him get a fair start in life.

It's always better to be a person who believes in helping others, because living up to such values is what makes life worthwhile. Besides, it makes you a good person, which is the only legitimate reason for self-esteem. The key to being helpful, however, is knowing when it's impossible or dangerous. Saving Assholes is usually both.

Before taking on responsibility for someone else's pain and problems, do a careful risk assessment. It doesn't require you to be cynical or negative about the person you wish to help, but it does mean gathering and paying attention to facts, regardless of your feelings.

If someone says she's been abused, for instance, you don't need to know whether it actually happened. You do need to know whether she can now tolerate the normal lumps and bumps of a relationship without reliving the abuse and getting paranoid about someone who is a not-so-bad friend, like you. If she's using drugs, you may assume she's using to self-medicate the pain of loss, anxiety, or depression, but nevertheless, you need to find out whether she can tolerate any pain and frustration without immediately doing whatever makes her feel better.

Get a little paranoid and ask yourself what's the worst that can happen if this Asshole decides you're the source of all her pain. It will obviously hurt like hell if she turns against you and bad-mouths you to all your friends, but with an Asshole, nasty gossip is only the tip of the iceberg. She's totally capable of reporting you to the authorities, be it for sexual abuse you did not commit or something illegal she involved you with. You've heard from her how many horrible things people have done to her in her crazy life; don't doubt for a second that, if you disappoint her, she'll see you as one of those people, deserving of the same treatment.

Don't lose your willingness to help the abused and downtrodden, but don't forget that some downtrodden people are, through no fault of their own, dangerous. If you don't carry out proper screening procedures, the damage can be disastrous, the fault is all yours, and when it comes to blowback, the sky's the limit with Assholes.

Quick Diagnosis

Here's what you wish for and can't have:

- To win the trust of someone who trusts no one
- To turn hate into love by giving love yourself
- To fill the emptiness in someone else's heart

Here's what you can aim for and actually achieve:

- Remain helpful while learning to protect yourself from the needy-but-potentially-nuclear
- Identify and help those who can actually use your help
- If you desperately need to help something, get a rescued pet, preferably one missing an eye or leg

Here's how you can do it:

- Do your due diligence on all those past "abusers"—don't assume they were all idiots, bad guys, or not as loving, sympathetic, or temporarily ignorant about due diligence as you
- Don't comfort someone's pain before you find out what he did and does when he's in pain, and whether it involves inflicting pain on others
- Keep your commitments to your old, unsexy obligations, including those to yourself and your family
- Avoid people who do bad things when they're in pain and don't expect themselves to stop unless they feel better

Your Script

Here's what to say to an Asshole who wants help (but isn't ready to stop being an Asshole).

Dear [Asshole-in-Need],

I sympathize with your mistreatment and your belief that it's caused you to [abuse drugs/bite your nails/get dolphin tattoos]. I wish I could help, but I can't see how anything I could offer could be helpful. If you ever get to the point where you don't feel the need to [abuse drugs/blow up at people/post racist comments on YouTube], I may be able to be helpful, but right now I just don't see anything I could do as a [friend/therapist/ not-drug dealer]. I'm rooting for you and I hope you'll get there.

Grammar for Defending Yourself against False Accusations of Bad Behavior

Don't Say	Do Say
That's not what happened!	Thanks for sharing that.
I can tell you what happened.	I'm going to think about that later.
You're wrong, you fucking jerk.	Friend, I've given it careful thought, and . . .
I want an apology right fucking now.	I'm afraid I'll have to disagree. Anyway.
I hope that cleared the air.	Agree to disagree? Great.
I'd like us to be able to communicate!	Next topic—do you watch *Suits*? I know it's on USA, but I swear, it's good stuff!

Living and Working with Inescapable Assholes

To paraphrase the old saying, opinions are like Assholes; everyone's got at least one really unbearable one in their house or office (or pants, at least depending on your hot sauce intake) and they usually stink. When an Asshole's behavior is out of control in what should be a quiet, controlled environment, it's often because whoever has leadership responsibility in the organization doesn't know how to use it. She's the one who is supposed to tell everyone else to keep their opinions/Asshole behavior to themselves.

Unfortunately, not even the strongest leadership can stop an Asshole from being an Asshole, but it can often limit the damage. By either firing or otherwise constraining an Asshole at work or by setting limits on his behavior at home he can be neutralized. If, without having the necessary authority, you try to limit an Asshole's bad be-havior, you may run into trouble and catch flak instead of gratitude. It's important to ask yourself why those who should be managing an Asshole's bad behavior aren't doing it, especially before you try doing something about it yourself.

It's natural to ask your boss or parent to protect you and limit the damage if an Asshole is messing up your work, belongings, head, etc. If the authorities don't have the strength and just want everyone to get along, however, they may well make you responsible for smooth-ing things over and stopping the bad behavior. They'll tell you that since you're more reasonable, they expect you to solve the problem. If you argue and imply the responsibility is theirs, you're also implying that they're doing a bad job (which they are, but bosses and parents are rarely keen on that kind of critique).

If you feel too responsible for the well-being of your workplace or family to suck it up, and instead try to clean it up, there's no way out of a vicious cycle. The more you try to change bad behavior when you don't have authority, the more everyone will wind up against you. Don't accept the idea that you need to make your family or workplace better when it's really impossible.

Instead, do your job and look for a new one while figuring out ways to stay polite and tune out the Asshole. Give yourself credit for work-ing in a sewer and use what you know about Assholes to find a better job with a good boss who's a better Asshole slayer.

How to know when an Asshole at home or work should be left alone:

- The Asshole has the same last name as the boss
- Your boss or parent wears a T-shirt saying "I'm EVER so nice and harmless!"
- Raising issues gets you sympathy for your feelings and jack shit in terms of action
- Conflict gets you treated as if you used your power to release the Asshole, Kraken-style

Among the wishes people express when they write us or come for treatment are:

- To stop the Asshole at home or work from making them miserable
- To understand why no one does anything about said Asshole despite her obvious jerkiness
- To figure out why speaking up about said Asshole causes nothing but trouble
- To get the powers that be to understand what said Asshole is actually doing—namely, something wrong

Here are some examples:

My sister and I never got along, and I'd like to say that we're fine now that we're in our twenties and living at home out of economic necessity, but it's gotten even worse. She's a weird person who doesn't really get along with anyone, and she has nothing better to do than to make sarcastic comments about me from the time I arrive home from work to the time I go to my bedroom to hide from her. When I complain to my parents, they tell me she's different and if I don't like it, I should find my own place. I don't yet have the money though because I'm paying them what I can every month for rent, but what my sister says to me is really awful. My goal is not to have to flee to my room every night when I'm really doing my best to get ahead and be a good, responsible person.

This guy at work is stupid and lazy, but he's good at joking with our male boss and the other guys on the team, so he gets away with murder. Meanwhile, he's dismissive with me and the other women on the team and has a way of passing the buck, losing what we give him, and then blaming our hormones if we complain. I like the job, but I'm afraid that complaining to our boss will seem petty and disloyal. I've tried telling this guy that I'm unhappy with his work and attitude, but he just makes excuses and tells me I'm not good at getting along. I don't want to be silent just because the boys don't respect what I'm saying. My goal is to figure out how to make this work.

My boss is downright abusive and my performance review was a joke, and I'm not the only person who feels that way, but going to HR about him has gotten me nowhere. I tried speaking to the big boss, who was very pleasant and said he'd look into it, but afterward nothing happened. Then my performance review got even pickier and I have the feeling they're trying to document me out. There's a nasty atmosphere, and it's really my boss's fault. I don't understand how he can get away with it. My goal is just to be left alone to do my job.

You're right to expect management to do something to stop Assholes from behaving like Assholes within your family or business organization. You're right to talk to management about the problem after making sure you've got your facts straight and don't sound too vindictive or emotional. Before you act, however, you should look around and wonder why no one has objected to the bad behavior before.

Unfortunately, the usual answer is that there's something wrong with the parent, boss, and others who tolerate bad behavior without stopping it. They may be far more likable than the Asshole, but they're the bigger problem and you're not going to get anywhere.

Don't keep on fighting. You'll just get more entrenched in a place you need to leave and a struggle you can't win. Use every tool you can think of to detach yourself from caring without compromising your principles. Keep on being polite, doing your job, and living up to your responsibilities, but start to cool your connection to this social or work world while heating up your search for the next one. Remember, your prime responsibility is to meet your own standards as an individual, not to save the family or team from itself.

An Asshole is like a managerial stress test; you can tell how solid the leadership is by how they deal with his bad behavior. The longer it's been going on and the more outrageous it is, the worse the weakness at the top.

If an Asshole is accustomed to getting away with bad behavior at your workplace, he may cross a line and do something nefarious. You can document it and use it for leverage. Don't expect it to happen, but be ready if it does. Seek out advice or do research that tells you where the line is and what your rights are if it's crossed. Remember, though, your goal isn't to get revenge or express your anger. As good as that would feel, your goal is to get what you think is right, if the fight is worthwhile and winnable.

Don't get distracted by Assholes and their bad behavior in your home or workplace. Look instead at how they're dealt with by the powers that be and decide what you need to do to protect yourself and find a better place to live and work.

Quick Diagnosis

Here's what you wish for and can't have:

- To be treated fairly and protected from bullying by the boss
- To see people who behave badly treated fairly, as the Bill of Rights dictates
- To be heard and understood when you have a legitimate complaint
- To be recognized for hard work and dedication, and not with a golden trophy or anything, just the basics

Here's what you can aim for and actually achieve:

- Become invisible and hope the Asshole picks on someone else, hopefully someone who actually has the leverage to get him axed
- Shift your office, partition, bedroom, career, etc., and get a white noise machine and a DVD on meditation
- Get permission to work at home so you can get your job (and new job search) done in peace
- Learn how to spot Assholes and ineffective bosses when you interview for a job or go on a date

Here's how you can do it:

- When you're sure that talking gets you nowhere, shut up
- Don't complain about the Asshole, nice-guy boss, or work because,

as cathartic as the temporary venting feels, it just makes them more important
- Don't threaten the Asshole or your boss/parent with criticism; chat with them about the weather or Greek yogurt
- Comfort yourself by doing a good job search or finding a good orphanage to grow up in

Your Script

Here's what to say to a boss or family member "in charge of" an Asshole who is making your life shit.

Dear [Nice-Guy Boss/Parent],

Thanks for listening to my concerns the other day. I really appreciate your [taking the time to listen/smart ideas/ability to fart so silently]. I now have a much better idea of how to respond to disagreements about [your job description/alleged bad behavior/my job performance (which is excellent)]. I now have an action plan that will include [being a dedicated part of the team/hearing my co-workers out/ doing all the stuff I'm already doing because I'm fucking good at my job]. I am optimistic that these measures will be helpful and effective. [Subconsciously implied: you are bad at your job. But don't insert that.]

Never expect to untangle your feelings about Assholes or whatever about them that ties you in knots. It will just get worse. If you try to "make things right," you will find yourself turning into an Asshole, driven to seek revenge, closure, and justice, instead of hanging on to your original goals and your original personality. You have a right to feel pain, injustice, and unfairness when Assholes collide with your life, but your goal is to keep going down the road that is most meaningful to you using whatever equipment still works. The more you can strengthen your personal philosophy and see meaning in the good things you do, the better. The Asshole will find a new source of blame. Focus on finding your old purpose, sticking to it, and riding out the shit storm.

fuck treatment

Even if you've read this entire book from cover to cover and learned all you can about managing expectations, accepting limitations, and wrangling Assholes, you may still be considering getting professional help, but not feel entirely confident you know what "treatment" actually entails.

So now that you've read a full guide to handling life's most common unsolvable problems, we offer you a guide to the most common forms of professional help, along with how to decide whether it's truly necessary, what kind might work best, what to expect, when to stop, and basically all the information you need to approach treatment without feeling helpless.

In any case, treatment usually provides partial help; the rest is up to you, so you need to get as knowledgeable as you can in order to decide whether more help is necessary or not, and what you can get out of it (that you can't get from just reading this book).

Getting Treatment

There are many suggested methods for problem solving in this book, from the pleasant, such as exercise and kindness, to the less pleasant, such as setting limits and shutting the fuck up. And then, of course, there's treatment, including medication and talk therapy.

Treatment happens to put food on our table, but it's rarely our first recommendation for any problem; it can be expensive and time-consuming, and if you enter it with unrealistic expectations, ineffective or even damaging.

Many people think therapy is a deeply emotional, somewhat spooky process whereby a compassionate, supportive Melfi/Gandalf hybrid therapist gets patients to recognize and experience painful thoughts, memories, and feelings. People assume this therapy gets at deeper reasons for emotional pain and irrational behavior and offers a more permanent and self-reliant solution to persistent unhappiness than just popping happy pills ever could.

Unfortunately, therapy of that kind, like most treatments, is rarely a cure, sometimes totally ineffective, and frequently effective to a limited degree. In any case, insurers would rather pay for you to get a third arm attached to your back to better facilitate the scratching of your ass than cover any kind of frequent, endless, goalless therapy.

As for getting at the root of issues, that's nice when it happens, but it usually only happens in movies (that aren't good) with results that are equally unrealistic. In real life, most problems have many causes and many of those causes can't be changed, even with blinding insight or a good, snotty cry, so if you expect that treatment will provide solutions, you'll feel like a failure.

People who recognize this simple fact, however, including both therapists and patients, do not see themselves as failures when therapy doesn't work. Indeed, therapists who recognize the limits of talk therapy have developed many new ways of using questions, ideas, suggestions, and coached behaviors to accomplish specific goals. When considering therapy, it's important to recognize that you have many treatment options beyond the classic couch scenario, ones that aren't mysterious, confusing, or interested in your mother.

Most therapies teach a specific technique for dealing with well-defined problems and have measurable goals for managing despair, eating disorders, or obsessive-compulsive symptoms. Very few invite you to describe how you feel about everything, or how your poor dating habits might be due to losing your hamster in sixth grade.

In any case, if you think you need therapy of any variety, there are simple ways to determine whether you need it, where to look, and whether it's working. Keep in mind, however, that as varied as your treatment options are, and they are extremely varied (see sidebar at the end of this section), all are limited and none guarantee a cure. If you can ask questions and figure out costs and risks, however, you can get the best out of what even we think is your last resort.

Here is what people wish mental-health treatment could provide (but it can't):

- A new you (or at least a you that you hate less than current you)
- No more urges to do or say stupid, self-destructive things
- A cure (to depression, anxiety, or most of life's problems)
- Better relationships (when the chemistry is bad and the other person is a jerk)

Among the wishes people express are:

- To get at the root of their problems
- To stop feeling the way they do
- To overcome depression and anxiety
- To no longer feel like they have to do self-destructive things

Here are three examples:

I often feel somewhat depressed, and have for short periods since high school, but anxiety is what's bothering me the most lately. I think it's related to losing my boyfriend, but I don't know if it means I choose the wrong kind of person and really need to explore why, or whether there's something wrong with me that ruins relationships, or whether it's part of a bigger problem that I've had since I was a teenager . . . all of which leads me to believe that I might need to talk to somebody. The problem is, even if my issues are worth talking out (and won't just pass on their own, like they always eventually do), I don't want to end up relying on drugs that make it impossible to feel anything. My goal is to figure out what kind of treatment I need, if any.

I don't think I need treatment, but my wife insists I do. She says I seem unhappy and depressed, and that I can be loud sometimes and intimidate people. Not her, clearly, but she worries about me and thinks it's affecting the way people see me at work, and when I asked a coworker, he agreed that I seem angry and down sometimes. I trust what they're telling me, but at the same time, I swear that I feel fine, and I'm never particularly cheery. I guess now that life has me a little stressed out for other reasons, I seem particularly sour, but I'm not sure a doctor can do anything about it. My goal is to figure out what they're talking about and get help if it's the right thing to do.

My marriage hasn't been going well since the kids arrived and nudged my husband to discover how much he likes to spend his evenings at the bar with his close, close drinking buddies. Still, I don't want to break up our marriage without trying to fix it first, so I finally got him to go with me and see a couples therapist. He talks about how he feels that I nag and criticize him until getting out of the house is the only way to prevent a fight, and I talk about why I'm angry having to hold the bag and be the grown-up all the time. The therapist encourages us to air our feelings and has suggested to him that he really isn't doing his job, but he doesn't get it and says we need to find a new therapist who takes his side instead of mine. So couples therapy really isn't working, but I'm still not ready to give up. My goal is to figure out why it's not working and whether we should continue or find another therapist (who doesn't take sides, period).

If you had a pain in your leg that wouldn't go away, you probably wouldn't hesitate to go to the doctor, and that doctor would help you pinpoint the pain and give you a variety of options to deal with the pain, and hopefully one would be simple and mostly successful, and ta-da: better leg.

Sadly, persistent psychic pain is less easy to pinpoint, and the brain is basically the human body's junk drawer; science has a rudimentary idea of what you can find in there, but the exact location of most things therein is unclear. That makes it hard for the doctor to provide you with new information or definitive treatment that will cure your pain, and even harder for you to know when it's smart to go to the doctor in the first place.

Still, even if brains are far more complicated and less understood than limbs, deciding whether you need mental-health treatment is basically like making any other medical resource decision, taking into account what you can afford, how much your problem interferes with your life, and whether obsessing about it will do more harm than good.

Perhaps because mental health treatment is misperceived as mysterious, people assume it has magical powers ranging from rooting out most kinds of unhappiness to turning you into a flake. In reality, of course, unrealistic expectations lock you into unachievable goals, so count on your own experience and judgment to decide whether treatment is meeting your expectations or likely to do so anytime soon.

If you have anxiety and depression after a loss, it's easy to assume that the loss caused your pain, and that talking with friends and healing with time is all you need. This may actually be the case if you haven't been depressed or anxious before, the loss is terrible, and there's no one around whom you can really talk to. To paraphrase R.E.M., everybody hurts sometimes, so not everybody needs to see a doctor about it.

Most likely, however, your symptoms aren't new and have persisted in spite of good talks with supportive friends and family. That's why it's wishful thinking to believe that treatment can stop symptoms quickly or entirely and prevent them from coming back. Instead, you can expect talk therapy to provide support—help you fight negative thoughts caused by depression, anxiety, and life—and give you a tool for managing your symptoms this time and after future episodes.

Since choosing the wrong person to love is often a key part of heartbreak, look for a positive coach or therapist who can help you nail down the lesson to be learned and figure out some new procedures to help you find better partners and keep you from making the same mistake, while also fighting negative thoughts arising from depression.

As far as looking for the right therapist, do remember to actually look; too many people make the mistake of picking the first name off the list provided by their insurance company and assuming that if things aren't working with that therapist that means therapy doesn't work for them, period. Finding the right therapist takes time, and it's like picking out a good mentor. Look for someone who is interested in teaching the topic you think you need to learn and who has a positive way of motivating you while accepting your particular learning style.

As for meds, it's always your choice to decide whether they're necessary; if you think that shrinks can hold your nose and force pills down your throat, you're mistaking them for veterinarians. Sometimes, the choice to try medication is simple; i.e., if your symptoms don't let you get out of bed in spite of warm support and good coaching. It's the same choice you would make for any chronic, severe medical problem, so don't get moralistic and blame yourself for whatever decision you think is negative.

If others say you need help but you don't really see what they're talking about, congratulations for being able to experience suffering without feeling any pain. Obviously, you care about the impact of your behavior on others, even if you don't have an instinctive ability to feel it or see what it is, and would rather make your wife happy than take your talents to the circus.

Ask yourself whether your grumpiness affects the roles you value the most and in which a little misplaced anger can do a lot of damage, to your parenting, partnership, and maybe leadership. If you don't think crankiness has much effect, then it's just an annoying-yet-harmless personality trait, like constantly soliciting high fives or ending every sentence with a question mark. If you do think being crotchety is holding you back, then look for a therapist who seems able to help you spot what you're doing when you're angry and manage your behavior more effectively.

If treatment changes your feelings and makes you less depressed and irritable, more power to you, but don't consider yourself or treatment a failure if that doesn't happen. Some people are grumpy and poor at self-observation, even when they're also smart and life is going well. If treatment doesn't change the source of your problems, you deserve great credit for deciding to improve how you manage them.

If you can't get a treatment like couples therapy to persuade your deadbeat spouse that he needs to stop drinking and come home after work, remember that your treatment goal is not to change him, because it's impossible, but rather to see whether he can be encouraged to change. And of course, despite how much your therapist might encourage sharing, remember that insults and character attacks, no matter how justified, rarely make for good persuasive tools.

In this case, your therapist agrees with your complaints but can't get through to your spouse any more than you can, even without the insults, so stop blaming yourself for feeling needy and angry and not getting your husband to see your point of view. A professional couldn't get a better result, and they needed nothing but the copay.

Now, instead of trying harder to get him to see the problem, figure out what you want to do about his faults. Find a therapist who blocks you from ruminating about could-haves and should-haves or sharing anger, helplessness, or complaints about your husband, and instead helps you build up your resources and consider your options.

Whether it's your current couples therapist or a new one, choose someone who can help you announce your intentions to your husband without further efforts to persuade, bully, or defend. Then, whether or not your announcement gets through, you'll know you've done your best to save your marriage while protecting yourself and your kids from an early-stage deadbeat alcoholic.

Try any kind of treatment you think might help, but don't try the same thing again and again or assume that it would have worked if it were done properly. Instead, use failed treatments to limit your expectations and teach you what you have to live with. Allow yourself to explore your options, whether that means different types of therapy or just different doctors.

If you've objectively assessed the severity and impact of your problem and decided it needs attention, it won't take you long to find out what you need to know about treatment, assuming you're not scared to read articles, ask questions, and weigh risks against benefits. Then you'll know what kind of expertise and personal qualities you're seeking in a doctor, as well as how to measure progress, so you can find the combination that will, ta-da, make you and your brain (mostly) better.

Quick Diagnosis

Here's what you wish for and can't (always) have from treatment:

- Insight to change your life and improve your behavior
- New, better, or more confidence
- A wrenching catharsis that will ease your sorrows and teach you to enjoy life, moment to moment, while you're still alive and not yet dead
- Happy, conflict-free relationships with the Assholes in your life

Here's what you can aim for and actually achieve:

- Identify how much control you have over whatever's ailing you, with or without treatment
- Develop a good idea of what treatment does and doesn't have to offer and what its risks and costs are
- Develop your own reasons for determining whether higher-risk, higher-cost treatment is worth pursuing
- Make treatment decisions that are worthwhile, whether or not they get you a good result

Here's how you can do it:

- Determine rationally whether your problems are worth getting treatment for, or would actually get worse with too much attention
- Ask questions and do a little research to figure out what treatments have to offer and the risk and cost of trying them
- Shop for a therapist thoughtfully
- Evaluate the effectiveness of a particular treatment, and its costs and side effects, without assuming that a poor result is anyone's fault
- List your criteria for considering treatment worthwhile, aside from its making you feel better
- List your criteria for stopping treatment to see whether or not you continue to need it

Your Script

Here's what to tell yourself/friends/your therapist about your treatment decisions.

Dear [Self/Concerned Friend/Therapist Who Would Like to Take Me On],

I feel like I should be able to [feel/do/relate/function/pitch] better than I do, but I won't let [frustrated ambition/comments of others/ peer comparisons] get me to waste time on treatment unless I believe my problems will possibly [cost me my job/drive away my spouse/cause me to burst into tears or rage in the middle of ordering a burrito]. If I think treatment is necessary, I have no doubt I can learn enough about it to decide what's [worth trying/inappropriate/total bullshit] and whether the risk and cost are worth it.

Basic Treatments, Defined

While we try to avoid shrinky jargon in this book, there's no way to avoid it when describing the different types of therapy, many of which (e.g., CBT, DBT, psychopharmacology) sound to the average person like the names of chemical weapons used in Vietnam.

Below we explain these terms by giving a brief description of several therapies, including how likely they are to be covered by insurance, who performs them, their negative aspects, and a one-to-ten rating on the BTPS, aka, the "bullshit-to-pragmatic scale." According to the BTPS, a therapy with a rating of one is totally flaky and subjective (e.g., new age crystal-type bullshit, relying on willpower, etc.), and a therapy with a rating of ten is supremely objective, measurable, and unbiased (e.g., a kind of therapy that hasn't been invented yet and is performed by a robot, but some existing therapies get close). Ratings are based on the assumption that the patient is a willing and eager participant in therapy; if not, he'll rate everything as 100 percent bullshit anyway.

Of course, you can always learn more about each treatment by discussing it with your primary care doctor, looking online, or talking to friends about their own therapy experiences, but for now, here are the basics.

Therapy Basics	Done By	What It Is	Drawbacks
Old-School Talk Therapies Insurance Friendly?: Sworn enemies— insurers think it's unfocused and endless and its therapists believe insurers want to rip off patients. BTPS: 3 or 4	Psychiatrists (MDs), psychologists (PhDs), social workers, nurses, the professional hand-holders on *Hoarders* (see chapter 4). Hereafter referred to as "those in all major clinical disciplines."	Therapist asks "How do you feel?" followed by painful silence, followed by the therapist's suggesting squirm-inducing reasons for what you did or didn't say or why you get angry when you're really sad or vice versa or something about your mother, etc.	Still popular on TV and among older clinicians, but younger clinicians have more faith in cognitive and behavioral techniques. Not very popular among most patients, who want direct answers and have less patience for painful processes that take forever to show results, especially when it's on their dime.
Current Talk Therapies Insurance Friendly?: Yes, but only if there's a measurable goal and a willingness to stop every few sessions for progress reports. BTPS: 4 to 6, depending on the therapist	Those in all major clinical disciplines, but talking more like consultants or teachers than stereotypical shrinks.	Therapist asking questions and giving advice, support, and criticism. Basically a professional friend who is legally prohibited from gossiping to others or even acknowledging they know you.	It isn't standardized— very dependent on the talent and steadiness of the shrink and whether you're on the same wavelength.

Therapy Basics	Done By	What It Is	Drawbacks
Psycho-pharmacology Insurance Friendly?: Yes, if the prescriber doesn't overuse expensive medications when cheap generics are available. BTPS: 7	Psychiatrists and nurses only, at least in most states.	Quick visits centered on assessment and prescribing medications that can reduce depression, anxiety, distractibility, crazy thoughts, and hallucinations.	Visits should, but don't always, include talk therapy about your attitude, illness, and medication. Also, medications are frequently unreliable (fail to work), weak (some symptoms remain), and have side effects.
CBT (Cognitive Behavioral Therapy) Insurance Friendly?: Usually, at least for a few months. BTPS: 7	Those in all major clinical disciplines, but more often psychologists and social workers than MDs.	Identifies standard negatively distorted thoughts usually caused by anxiety, depression, and other conditions, and then teaches you mental and behavioral exercises for fighting their impact on your beliefs and habits.	No quick relief, but makes you feel stronger if you do CBT exercises, negotiating with and dismissing the negative thoughts that make you feel bad in the first place.

Therapy Basics	Done By	What It Is	Drawbacks
DBT (Dialectical Behavior Therapy) Insurance Friendly?: Same as above. BTPS: 7	Those in all major clinical disciplines, with special DBT training.	A kind of CBT that focuses on thoughts of despair, self-hate, and self-injury and teaches a set of thought-and-behavior exercises for staying positive and not giving in to dangerous impulses.	Doesn't immediately reduce your *urges* to hurt yourself, leave your family, or generally blow up your life. Instead, makes you less likely to actually do any of those things.
ECT (Electroconvulsive Therapy) Insurance Friendly?: Surprisingly, yes. BTPS: 9 (Was once low—it was tried for whatever ails you until the 1970s—but now very high)	Doctors in hospitals.	A method for causing seizures in people who don't have epilepsy, because seizures tend to clear up depression (as was probably discovered thousands of years ago). Only administered in hospitals under anesthesia.	Impairs recent memory and requires lots of time and money, because you need to be anesthetized first so the seizure won't hurt you. However, trust that it is nothing like the bullshit shown in *One Flew over the Cuckoo's Nest.*

Therapy Basics	Done By	What It Is	Drawbacks
TMS (Transcranial Magnetic Stimulation) Insurance Friendly?: Nope—high price, hard-to-prove success rate. BTPS: Probably higher than insurers think	Those in all major clinical disciplines.	A painless method for applying intense magnetic fields to specific areas of the brain, it may help depression without requiring anesthesia or causing memory loss.	Not cheap, not welcomed by insurance, not backed by tons of research. It may require many daily sessions followed by refresher sessions.
Couples or Family Therapy Insurance Friendly?: Again, depends on whether there's a focus and time limits. BTPS: 6 (Was low at 4, when all individual problems were blamed on the family. Now not so bad at 6, but still, depends on the therapist)	Those in all major clinical disciplines.	Meeting as a couple or family, uses many different techniques to identify problems and conflicts and get people to work together on solutions.	Not guaranteed to keep things from exploding (think Jerry Springer), particularly if the therapist gives people too much encouragement to air, or fart out, their grievances and share their feelings (see analogy on page 234).

Therapy Basics	Done By	What It Is	Drawbacks
Freudian Psychoanalysis Insurance Friendly?: Not even a little bit. BTPS: Just check out a book of *New Yorker* cartoons	Used to be psychiatrists (MDs), now those in all major clinical disciplines who have received years of training in specialized institutes that teach the theories of Sigmund Freud (1856–1939), granddaddy of talk therapy.	Lying on a couch, usually several times a week, with your back to a relatively silent therapist, you are asked to talk about whatever comes into your mind and then analyze it with the invisible therapist's guidance. Just as Freud did it. Mothers are a frequent topic.	Costly and slow, but impresses some people as very interesting and stimulating, so if you like that kind of thing and have the money ($50K/year) to spend, enjoy.
Jungian Analysis, aka, Analytical Analysis Insurance Friendly?: Insurance providers are allergic to anything analytic, so no. BTPS: Let's call it creative and interesting	Those in all major clinical disciplines, but with years of training at specialized institutes that teach the theories of Carl Jung (1875–1961), frenemy of Freud.	Like Freudian analysis, except Jungian analysis asks the patient to focus on dreams, myths, and folklore-based archetypes so they can become one with the unconscious. PS: Jung might have had schizophrenia.	Equally costly and slow as Freudian analysis, but impresses some people as very interesting and stimulating, if you like that sort of thing (and the Deptford Trilogy by the legendary Canadian author Robertson Davies).

Therapy Basics	Done By	What It Is	Drawbacks
Primal Scream Therapy Insurance Friendly?: NO! AARGH! I HATE YOU, MOMMY! BTPS: Calibrates the low end of the scale, along with Scientology	Those in all major clinical disciplines, but mostly well-meaning psychologists with MAs or PhDs.	Nearly extinct method (popular in the 1970s), held mostly in padded rooms where patients were encouraged to work out their childhood trauma by having tantrums and generally losing their shit.	Loud, dated, and probably not effective. The padded rooms, however, are great fun for kids.

Getting Your Fill of Treatment

Therapy is a lot like dating someone; the only thing harder than knowing when to get involved is knowing when to walk away. There is no marriage in the therapy analogy (just among therapists, as with a certain author of this book), so at some point down the line, your current course of therapy must end.

Most people assume, logically, that treatment doesn't last forever, but as long as they expect it to make them feel better and gain more control over their lives, they find themselves engaged in a process that never seems to end.

The reason, of course, is that treatment is seldom completely effective, and expecting it to be so means you can stop therapy only when all your pain goes away; i.e., when you stop living. Quitting before you get there, even if "there" doesn't exist, makes you feel more responsible than ever for the things about your life you'd most like to change.

Similarly, if treatment lifts your spirits and gives you perspective that rapidly disappears when you stop for even a week because your shrink needs bunion surgery, it's natural to feel you're not finished yet and won't be until your good feelings last longer and you're able to maintain a positive, realistic perspective on your own.

Since treatment of any kind, no matter how frequently it occurs or how deeply it delves into your hidden feelings and painful issues, seldom achieves the kind of change that people expect, it's reasonable to stop at any time you think you're no longer benefiting, regardless of whether there's lots that's still wrong with you.

Your goal is to get what you can out of treatment and accept whatever ills you can't solve. Don't cling to the idea that it has more to offer if you just try harder and longer. You haven't failed; treatment just isn't that powerful, and maybe not that necessary.

It's also reasonable to stop treatment (or at least pull back) if it's not bringing about measurable improvement, even though you still feel you need it. After all, it's costly and you may do fine without it, regardless of how anxious you are not to lose it. Ideally, treatment should show you that you don't need certain things as much as you feel you do, even though it hurts to let them go—like finding the strength to leave an abusive partner or quit drinking—and gaining the courage to quit treatment itself is often a sign of success.

Of course, just because treatment stops doesn't mean you should ever give up on managing bad behavior or getting on with life in spite of bad symptoms, without a therapist; there are plenty of tools out there, including readings and support groups, that can fill the therapy void. Don't rely on treatment unless you see strong evidence that it's making a difference and doing so in a way you can't replicate otherwise.

Sometimes you'll find that continued treatment is, indeed, necessary to maintain stability and prevent you from relapsing. If so, use it only when necessary, as measured by how well you do as you cut back. Never depend on treatment for support if you can find another source, because therapy is the high-maintenance ex you can stay friends with only if you don't fall into old habits again.

Of course, people who know about your problems will always think you need treatment, but that's their worry talking. You must rely on your own knowledge of available treatments and your experience with them to tell you whether or not you do need treatment again.

In the end, you probably don't need treatment for a long period of time and are better off relying on what you've learned and other sources of strength, knowledge, and comfort to manage problems. In other words, you may have moved on, but the time you and treatment shared together will always be special.

Here are reasons for stopping treatment that you'd like but probably can't have:

- Removal of the angst center of your brain
- An acquired immunity to criticism
- A learned inability to bicker or create conflict
- Solid confidence in your ability to take care of yourself, regardless

Among the wishes people want to fulfill before stopping treatment are:

- To first get better control of symptoms
- To first figure out why they can't stop their troubling behavior
- To completely finish healing
- To find a way to hang on to the one thing that has helped them; i.e., therapy

Here are three examples:

I like seeing my therapist and she has helped me get over my shyness, but my social life is fine now and I'm just not unhappy, so I wonder whether I really need to see her anymore. She says we haven't gotten to the root of my problem, so my shyness will probably return and get in the way of having a serious relationship, but I just don't know. My goal is to figure out whether I need to continue and why.

My therapist has been my lifeline for the past five years and I don't know what will happen if I have to stop seeing him. I can tell he's worried, too, but my insurance says that it's not "medically necessary" and won't pay for it. Before I saw him I was very depressed and made a sui-cide attempt. Now I'm still depressed, but I've been working steadily and have a couple friends. I've got a long way to go, and I'm afraid of going back to the way I was before. My goal is to get the insurance company to see that my treatment is medically necessary to keep me from sliding back into the pit.

I was put on two antidepressant medications a year ago when I was very depressed, but I'm not sure I need them anymore, and I think they do nothing but make me fat and tired. I'm back to my usual blah mood, and I don't see why I should continue medications that may be doing me no good and are probably making me feel worse by making me look and feel like a hibernating bear. My goal is to get off medication.

Treatment and its results may always feel personal—and how could they not, given how they focus on your private thoughts, hon-esty, and commitment—but when assessing therapy's effectiveness, it's best to imagine that you're a management consultant, your thera-pist is an employee, and the client is your life. It's your job to fig-ure out whether your therapist is still a valuable part of You, Inc., or whether, based on his performance, it's time to let him go.

As you may have learned from films (*Office Space*, *Up in the Air*) or from the personal experience of being brutally laid off from your job, management consultants are neither sentimental nor compassion-ate. That kind of objectivity can be difficult when reviewing your own treatment, but if you can accept the evidence of your own experience, even if it's disappointing, you can make hard choices the smart way.

Other people may urge you to continue treatment because they wish you didn't have to suffer so much, and while it's easier to dismiss those people when they're friends and relatives, it's harder when the main per-son who believes you need more from therapy is your actual therapist.

It's important, of course, to value your therapist's advice—if you'd never taken his advice to heart, you probably wouldn't have made any gains at all—but ultimately, you're the only one who can evaluate therapy's effectiveness, both for your life and your wallet, and decide whether it's still worthwhile. He may be a problems expert, but you're the only *you* expert, and your opinion on your progress is the final authority.

Ask yourself whether the lingering fears and insecurities that therapy hasn't alleviated are doing you any harm, other than causing you to be anxious, unhappy, and self-doubting. Sure, these are not enviable emotions, but at normal levels, if they don't impair your ability to work, be decent, or live, they can actually be beneficial, since fear can help you be aware of dangerous situations, and self-doubt can get you to double-check your results. Simply put, feeling bad is sometimes good for you.

You're doing a respectable job proving to yourself, day by day, that you can take risks, do new things, and become accustomed to doing things that scare you but won't bother you nearly as much after you get used to them. Your therapist did a good job, too, which is why you should feel confident telling him it's over.

If you feel your therapist is doing a job for you that no one else could and are worried that something—running out of money, an insurance decision, your therapist's departure—will cut off your therapy and your lifeline, remember that feelings are not necessarily reality, and that severe depression and anxiety have their own way of making you feel like you're much more vulnerable and dependent on treatment than you are. If your therapy is making you feel even less independent, it's also less beneficial than you think.

Test out the reality of your need for treatment by cutting back on the frequency of your visits and finding other sources of encouragement, like twelve-step groups, depression-support groups, and friendships with people you can count on. If you haven't done it already, educate yourself about DBT exercises that you can practice when you're feeling self-destructive and hopeless. Yes, you may not feel comfortable sharing intimate information with anyone other than your therapist, but it's something you can learn and it's well worth doing.

Whether it's your own bank account or your insurance benefit that's running dry, don't let panic discourage you. Create a program for shifting your sources of support and, almost always, you'll find you can reduce your dependence on weekly treatment. Even if you continue to need treatment, you will probably not need it regularly or weekly, so you will lower your costs and make it easier to negotiate continued support from your insurer.

If you're less worried about becoming dependent on a therapist and more worried about dependency on medication, then your assessment requires slightly more objectivity, since you're trying to ignore not just feelings of panic but also the stigma of psychotropic medication.

Assessing medication also requires you to weigh a whole new set of costs and benefits; i.e., is not being miserable/anxious/paranoid worth not being thin or able to stay awake or capable of getting a boner?

Since you're the one who knows best whether your symptoms are severe enough and happen frequently enough to be worth preventing, you're also in the best position to decide whether the medication is effective enough to justify the side effects. If you're not sure, talk to your doctor about stopping your meds, at least temporarily; it may give you an opportunity to test the medication's effectiveness and also to see whether it's responsible for symptoms that may be side effects. (Just don't go cold turkey on your own, because some medications can be harmful if discontinued too quickly.)

Another thing you might learn from talking to your doctor is that, if a medication is obviously effective and you tend to get relapses without it, taking it forever as a preventive may actually protect your brain from subtle damage that occurs to some people who have chronic depression over many years. If the idea of being dependent on a medication that long is unacceptable, just think of your meds as brain insulin; diabetics aren't ashamed that they require a lifelong drug treatment, and neither should you be.

The higher the risk from side effects (like the tendency of certain antipsychotic drugs to actually cause diabetes), the more important it is for you to stop the medication as soon as you know it's ineffective or you find a less dangerous substitute. Your job is to consider the risks of stopping medication versus the risks of continuing it. Then, whatever decision you make will be a good one, even if it's not good for your waistline.

Don't make decisions about stopping treatment any more emotional, frightening, or mysterious than they have to be. If you trust your own observations and accept the fact that all treatments have limitations, you can be sure you'll get the most out of whatever treatment you're evaluating and do whatever's best to make You, Inc., as successful as possible.

Quick Diagnosis

Here's what you wish for and can't have from treatment:

- Relief from all intractable, no-good-reason-to-have-it depression and anxiety
- An understanding of why you do unreasonable things that actually gives you power to control those things
- Elimination of the dark, nasty, angry, obnoxious, addictive, and otherwise self-destructive parts of your personality
- Better relationships with people who don't want or expect to have a good relationship with you

Here's what you can aim for and actually achieve:

- Develop rational methods for determining what you really control
- Rate yourself according to how well you cope with what you don't control, regardless of what your instincts tell you
- Learn tricks for managing your weaknesses

Here's how you can do it:

- Use treatment as a tool to discover the limits of what you control
- Find out what treatments are available, what they offer, and what risk they pose

- Define the conditions of illness or disability that, in your opinion, make looking for treatment necessary
- Define the conditions for progress that, in your opinion, make treatment effective and worth continuing
- Stop, suspend, or reduce the frequency of treatment if you don't see your problem improving

Your Script

Here's what to tell yourself/your shrink when you're considering starting or stopping treatment.

> Dear [Self/Shrink/Concerned Friend],
>
> I often feel that my life is a [mess/sewer/vale of tears], but even so, I'm actually coping pretty well overall. I want to find out whether treatment can help me stop [crying/swearing/being afraid of everything, including my own shadow] and I've read up on what's available. I will continue to look for help until it's clear that I'm as [antonym for "broken"] as I'm ever going to be, and then I'll know I've done my best to manage my psychiatric/life problems.

Lower-Cost DIY Treatments

Before you commit to therapy, or if you just can't afford it, we recommend you try less costly alternatives to professional treatment. Below is a sampling of such alternatives, listed in order from those with the highest benefit-to-risk ratio to those with the lowest (and highest absurdity factor).

	Useful For	Effectiveness	But
Exercise	Depression, anxiety	Reduces anxiety and depression within hours, or at least distracts you from them for a while	Relapse is rapid after an injury (as if you weren't already hurting)
Diet, Vitamins, Health Foods	Depression, anxiety	Very hit-and-miss, so you don't know until you try it, but diet means what you eat, not necessarily eating less; nobody feels happier when they're starving	Don't get superstitious about all the things that seem to hurt or help, with very little real evidence, and wind up on an all-Cheerios diet because your depression cleared up the morning after you had a bowl
Twelve-Step Groups	Almost everything	Helps you fight addiction of any kind, or even just negative thoughts when they're not rooted in addiction	You have to find a group that has what you need, and some don't
Meditation/ Yoga	Anxiety	Definitely helps a little bit, and some people are helped a lot	Doesn't help everyone, the effect is limited, and like exercise, yoga has an injury factor
Scientology	Gives a certain kind of person a feeling of meaning and community	May fill a void? Or at least get you closer to Tom Cruise.	It's not cheap, and it's not, shall we say, inclusive to outsiders or forgiving of insiders who decide to leave

	Useful For	Effectiveness	But
Lobotomy	Stops life-threatening symptoms, like depression and suicidal urges, but may leave you with seizures from just a wee bit of brain damage	Very often effective when nothing else is, but we're talking serious Hail Mary here	Not without risk of taking away some function or part of your personality you value, so not administered by almost anyone since the 1960s. That's why it's available only if you do it yourself with a chopstick or golf pencil (but never, ever do that).

Getting Treatment for the Unwilling

If "Things You Can't Control" was a round on *Family Feud*, then the number one choice, above "natural weight" and "the weather," would be "other people's will." When you want to get mental-health treatment for someone who believes they don't need it, it's natural to push them in any way you can, but if you thought controlling someone was difficult, try controlling someone who can't control his own mind. Your urge to drive him to treatment may just drive you nuts.

Perhaps your hope is that once he's "in treatment," even if he feels coerced and reluctant, something about the shrink or treatment process will grab him, change his mind, and allow him to be helped. Then he won't just forgive you for pushing, he'll thank you for your lifesaving heroics.

Unfortunately, treatment for mental illness is the same as for medical problems and usually requires patients to be actively motivated. Push too hard, and she won't be thanking you, just ignoring you out of frustration and even rage; if you're trying to help a relative, you'll have an actual family feud on your hands.

The problem is that if someone enters talk therapy reluctantly, they wait for it to do something *to* them rather than *for* them, passively complying rather than getting involved and doing the homework. If she complies with medication prescriptions, she will quickly object to side effects and stop taking them before they might be effective. If your goal is to show her that treatment can save her, her goal then is to show you that treatment won't work, and she will usually succeed.

There are exceptional circumstances, however, when forcing someone to get help may be worthwhile, and there are other circumstances when advising someone to get help may pay off in the long run, even if your advice is ignored for the time being. Knowing those circumstances, and accepting the limits on your ability to get people to accept treatment, will make you much more effective than if your philosophy is to push hard whenever you see someone who needs help.

Exceptional circumstances always exist when you think someone might hurt themselves or someone else; that's the only time that the police and mental health clinicians have the power to put someone in a mental hospital against their will and keep them there for what is usually a short stay. Even then, it's up to a judge to review the case and decide whether the risk of harm is severe enough to force them to stay there and accept treatment. If there's a risk of harm, you should know what you need to observe and do to start the ball rolling on a commitment evaluation.

(Please note: in most Western countries, the days of having someone hauled off and involuntarily and indefinitely committed to a white-tiled asylum ended long ago; the laws have changed dramatically in favor of preventing unnecessary commitment, and almost all of the long-term state hospitals have been demolished or turned into fancy condos.)

Adolescents who have never been treated sometimes respond well when they're forced to try it, so if you know what treatment he's had before, and have leverage, you can sometimes get an adolescent to get the help he really wants but has been too angry to accept.

In any case, you can learn how to sell people on the advantages of getting help and even covertly offer some ad hoc therapy yourself without bullying or implying she should do it to make you happy.

First, however, you must learn to control your helplessness so you don't wind up expressing anger or fear.

While it's usually impossible to make someone get help, it isn't always, and learning how to describe treatment as a valuable choice, rather than a punishment or obligation, is your best approach. Aim to teach someone, not control them, and she may make the right choice on her own.

Here's what you would like to offer (but can't) for those who refuse treatment that they obviously need:

- A guarantee that going to therapy will make their depression, anxiety, drug addiction, etc., all better
- Treatment that promises a reliable cure without any effort on the patient's part
- A mental hospital/rehab facility that feels like the Four Seasons and doesn't smell like Lysol and pee
- The one, magical therapist who need only make eye contact with them to make them want treatment

Among the wishes people express are:

- To get someone help before they hurt themselves, lose their jobs, and drive their families away
- To get someone to see what his symptoms are doing to him
- To stop addictive, self-destructive behavior
- To prove to someone that treatment won't fail this time

Here are three examples:

My father has been depressed and irritable for the past two years, since my mother died, but he won't get help. He was always a gruff guy, but my mom would balance him out and reveal his lovable side. Now he's just a miserable bastard. I think he might even admit to himself that he's become unbearable—that's part of why he's miserable, maybe—but when I bring up the idea of talking to someone, he just says that therapy is gay and shrinks are lying crooks. Meanwhile, he has driven some of his friends away and my kids dread visiting him. My goal is to get him to get help.

My girlfriend admits that she's depressed, but she insists that there's no point in getting treatment because it's never helped her in the past. Her parents first sent her to a therapist when she was eight, and even after getting treatment off and on for years, it didn't change anything. She only agreed to go back to therapy as a condition for being readmitted to college after dropping out, but it had no impact. I keep catching her crying and I see the cuts on her arms, but if therapy isn't an option, I feel totally helpless. She can be so smart and sensitive and fun when she's not depressed, so I know she can feel better, but she insists she's powerless to change her moods. My goal is to figure out why therapy doesn't help and find something that will, because if I can't help her, I don't know if she'll survive, let alone if our relationship will.

I don't think my brother has ever gotten the help he needs. He has been in and out of hospitals for the past ten years with multiple diagnoses—depression, psychotic depression, schizophrenia—and he's had years of therapy and many medications, but nothing seems to work, and nobody can say definitively what's wrong. Now he's suicidal again, but I don't know if he's on any medication, or been prescribed meds and is just not taking them, or even if he has a therapist at the moment. I just know that I can't force him to get one or take his pills, and that he's gotten so good at hiding things from me, even the crazy thoughts he's probably having, that if he's determined to die, I can't do anything to stop him. My goal is to figure out where he can find someone who can really help him and then make him get an appointment and stay alive.

Since mental illness is in so many ways a total mystery, it's odd that people assume that it can always be solved with treatment.

Total mysteries don't have absolute solutions, so if treatment doesn't work, the answer isn't always to keep looking for new treatments, but to look beyond treatment entirely.

After all, some of those in great distress may have already given treatment a good try with no (or not enough) results, and others may believe they're the only sane person and everyone around them needs professional help. You can't close your investigation and push someone who is unwilling into treatment if it's already clear that it isn't going to help.

On the other hand, if you think someone is in danger but too sick to take care of himself, then that's not a mystery, just a nightmare, and you may decide he needs to be hospitalized regardless of whether he agrees. The only question is whether someone is likely to hurt himself, and if the answer is yes, then close your investigation and ask the real police to come running.

In short, don't be afraid to get creative and use your own judgment. If you can gather a little information and ask yourself a few simple questions, you'll often know whether treatment is worth pushing and how hard to push, or whether you need to turn your inquiries elsewhere.

If someone you love is suffering from depression and loss, it's natural to urge them to get help with their grief. If that depression has turned them into a nasty Asshole, however, urging them to do anything will just allow them to give that grief to you.

To paraphrase the old saying, if you can't get the nouveau Asshole to go to therapy, the therapy must come to the Asshole. Make like a therapist yourself and find a positive way to describe his negative behavior and what it's doing.

After all, your advice and encouragement are perhaps as valuable as anything a therapist could offer. Very often, therapists are in no position to observe how a patient behaves with other people and only know what their patients tell them. You may be in a much better position to observe the problem and give particularly relevant advice.

As such, you could say his irritability, which he used to express in a way that was funny and warm, now drives people away, including those he obviously loves and who love him. You wonder if he sees the problem and, if so, whether there's anything you can do to help. You can think of several promising possibilities, beginning with a talk with his regular doctor about a variety of treatments. That way, you cover all the bases any counselor would, only you don't get paid for the referral.

Like any decent therapist, don't promise that he'll feel better. Indeed, he may feel worse, in the short run, if he stops being mean. Instead, promise him that he'll have better relationships in the long run and like himself more.

Protect yourself by limiting your exposure to uncontrolled irritability, making it clear that you're stepping away reluctantly and not punitively while respecting his decision and conveying confidence in your own view. You may never get him to get treatment, or get everything possible out of your excellent amateur treatment, but you'll know you've given him a respectful, positive push and done all you could.

When someone declares that treatment for depression hasn't worked and isn't worth pursuing, you're right to wonder if she's really tried every reasonable option or if irrational pessimism is controlling her. At that point, try to learn enough about possible treatment options to judge for yourself.

If you think there are treatments she hasn't tried, tell her your opinion and see how she responds. If she's too fed up with treatment to listen, don't feel responsible for getting her to change or you'll go from being her pleasant partner to her overbearing parent in record time.

Instead, accepting the fact that change is highly unlikely, ask yourself whether she has a problem with negative, rigid thinking in other areas of her life. Then decide how much it's likely to affect your relationship if you spend more time together and what kind of limits, if any, to put on your relationship.

Announce your limits in a positive way. Let her know that you respect her ability to tolerate depression, but you think her treatment decisions are too negative and have deprived her of opportunities for help. You can accept a partner who has depression, but you can't accept someone who doesn't take good care of herself. If she can't accept *that*, you know you've done your best and can move on.

If someone you love is very sick and might be at risk of suicide, don't distract yourself by blaming the failure of prior treatment. Like all illnesses, there are forms of mental illness for which modern treatment, no matter how well done, is inadequate. Forget the past and do what's necessary now.

Ask yourself whether you've heard him talk about death, murder, or escaping unbearable pain, or seen him running into traffic or grabbing extra pills "by accident." If you have, tell it to the police and then to the nice emergency room shrink who will decide whether or not to lock him up. Don't worry about whether he'll blame you for stealing his freedom and giving him nightmares; just do the right thing and make sure he lives to be angry at you another day.

If something bad happens, don't focus on who's to blame. Respect the fact that severe mental illness is tough to live with and value the many ways you and others have tried to help. Some people say that suicide is a result of cowardice or failure on the part of loved ones to act, but those people are, to use the clinical term, fucking idiots; there's is no such thing as failure when you continue to love and care for someone who is desperately ill and has lost much of his original personality. There's no such thing as cowardice when someone bravely fights a disease just by getting out of bed every day, even if they eventually can't do it anymore.

Never assume that treatment is the solution when all the clues point elsewhere. Give yourself the opportunity to decide for yourself whether additional treatment is likely to help, whether it will ever be accepted, and whether you're morally obliged to call the cops if it isn't.

You may feel like you're trapped in an impossible enigma, but in reality, some solutions are impossible and some mysteries can't be solved. Still, helpless feelings need never stop you from doing everything you think is necessary to help out and find answers, even if they aren't the ones you were originally looking for.

Quick Diagnosis

Here's what you wish for and can't have:

- The ability to scare people into doing what's necessary to help themselves, since reason doesn't work
- The power to make treatment work if they reluctantly agree to try it
- Relief from fears of what will happen if he doesn't get help
- The ability to retain his trust while you tell him what he doesn't want to hear

Here's what you can aim for and actually achieve:

- Trust your own assessment of the quality of a person's treatment decisions
- Urge better decision making without becoming negative or emotional
- Ask the police and emergency room doctors to take over decision making when you decide it's necessary

Here's how you can do it:

- Ask about wishes to die, give up, kill, ingest, or punish
- Urge someone to consider what she wants treatment for, rather than what she wishes treatment would have done for her
- Gather information about past treatments to determine whether this one has something new to offer
- Warn about the power of depression to cause negative thoughts about the value of treatment
- Hand responsibility to crisis responders if you think someone's at risk of harm

Your Script

Here's what to say about a suffering person's refusal to accept treatment.

> Dear Miserable [Relative/Partner/Guy on the Rail of the Golden Gate Bridge],
>
> I hate to see you [suffering/drinking/sleeping all day] and would love to see you get [help/medication/therapy/your ass kicked/a much better attitude], but I know you won't. From what I know about your past treatment and treatment in general, there are treatments that [might help/won't help/couldn't hurt], and I think that, after considering the benefit-to-risk ratio, you [do/don't/could] owe it to yourself to try them. I will always respect the fact that you have [synonym for "heavy bullshit"] to deal with, but will [say nothing more/doubt your ability to make smart decisions/call the cops] if you don't get more help for yourself.

If you equate treatment with a cure, you're bound to be shocked, helpless, and dismayed when it underperforms. If you take the trouble to find out everything you can about what's available, what it can do and can't, and who can do it to your liking, you'll find yourself making better use of treatment and managing your problems well on your own when treatment has nothing more to offer.

well, fuck me

Ultimately, there's no perfect way to find *the* professional who will be the ideal ear. Personally, I think two important qualities to look for in any clinician are a sense of humor and, while this might seem unbelievable given my tone in the previous pages, a touch of humility.

If you're supposed to embrace the uncontrollable nature of life and human suffering, your doctor should be able to do the same, and some MD/PhD who acts like a master of the universe probably has too much hubris to understand that sometimes we are simply life's bitch.

While I have two Harvard degrees ("the deuce"), a loving family, and a job that allows me to spend my days telling patients when they're being stupid, I've also had to eat a fair number of shit sandwiches in my time. Not long after I turned forty, my father died after years of suffering from dementia that continued during my years in high school and college (a place where, I admit, I was often struggling to keep up with my classmates). For years he had been the wise, calm rock of our family. His dementia, together with an injury that thwarted my mother's musical career, transformed my parents' marriage from ideal to, in a word, unpleasant.

I know now there was no helping them, because many people tried, including, of course, my sister and me (a dysfunctional family is the usual reason for wanting to become a therapist). For many years, I searched for the right words or an illuminating insight that would allow me to alleviate their pain. Finally, as I realized there was nothing I could do, I began to appreciate what they had really achieved.

During all those conflicts, my father never lost his temper, and despite her frequent frustration and anger, my mother never abandoned her family. Their unhappiness never induced them to forget what was important. My respect for them knows no bounds, nor does my appreciation of how un-fucking-fair life can be.

This book is not truly complete until I make one more thing as clear to you as I do to my patients: that I am as prone as anyone to the stupidity of wishful thinking and the humiliation of owning various permanent emotional and behavioral handicaps. I enjoy adopting a scathing and condescending tone when addressing you, and them, because I take great pride in being, myself, the sometime king of stupid. Like all human beings, I am fucked, but I am proud.

So no matter what you plan to do—who you plan to seek treatment with, or if you don't seek treatment at all—remember that there's no such thing as "fair," feelings are stupid, life is hard . . . and you're going to be relatively okay, even if you won't be happy, because your goals are realistic and your efforts to reach those goals will make you proud. Then, the next time life gives you a shit sandwich, slather that puppy in ketchup and enjoy. They're on everyone's menu. Even at the fine dining halls at Harvard.

—Dr. Bennett

suggested bibliography

(The following works were not cited directly in this text, but contain ideas or inspiration that informed this book.)

Michael Bennett:

Austen, Jane. *Pride and Prejudice*. London: Random House UK, 2014.

Burns, David. *The Feeling Good Handbook*. New York: Plume, 1999. Revised edition.

Conrad, Joseph. *Heart of Darkness*. Mineola: Dover Publications, 1990. New edition.

Crews, Frederick. *The Pooh Perplex*. Chicago: University of Chicago Books, 1964.

Hallowell, Edward M., and John J. Ratey. *Driven to Distraction*. New York: Pantheon Books, 1994.

Kushner, Harold. *When Bad Things Happen to Good People*. New York: Knopf Doubleday, 1987.

Linehan, Marsha. *Skills Training Manual for Treating Borderline Personality Disorders*. New York: The Guilford Press, 1993.

Maclean, Norman. *A River Runs Through It*. Chicago: University of Chicago Press, 1989.

Mason, Paul, and Randi Kreger. *Stop Walking on Eggshells*. Oakland: New Harbinger Publications, 1998.

Nadelson, Theodore. *Trained to Kill: Soldiers at War*. Baltimore: Johns Hopkins University Press, 2005.

Nolen-Hoeksema, Susan. *Women Who Think Too Much*. New York: Holt Paperbacks, 2004. Reprint edition.

Prine, John. "Dear Abby." *Sweet Revenge*. Atlantic Records SD 7274, 1973, LP.

Reiner, Carl, and Mel Brooks. *The 2000 Year Old Man in the Year 2000: The Book*. New York: HarperEntertainment, 1997.

Strout, Elizabeth. *Olive Kitteridge*. New York: Random House, 2008.

Sarah Bennett:

Aldon, Pamela, Dave Becky, Blair Beard, Louis C.K., et al. "Pregnant." *Louie*. Directed by Louis C.K. Aired June 23, 2011. New York: 3 Arts Entertainment, 2011. Television broadcast.

Brosh, Allie. *Hyperbole and a Half: Unfortunate Situations, Flawed Coping Mechanisms, Mayhem, and Other Things That Happened*. New York: Touchstone, 2013.

Davies, Robertson. *Fifth Business*. New York: Penguin Classics, 2001.

Fisher, Carrie. *Wishful Drinking*. New York: Simon & Schuster, 2009. Reprint edition.

Forrest, Emma. *Your Voice in My Head*. New York: Other Press, 2011.

Gay, Roxane. *Bad Feminist*. New York: HarperPerennial, 2014.

Gethard, Chris. *A Bad Idea I'm About to Do: True Tales of Seriously Poor Judgment and Stunningly Awkward Adventure*. Cambridge, MA: Da Capo Press, 2012.

Loder, Kurt, and Tina Turner: *I, Tina: My Life Story*. New York: William Morrow & Co., 1986.

Maria Bamford: The Special Special Special! Directed by Jordan Brady. Burbank, CA: New Wave Dynamics, 2014. DVD.

Poehler, Amy. *Yes Please*. New York: Dey Street Books, 2014.

Saks, Elyn. *The Center Cannot Hold*. New York: Hachette Books, 2008. Reprint edition.

Sheindlin, Judith. *Don't Pee on My Leg and Tell Me It's Raining: America's Toughest Family Court Judge Speaks Out*. New York: Harper-Perennial, 1997. Reprint edition.

Styron, William. *Darkness Visible*. New York: Vintage, 1992.

Whedon, Joss, Gail Berman, Sandy Gallin, David Greenwalt, et al. "Amends." *Buffy the Vampire Slayer*. Directed by Joss Whedon. Aired December 15, 1998. Beverly Hills: Mutant Enemy, 1998. Television broadcast.

acknowledgments

Both Bennetts:

We owe special thanks to our agent, Anthony Mattero at Foundry, who immediately got what we were trying to say (as well as our sense of humor), then got us to say it so everyone could understand, then got us a book deal.

Thanks to Liz Gallagher, who introduced us to Anthony, and Quinn Heraty, our lawyer, who has nothing to do with Anthony, but is still great.

We are also grateful to Trish Todd, our editor at Simon & Schuster, who is so smart, kind, and insightful, we spent a long time thinking we had dreamed her. And she let us keep the title, which was also a total fucking dream come true. Thanks also to the rest of the Simon & Schuster team: Kaitlin Olson, Stephanie Evans, Navorn Johnson, Andrea DeWerd, Amanda Lang, and Jon Karp.

In the book, we often refer to the rules for choosing friends that you can accept as family, and these are the friends/families who occupy that special position in our lives: thank you Cottons, Steins (and Kelders, and Carmels), and Nadelsons (and Glebas). Thanks also to actual family who are nevertheless friends, some of whom (Peter Blei-berg, Naomi Bennett, Vicki Semel, and Dee Robinson) were willing to talk with us at great length and help us work out the ideas in this book.

Thank you, Eudora Prescod, for helping to raise the younger Bennett and keep the elder Bennett on his toes.

Here's where we lovingly acknowledge the other Bennett off-spring, Rebecca, who has not written a book, but has done one better by carrying on the family traditions of becoming a skilled doctor and, with her amazingly good-natured husband, Aaron, having a family. We also want to thank their brood of boys, none of whom are cur-rently old enough to look at the cover of this book, let alone read it.

The biggest thanks goes to Mona Bennett, MD, mother/wife, who is not only the head and heart of the family but this book's spiritual adviser and unofficial third author. This book would not exist without her, period (nor would one of the authors). Her expertise—in psy-chiatry, poetry, rustic furniture building, small-dog wrangling, camp-fire songs from Camp Navarac, etc.—is too vast to be contained in any book. In short, M, we love you, and we thank you, for this and everything else.

Do we have to thank each other? That seems tacky. Never mind.

Dr. Michael Bennett:

I thank my college mentor, Professor Robert Kiely, for encouraging me to see a moral force in the magic of a work of art that, however powerful, could be constructive, destructive, or both.

I thank Joseph Conrad, who taught us that every therapist and idealist must beware his inner Kurtz.

I thank my Beth Israel hospital therapy supervisors, whose well-coached scripts helped us shrinks-in-training to respond to a patient's deeper needs while side-stepping expected feelings and conversa-tions: Ted and Carol Nadelson, Paul Russell, John Backman, Alicia Gavalya, Malkah Notman, and Joan Zilbach. Without being overly optimistic about treatment, they believed strongly in the value of *trying* to make your life better, even when it sucked and was likely to stay that way. Particular thanks to Carol, my mentor and matchmaker, who insisted that I had a book to write if I had something I really wanted to say.

I thank my old Upper Canada College buddies, Bill Johnston, George Biggar, Jim Arthur, and Brian Watson, for warm friendship, and my newer Toronto buddy Gail Robinson, who assures me that Canada is much more sensible about psychiatry than the U.S.

I thank my colleagues and friends at the old Massachusetts Mental Health Center who aided, abetted, and debated the views in this book when they ran against the prevailing culture: Jon Gudeman, Laura Rood, Steven Kingsbury, John Vara, Annette Kawecki, Robert Goisman, Dan Pershonek, Paul Riccardi, Barbara Dickey, Sondra Hellman, and Josephine Nazzaro.

I thank my patients who, by and large, give me the benefit of the doubt when I seem offensive and take it on faith that my intentions are good. Although we have taken great pains to remove any and all specific, personal information, the spirit and energy from their part of our conversations is what makes this book a dialogue.

Sarah Bennett:

Thank you to the following people I don't know, but admire, and whose work I found especially encouraging and cathartic during the writing process: Joss Whedon, Jason Isbell, David Ortiz, Jill Soloway, Maria Bamford, Roxane Gay, Rob Delaney, and Amy Sherman-Palladino.

In addition to the family co-thanked above, extra thanks to the cousins Mitchell—Mary-Jane, Eyan, the Mitchell brothers (yes, just like on *EastEnders*)—my caring local family in Fort Greene, and Eilene and Bill Russell and Sherry Lee, my devoted local (unofficial) family in NH.

Thanks to these excellent friends, in order of seniority, because that seems fair: the five-ish-year club is small, because women over thirty rarely make new friends unless they have kids or join a cult. So thanks Mary Lordes and Tabitha D. Lee, and thanks again to Liz Gallagher, the rare hippie with a good sense of humor, for her generosity, positivity, and occasional futon use.

The ten-to-twenty-year club: Angela Boatwright, Lizzy Castruccio Kim (and the *familia* Castruccio) and Jimmy Kim, Jon Hart, Ashrita Reddy, Melissa Ragsly, S.D. Gottlieb, Simon Goetz, Ali Chenitz, Paisley Strellis, Amanda Nazario, and Kesone Phimmasone. Never did I think I'd have such long friendships with people I'd originally baited with mixtapes.

Thanks to even more friends of various vintages: Molly Templeton and Steve Shodin, Tobias Carroll, Alex Eben Meyer, Sarah Bridger, Diana Rupp, Quinn Heraty (again! Never too many times!), and Ben Strawbridge, who get their own special grouping because they haven't just logged many friendship years but helped with this book specifically, whether they know it or not.

Amy Baker helped so much with the proposal, plus she ran a hockey league with me and has an unofficial medical degree, so she knows she's hot shit (or at least she does now).

The twenty-plus club; i.e., those ladies with whom I survived high school: Elanor Starmer, Julia Turner, Dr. Rebecca Onion, and Dr. Cristie Ellis. I did many, many stupid things between the ages of twelve and fourteen that would have made anyone think twice about starting a friendship with me, yet these ladies did and we've since had the privilege of doing many stupid (and not-stupid) things together. I thank them (and their families, old and new) for their love and support in this and everything else.

For her friendship, love, and generosity, Emma Forrest is filed under "timeless." She's the goddess of chutzpah, the lady of the canyon, the woman who originated the phrase "Seth Green is so short that Prince uses him as a vibrator." I love her and her family, both in the UK and in LA, and she is one of the funniest people in the world.

Maysan Haydar is the kind of friend who will never ignore your call, surprise you with tickets to see Soul Side, and load her husband and three genius, exquisite young children into a minivan to drive from Ohio to New Hampshire to visit you, and during that visit, she will bake a spinach pie, and it will be *excellent*. Maybe she'll just do all that for me, along with so much more I can't repay, which is why my last acknowledgment, to her and the thousands of Haydars everywhere, will have to do.

index

about the authors

DR. MICHAEL I. BENNETT, educated at both Harvard College and Harvard Medical School, is a board-certified psychiatrist, a Canadian, and a Red Sox fan. While he's worked in every aspect of his field from hospital administration to managed care, his major interest is his private practice, which he's been running for almost thirty years. The author of *F*ck Feelings* with his daughter Sarah Bennett, he lives with his wife in Boston.

SARAH BENNETT has written for magazines, the Internet, television, and books. She also spent two years writing for a monthly sketch comedy show at the Upright Citizens Brigade Theater in New York. When not living by her philosophy of "will write for food," Sarah walks her dog, watches Red Sox games, and avoids eye contact with other humans. Somehow, she lives in New Hampshire and works in New York. *F*ck Feelings*, written with her father, Dr. Michael I. Bennett, is her first book.

"I keep telling myself that she just can't get much better, but with every book she amazes and surprises me!" —*The Best Reviews*

Praise for the futuristic fantasy of
Robin D. Owens

Heart Search

"Will have readers on the edge of their seats . . . Another terrific tale from the brilliant mind of Robin D. Owens. Don't miss it."
—*Romance Reviews Today*

"A taut mixture of suspense and action . . . that leaves you stunned."
—*Smexy Books*

"Thank you, Ms. Owens, for this wonderful series."
—*Night Owl Reviews*

Heart Journey

"Sexy, emotionally intense, and laced with humor . . . Draws readers into one of the more imaginative otherworldly cultures."
—*Library Journal*

"[A] skillfully crafted read for any lover of futuristic or light paranormal romance."
—*Fresh Fiction*

"It is no secret that I love Ms. Owens's Heart series . . . [A] wonderful piece of fantasy, science fiction, romance, and a dash of mystery. *Heart Journey* is no different, a delight to read." —*Night Owl Reviews*

Heart Change

"The story accelerates as new dangers to Avellana crop up, and the relationship between Signet and Cratag develops, making for a satisfying read."
—*Booklist*

"Each story is as fresh and new as the first one was. I am always delighted when a new Heart book is published!"   —*Fresh Fiction*

"A satisfying return to an intriguing world. Cratag and Signet will leave you wanting more."   —*The Romance Reader*

Heart Fate

"A true delight to read, and it should garner new fans for this unique and enjoyable series."   —*Booklist*

"[This] emotionally rich tale blends paranormal abilities, family dynamics, and politics; adds a serious dash of violence; and dusts it all with humor and whimsy."   —*Library Journal*

"A wonderfully delightful story . . . The author's creativity shines."   —*Darque Reviews*

Heart Dance

"[A] superior series."   —*The Best Reviews*

"I look forward to my yearly holiday in Celta, always a dangerous and fascinating trip."   —*Fresh Fiction*

"Sensual, riveting, and filled with the wonderful cast of characters from previous books, as well as some new ones, *Heart Dance* is exquisite in its presentation."   —*Romance Reviews Today*

Heart Choice

"The romance is passionate, the characters engaging, and the society and setting exquisitely crafted."   —*Booklist*

"Maintaining the 'world building' for science fiction and character driven plot for romance is near impossible. Owens does it brilliantly."   —*The Romance Readers Connection*

"Well-written, humor-laced, intellectually and emotionally involving story, which explores the true meaning of family and love."   —*Library Journal*

Heart Duel

"[A] sexy story . . . Readers will enjoy revisiting this fantasy-like world filled with paranormal talents." —*Booklist*

Heart Thief

"I loved *Heart Thief*! This is what futuristic romance is all about. Robin D. Owens writes the kind of futuristic romance we've all been waiting to read; certainly the kind that I've been waiting for. She provides a wonderful, gripping mix of passion, exotic futuristic settings, and edgy suspense. If you've been waiting for someone to do futuristic romance right, you're in luck, Robin D. Owens is the author for you." —Jayne Castle

HeartMate

**Winner of the 2002 RITA Award
for Best Paranormal Romance
by the Romance Writers of America**

"Engaging characters, effortless world building, and a sizzling romance make this a novel that's almost impossible to put down." —*The Romance Reader*

"Fantasy romance with a touch of mystery . . . Readers from the different genres will want Ms. Owens to return to Celta for more tales of HeartMates." —*Midwest Book Review*

"*HeartMate* is a dazzling debut novel. Robin D. Owens paints a world filled with characters who sweep readers into an unforgettable adventure with every delicious word, every breath, every beat of their hearts. Brava!" —Deb Stover, award-winning author of *The Gift*

"A gem of a story . . . Sure to tickle your fancy." —Anne Avery, author of *A Distant Star*

Titles by Robin D. Owens

HEARTMATE

HEART THIEF

HEART DUEL

HEART CHOICE

HEART QUEST

HEART DANCE

HEART FATE

HEART CHANGE

HEART JOURNEY

HEART SEARCH

HEART SECRET

Anthologies

WHAT DREAMS MAY COME
(with Sherrilyn Kenyon and Rebecca York)

HEARTS AND SWORDS

Heart Secret

Robin D. Owens

B
BERKLEY SENSATION, NEW YORK

THE BERKLEY PUBLISHING GROUP
Published by the Penguin Group
Penguin Group (USA) Inc.
375 Hudson Street, New York, New York 10014, USA
Penguin Group (Canada), 90 Eglinton Avenue East, Suite 700, Toronto, Ontario M4P 2Y3, Canada
(a division of Pearson Penguin Canada Inc.) • Penguin Books Ltd., 80 Strand, London WC2R 0RL,
England • Penguin Group Ireland, 25 St. Stephen's Green, Dublin 2, Ireland (a division of Penguin
Books Ltd.) • Penguin Group (Australia), 250 Camberwell Road, Camberwell, Victoria 3124, Australia
(a division of Pearson Australia Group Pty. Ltd.) • Penguin Books India Pvt. Ltd., 11 Community
Centre, Panchsheel Park, New Delhi—110 017, India • Penguin Group (NZ), 67 Apollo Drive,
Rosedale, Auckland 0632, New Zealand (a division of Pearson New Zealand Ltd.) • Penguin Books
(South Africa) (Pty.) Ltd., 24 Sturdee Avenue, Rosebank, Johannesburg 2196, South Africa

Penguin Books Ltd., Registered Offices: 80 Strand, London WC2R 0RL, England

This book is an original publication of The Berkley Publishing Group.

PUBLISHING HISTORY
Berkley Sensation trade paperback edition / August 2012

Library of Congress Cataloging-in-Publication Data

Owens, Robin D.
Heart secret / Robin D. Owens.—Berkley Sensation trade paperback ed.
p.   cm .
ISBN 978-0-425-25314-4 (pbk.)
1. Life on other planets—Fiction.   1. Title.
PS3615.W478H475   2012   2012015839
813'.6—dc23

PRINTED IN THE UNITED STATES OF AMERICA

10 9 8 7 6 5 4 3 2 1

To those who enjoy visiting Celta.
Thank you.

Characters

The Mugworts:

Artemisia Mugwort: SecondLevel Healer assigned temporarily to Primary HealingHall, who caretakes and lives in the secret sanctuary of Druida City that only lets in the desperate, BalmHeal estate.

Tiana Mugwort: Younger sister of Artemisia and good friend of Camellia Darjeeling D'Hawthorn (heroine of *Heart Search*), a FirstLevel Priestess at GreatCircle Temple.

Sinjin Mugwort: Artemisia's father, ex–GraceLord Mugwort, ex-judge, author of legal treatises, caretaker of BalmHeal estate/FirstGrove.

Quina Mugwort: Artemisia's mother, a SecondLevel Healer and caretaker of BalmHeal estate/FirstGrove.

Randa: Artemisia's Fam.

Garrett Primross: Private investigator and owner of Prime Investigations. Sole survivor of the first people infected with the dreaded Iasc sickness.

Rusby: Garrett's Fam.

Note: Garrett's feral Fam informants are not listed here by name since their numbers are always in flux, but include a gang of cats, at least two dogs, foxes, and the occasional housefluff (rabbit).

The Hawthorns, Garrett's Friends:

GreatLord Huathe Laev T'Hawthorn: Entrepreneur and Garrett's best friend. Laev is nephew to Lark Hawthorn Holly, a FirstLevel Healer (*Heart Search*).

Camellia Darjeeling D'Hawthorn: Wife of Laev, friend of Tiana and Artemisia. Owner of Darjeeling's Teahouse and Darjeeling's HouseHeart. (*Heart Search*)

Brazos: Laev's Familiar Companion, a young long-haired black cat.

The Healers:

FirstLevel Healer Ura Heather: Head of the Primary HealingHall.

FirstLevel Healer Lark Hawthorn Holly: Works at Primary HealingHall and All Class HealingHall, niece to Ura Heather (*Heart Duel*).

GrandLord T'Heather: Retired head of Primary HealingHall, patriarch, father of Ura, MotherSire (grandfather) of Lark Hawthorn Holly.

The Guards:

Captain Black Ilex Winterberry: Captain of the Druida City guards, liaison with the FirstFamilies, wed to Trif Clover Winterberry (*Heart Quest*). He handled the original investigation of the Black Magic Cult.

Fol Berberis: A guard who investigated the original Black Magic Cult.

Rosa Milkweed: A guard who investigated the original Black Magic Cult.

Others/Suspects:

GreatLord Muin T'Vine (Vinni): The prophet of Celta, who has a Fam (Flora) who was nearly sacrificed by the Black Magic Cult.

Avellana Hazel: Mural artist and prodigy. She has a Fam (Rhyz) who was nearly sacrificed by the Black Magic Cult.

GreatLady Danith Mallow D'Ash: HeartMate of T'Ash, an animal Healer. (*HeartMate*)

A. Gwydion Ash: Second son of GreatLord T'Ash and D'Ash, an animal Healer.

Straif T'Blackthorn: GrandLord T'Blackthorn, FirstFamilies Grand-Lord, best tracker on Celta, married to Mitchella Clover D'Blackthorn. (*Heart Choice*)

Trif Clover Winterberry: Wife of Captain Black Ilex Winterberry, surviving victim of the Black Magic Cult. (*Heart Quest*)

Dufleur D'Thyme D'Willow: Wife of GreatLord Saille T'Willow, surviving victim of the Black Magic Cult (*Heart Dance*), cousin to Captain Black Ilex Winterberry.

Sedwy Grove D'Clover: Wife of GrandLord Walker Clover ("Noble Heart" in *Hearts and Swords*), dupe of the Black Magic Cult.

Barton Clover: Brother of GrandLord Walker Clover, head of security of Clover Compound.

One

Nightmares and a sense of foreboding woke him, so Garrett Primross walked to work as dawn broke hoping the infrequent uneasy feeling of doom was wrong for the first time in his life. In his career as a private investigator, he felt in control. He knew what he was doing. And at work he might be able to avoid or mitigate any disaster that might be looming today.

As he approached the back entrance of his shabby office building located in a lower-middle-class neighborhood, a cat hissed and a group of seven intelligent feral cats slipped from the shadows within the alley. Animals that Garrett used as observers and informants, they were able to become Familiar Companions to people if they'd wanted. Most didn't. They preferred the wild and free life—with regular meals and occasional petting.

Garrett had contacts within the fox dens and with the rare wild dog.

Gar-rett! the current leader of the ragtag band of ferals shouted loudly in Garrett's mind.

I hear you, he broadcast to the group. Their milling around slightly decreased.

You promised first thing at office, We get FOOD! Black-and-White tom insisted.

I haven't broken that promise, Garrett said.

There is a MAN on OUR front stoop. He has big magic-Flair. He looks like he belongs around here, but he wears clothes that don't smell of him. He wants to talk to YOU.

At a little after dawn, septhours before WorkBell? Not a good sign. *How do you know?* Garrett asked telepathically.

He said your name to the door, but the door was quiet. Then he looked at Us and told Us, but We ignored him. You can talk to him, but We get Our FOOD first!

That's the deal, Garrett agreed, though his curiosity was ruffled. So were the hairs on the nape of his neck that warned of trouble.

The young and slinky short-furred black cat slipped around the corner of the building at the end of the alley. *I got close. He did not see Me.*

Maybe not, but if the man had great psi power—Flair—Garrett would have bet that the guy had sensed the intelligent animal.

He did NOT sense Me with any of his Flair, the cat, also a tom, insisted. *He smells like rich.*

Garrett grunted. Probably a Nobleman. A spot between his shoulder blades twitched and the damn foreboding increased. Sounded like a man with a problem. A high-class client usually meant a tough problem. The last one had included theft, kidnapping, and murder.

And he smells like a long-eared, ball-tailed housefluff Familiar Companion, the black cat that Garrett called Sleek Black continued.

More interesting, but still not enough data for Garrett to figure out who the guy might be.

And he smells like RESIDENCE.

Only the greatest Nobles on the planet lived in Residences—Houses as intelligent as these animals, and a lot longer lived. Interested, Garrett asked, *What do Residences smell like?*

Cats would sometimes answer, but usually not unless they wanted something from him. He made it a point to always be in the credit column with intelligent cats, giving them information without expecting payment. It had irked him at first, then he'd shrugged and accepted it as a cost of doing business.

This time, again, there were many replies.

Special housekeeping spells for pee, said the brindled tom.

And for puke, said the fat brown tabby female.

Thick, rich, nose-stop smoke smells for rituals, said the leader, sniffing lustily, as if proving he could.

Expensive incense, Garrett translated. The twenty-five First-Families—descendants of the colonists who had funded the trip from Earth—all resided in sentient Houses. Garrett ran through the lords mentally, but didn't come up with any reason why a person so powerful would want to hire him.

A yowl went up, followed by more. *We get Our FOOD!*

Garrett winced. *FINE!* he yelled back at them telepathically. *Stop that caterwauling, NOW.*

They did, having learned by experience that when he gave such an order, the consequences of disobedience could be major. Like a delay in being fed.

Now they ringed his feet, staring up at him, narrow-eyed.

He said, *I will feed you in the back courtyard.* Then he'd see if he could come up from behind the Nobleman and check him out— begin the conversation on his terms. And whip his inner dread into shape, get control of the problem from the start.

Quiet, the cats trotted after his own soft-footed prowl to the back entrance of the office building. The area was paved with flag-stones as old as the building in the optimistic hope that the tenants would have gliders to park. No one who rented in the building was wealthy enough to do so.

He murmured the spellshields down and the locked door open with a few Words. Once inside he tilted his head but sensed no one else was there.

So he went to the small spellshielded storeroom off the one long main corridor. There he kept cat food, treats, a few toys, and a small canister of catnip. He'd left the back door open and returned to the courtyard with the bag of kibble and poured the daily amount into the trough.

As if they'd unconsciously expected him to renege on the deal, they all hurried up to the trough with minimal jostling for position and crunched up the food. The cats were his informers and observers, but he knew that more than one of them had gone hungry before they'd become his secret eyes and ears around the city.

Sleek Black finished first and sat back on his haunches, staring at Garrett. He'd only joined the band in the spring. Garrett got the impression that the tom might be considering becoming a Fam . . . if Garrett, as an example of a human, impressed the young cat. Garrett figured that the youngster would want a home and a warm hearth when winter came.

The black cat burped discreetly, flicked his whiskers. *What do you want Us to do for the food?*

Garrett shrugged. He'd find out who the Nobleman was soon enough. After that, if he felt he needed more information, he could have the cats check the guy out.

Ears swiveled in his direction. *As always, keep your eyes open and listen.* He continued to speak mentally. He didn't know what the man might be able to hear; his psi power Flair might have gifted him with augmented hearing.

Sleek Black nodded and vanished into the deep shadows of the morning. The rest left the food trough, some stopping to clean themselves, some shooting away like they had their own business or something that might bring them an extra treat from Garrett. Dogs and the other ferals would come to eat now.

Going back inside, he closed and locked the door with a Flaired Word and padded softly along the dingy corridor with offices on either side toward the front door. His sword was heavy on one hip, his blazer on the other. They were emotionally comforting, but they'd never been much use in the three events that had come after the warning dread had hit.

He stopped at the front door and used Flair to make the small window panel in the door transparent on his side.

The Nobleman in disguise was younger than he by about a decade. But his young face still had lines beginning to etch deeply in his skin, and his long dusty brown hair showed silver threads—careworn. His eyes were a muddy green. He was more even-featured, of course, than Garrett and held himself well. The man was nearly as tall as Garrett, who was a big man, but the guy wasn't as muscled.

Garrett yanked open the door. The Nobleman whirled, set into his balance, raised his arms ready to defend.

"Good reflexes." Garrett nodded to him. "I'm Primross." He gestured the Noble to proceed ahead of him down the hall.

"Vinni T'Vine," the man said as he stepped inside. He waved the door shut, but made no other move.

A great Noble, highest of the high. And *the* prophet of Celta. No one wanted Vinni T'Vine to show up on his doorstep with the knowledge of his future in his eyes.

Close up, Garrett noted strain on his face, his sunken eyes. A hint of darkness in the tender skin under them showed T'Vine hadn't gotten much sleep lately. Garrett really didn't want to contemplate what might keep a man who saw visions of the future up at night.

The Noble continued in a low voice that held more rough than smooth, "You must have figured out by now, Garrett Primross, that you are a point the fate of Celta circles around."

Garrett's mouth dried and his bowels went sloshier than he'd ever admit. "Haven't thought of that much," he lied. Ever since he'd lived through a sickness when everyone else around him had died, he'd been considered unique by most.

"I don't like to try and guide the future." An unamused smile from T'Vine. "Bites me in the ass more often than not." His gaze drilled into Garrett with nearly tangible force. T'Vine examined him, shook his head. "But sometimes I have to take the chance." His nobly sculpted mouth flattened, he dipped his head in what might be respect.

All of Garrett's nerves twined tight as he waited. The moment took on the glassy and acute atmosphere of danger.

"You should cooperate completely with the FirstLevel Healers," T'Vine said.

Healers. Hell. Garrett didn't like Healers, too much poking from them during the epidemic as he gave blood and Flair to help stop the sickness.

He and the prophet stared at each other for a full moment of silence, until Garrett dragged out words. "That all?"

Vinni inclined his head. More heavy silence. More matched stares. Breath stopped in Garrett's lungs until his ears rang from the lack and he knew from the hair rising on the back of his neck that he had to listen to the prophet. Probably follow T'Vine's advice. "I hear you."

The Nobleman's head tilted. Garrett felt his own eyes widen as he watched T'Vine's eyes change color from dull green to hazel, a better tint for the guy. The Noble's shoulders relaxed and Garrett heard the puff of relieved breath. Then he smiled and his gaze warmed. "You'll do." He paused and his grin spread. "You and your HeartMate." Another dip of his head and T'Vine teleported away.

Leaving Garrett to stagger and lean against a wall.

Healers. Hell.

He'd almost forgotten his HeartMate was a Healer, he'd avoided her for so long. He wasn't a good bet for a husband or father. Not to mention that he still mourned the woman he'd wanted as a wife.

Healers. HeartMate. Doom. Damn.

*A*rtemisia *Mugwort Panax stood with two FirstLevel Healers in* Primary HealingHall looking down at the sweaty and panting boy of six, Opul Cranberry.

The room was tinted a rich cream and furnished comfortably, but it was still in an institution and the faint odor of sickness underlaid even the cleansing herbs.

Her heart thudded hard as she waited for the verdict.

"Yes, it is the Iasc sickness. The first outbreak we've had in eighteen months," Ura Heather said flatly.

"We can't Heal him with our regular psi Healing, our Flair." Sympathy with a touch of fear laced Lark Holly's tones. No doubt she was thinking of her own children.

The middle-aged Ura Heather turned away. She was the best Healer on Celta since her father had retired, and was in charge of all Healers. "Get that guard guy. Primross? Only survivor when everyone in the first group hit by the virulent illness died. Maybe his blood and the Flair in it can help.

"No one except you two and the guard are allowed in this room. Lark, you and SecondLevel Healer Panax must take all care. We can't afford another epidemic." Ura Heather strode through the sterilization field Artemisia had erected, grunting as it affected her. Then her Flair spiked as she killed any lingering germs before she walked from the room.

Artemisia took the child's hand and stroked the back of it with her thumb. "Easy, Opul, we'll help you."

The child tossed and turned, whimpering.

Lark sighed. "I'll contact Garrett Primross and let you know when you should meet with FirstLevel Healer Heather and me."

That was moving in circles Artemisia had only dreamt of. "Why do you need me?"

Lark blinked lavender eyes. "Because Opul Cranberry is your patient."

"I was manning Private Intake Room Six a septhour ago when he was brought in," Artemisia agreed. "But I work for the HealingHall." And glad she was that she'd been accepted temporarily on the Primary HealingHall staff. "I don't have him as a private patient."

"Now you do," Lark said. "All his fees will be paid to you by the council." Lark met Artemisia's eyes and smiled. "Since you don't get a NobleGilt salary."

Not since Artemisia's Family, the Mugworts, had been smeared with scandal. Her father had lost his title and judgeship, her mother, her Healing practice. Everyone knew Artemisia was a Mugwort, but since she went by a distant Family name on her mother's side, everyone could pretend she wasn't touched by the ruin of her Family.

Lark glanced at her wrist timer. "I must put this in motion; Ura Heather isn't a patient woman. If she hasn't spoken with the boy's parents, I'll talk with them, too."

If it had been Artemisia's son, she'd want the more sympathetic Lark Holly rather than Ura Heather to brief her.

"I'll see you later," Lark said.

"Yes," Artemisia agreed. She pulled up a chair and sat by the elevated bedsponge. Even as she wiped the boy's face with a tepid cloth, deep inside she experienced mixed emotions. A whisper of happiness that she was advancing in her career, along with the dread of every Healer, every Celtan, that the sickness that had claimed too many people was back.

Two

$\mathcal{M}$inutes *later, standing outside Heather's office, Artemisia smoothed* her tunic and said spell Words to tidy herself. She'd been through three sanitation and germ-sterilization procedures. The large windows on one wall of Opul's room were uncovered, with a staff member observing him until she or Lark Holly returned. Artemisia touched the monitoring bracelet that matched the one on Opul's wrist. All was fine with him.

Her pulse was fast and she was flushed. She was rising in the world, and though she didn't have great ambition, she wanted to find her place and keep it. This was another minor step, a consultation with the Healers because she had a patient with Iasc sickness.

She rapped on the door and Lark Holly opened it.

"GentleSir Primross doesn't seem as angry about being called as before," Lark murmured. "Yet."

"I haven't met him, but I've heard of him."

Lark gave an ironic half smile. "Every Healer has. He's mostly refused to let us . . ."

". . . Experiment with his blood?"

Now Lark's smile was full. "Yes."

"I've heard he's been difficult."

Lark's breath was audible. "Also true, but he helped us stop the sickness." She slanted Artemisia a glance and said, "FirstLevel Healer Ura Heather has a plan. I think we'll find out how difficult GentleSir Primross is. He's already here." She opened the door wider and stepped aside.

"Thank you." Artemisia straightened her shoulders. She wanted to be a solid, permanent member of the Primary HealingHall staff. If she followed Heather's instructions, she'd get that position and prove herself. She'd have allies who would look beyond her name and the scandal. She'd be set exactly where she wanted to be in her career for the rest of her life.

The paneled chamber was richly furnished with a large carved desk and several cushy chairs set on a thick rug of dark purple and gold. The scent of expensive herbal housekeeping spells permeated the room. Long curtains of gold gracing the Palladian windows were pulled aside to let in the sunlight. The torpid heat of summer didn't reach here.

Outside showed the lush green of the Healing Grove and Artemisia wished she were there. All she'd ever wanted was to be a Healer, and she disliked having to play politics to get what she wanted. She preferred to avoid confrontation and risk.

Lark Holly sank into a chair. Since the man was propped against a wall with crossed arms, and his scowl deepened as Artemisia came in, she decided he had no intention of taking a seat. So she angled a chair to see him and FirstLevel Healer Ura Heather.

He was not a handsome man, but there was something about him that made her catch her breath. He was tall and extremely well built—not slender nor thick bodied. His face wasn't well proportioned. He had heavy brows, amber eyes set deep, jutting cheekbones, and a nose and mouth wider than was considered good-looking. His natural skin tone was a couple of shades darker than the average Celtan and went well with his sandy brown hair.

His hair was tousled as if his fingers had plunged through it. He wore an air of supreme competence as well as sturdy brown work trous tucked into black boots and a top that appeared to be more like leather armor than a shirt. The masculine scent of him went straight to her core.

"GentleSir Primross, you know FirstLevel Healer Lark Holly; this is SecondLevel Healer Artemisia Panax, who is treating the patient with the sickness," Ura Heather said. She didn't rise from her seat behind her desk.

He hadn't been fidgeting but now went completely immobile. "It's back."

Ura Heather lifted her index finger. "One case."

His shoulders shifted, drawing Artemisia's attention to their broadness. "Not good."

"No," Lark said quietly.

"What do you want?" Primross asked, still not moving from the wall.

Heather smiled sharply. "Quite a bit. Please, take a seat."

His eyes narrowed and his face took on a lack of expression that was wary in itself. "One case. I'll donate my blood if it will help."

"Opul Cranberry, age six, will thank you for that," Artemisia said.

He winced. "Starting with kids again?"

"Maybe," Heather said. "We know how he was infected." She snorted. "Luckily the Cranberrys have stayed on their estate outside the city for the summer and didn't have much contact with anyone else, and none when they guessed what the sickness was. The three of them teleported here immediately. We think we can contain the malady."

Primross grunted, nodded. "You want to increase my blood production?"

"Much more." The gleam in Ura Heather's eyes was sharp.

"What?" Primross asked.

Heather glanced down at a papyrus file, then at Primross.

That scrutiny wasn't reassuring, either. Artemisia was shocked that the woman didn't cultivate a better bedside manner.

Primross pushed away from the wall, eyeing the premier Healer of Celta.

"I have the details of your history." Heather tapped the file. "But I'd like to hear them from you."

Pain flickered on his face, then was buried under impassivity. He jerked a nod at the folder. "I went over every fact many times, with many people, including your father, T'Heather himself."

Ura Heather's mouth turned sour. Artemisia realized the head of Primary HealingHall doubted whether her reputation would ever equal her father's, and that mattered to her. Artemisia shifted. Again, she didn't want to be here, taking part in a conflict.

The man's gaze switched to her and she flinched at the storm in his eyes. Then his glance seemed to soften as he stared at her.

"You're a private investigator," Ura Heather gritted out. "Surely you must prefer to talk to witnesses yourself and not rely on others' reports." She opened the file.

Lark Holly stood and walked to him, held out her hand. "Please. We need you."

He flinched. "That's pretty much what the Healer in Gael City said to me when all this started." His voice, too, was rough.

Lark gestured to her seat. As a shroud of dread enveloped her, Artemisia wondered if she could get out of hearing the tragedy. She knew Primross's story vaguely and was sure the details would be much worse. Everyone had died except him.

The skin on his face had tightened and he appeared haunted.

Ura Heather looked at Lark Holly, her niece. Lark was of greater status and had a more sympathetic outlook. Primross would be an individual to Lark, and only a case and an informant to Heather.

Primross stood on the balls of his feet, as if he might break away. Artemisia thought of Opul's suffering. "Please," she added.

Once again his dark and brooding gaze touched her; a corner of his mouth curled. He snorted and trod to the chair and sat straight in it, challenging Heather. "Yeah?"

She leaned forward over her desk. "We have new information. After three years of decontamination, we retrieved the locking mechanism of the door for the body storage in the back of the transport vehicle that you drove." She touched a hand-sized panel that ran with the slight orange light of Flair tech along the curving lines of spell algorithms. "Its recording mechanism of when and how often the door was opened is intact. So we have better details of how the sickness progressed that we would like you to confirm."

Garrett stared at the small piece of the bus he'd driven, and his brain played back Old Grisc in the driver's seat when they'd smelled the first scent of death. He'd reached over and pressed the red button . . . setting the recorder as well as unlocking the door, Garrett now understood.

Beads of sweat formed along his spine, were absorbed by his padded and Flaired armor. Now he knew why he'd worn it. More for emotional protection than physical. Primary HealingHall was in a well-protected part of town—not to mention that many of the less advantaged had died during the sickness that swept through the land two to three years before.

"GentleSir Primross, can you give us more details about your experience?" prompted Lark.

Nothing he enjoyed more than reviewing the worst days of his life. He felt his impassive expression stiffen into a stone mask. He'd made this report before . . . more times than he wanted. Doing so now just hurt because he hadn't been expecting it. The scab had been ripped off his inner wounds. He wouldn't let the tear or the inner bleeding show.

"No." He stood and walked back to the door.

"Of course you do not need to help us," FirstLevel Healer Ura Heather said. "We are only facing an epidemic again. One that you can stop."

He slammed his hand against the door and muttered curse words that should have singed the air with his frustration at having to fall into line with someone else's plans.

"Yes," the Healer nearly purred, though he'd have expected more of a satisfied snake hiss. "Anyone else who dies of this sickness could be due to you."

"You shouldn't say such things," the SecondLevel Healer protested.

"Stop this, Aunt!" demanded Lark Holly.

"It's true." Heather's voice was smooth, like she was a fighter who knew she had him by the balls.

Guilt always gnawed. He'd start off as usual. "The Iasc sickness was traced to an unknown fish with an unknown infection that washed ashore on the beach of the Smallage estate near Gael City."

"We know that." Ura Heather's brows snapped down.

Garrett angled his thumb at the thick folder. "You know all that I have to tell you." He put his hand on the door latch.

"Please, stay, GentleSir Primross. We understand this is hard for you," Lark Holly said. "We'll take it in chronological order so you can settle before we ask about the new information."

His gut twisted. It was hard for him and he didn't want any of the women—especially his HeartMate—to pity him.

Yeah, he hadn't seen her for a while, a year maybe, since he avoided her. They'd never met. He didn't think that she knew they were destined mates, and he couldn't legally tell her and limit her choices. Not that he wanted to tell her anyway. Not that he wanted her.

Maybe his blood was humming because they were in the same room, but that was his body. His emotions were . . . Who the hell cared?

"The Iasc sickness was traced to the discovery of the large fish on the former Smallage estate," Ura Heather repeated.

There was no more Smallage estate. The house had been demolished, the land sterilized, remotely. There were no more Smallages.

Garrett stood where he was. He didn't want to be sucked back into that dark time. But words came from his mouth. "People from the estate got sick, a group went to a research HealingHall on the edge of Gael City for help. By that time, they were sick, too," he began in a monotone.

Rushing air pounded in his ears, matching an inward, rumbling shudder. Even if he left this office, memories would slice him. He might fall apart in bits before he left the HealingHall.

Someone made a soft noise of concern. Not someone. He knew

who, the SecondLevel Healer. She was there, standing beside him, her fingers light on him near his elbow, nudging him back to the chair. He picked up his feet carefully, let the pressure on his arm guide him since he was having trouble seeing. Seeing outside. Inside, his mind flashed vision after vision of those terrible days.

He bumped the edge of the chair, sat back down. His face felt cold. But the memories were fever hot. Like the sickness he'd survived.

Heather said, "The research HealingHall determined the sickness was unknown and virulent. They took samples and wanted the infected moved to a quarantine clinic in the hills. You were called in to guide the off-road quarantine vehicle."

"Me and the driver of that bus, Old Grisc," Garrett said. Old Grisc had been tough, but not tough enough. "We both knew the rough back trail to the clinic." Little used, and since one part of the shelf road had crumbled behind the heavy vehicle, never to be used again. The trip had been hazardous. More from the sickness than the rugged terrain.

"There were twenty-three who left on the journey. It was supposed to take six septhours?" Lark Holly asked in her calm voice. Not as pleasing to his ears as the younger woman's, who he didn't want to name.

Pain razored through him as he was back again in the Gael City HealingHall. He saw the fearful expression of Dinni, his childhood friend. They'd been each other's first lover. But Dinni was the girl who'd rejected him because he'd had a HeartMate somewhere and Dinni believed in that kind of love. She hadn't wanted to take a chance on him and the love between them.

Dinni had cradled her fretful and sick baby. Her son, no more than two months old, his father already dead of the sickness. She had begged Garrett to take the job, to go with them. Had the utmost faith he would save them.

His Dinni. More memories—sweet, laughing, as sunny in nature as her blonde hair, as a child, a girl. He'd have done anything for her. So he'd agreed.

"GentleSir Primross?" Healer Lark Holly prompted with an underlying command that greatly Flaired and greatly Noble people used to get results.

Something warm brushed against the back of one of his fists and he saw it was a steaming mug of caff. Strong and dark. He took the cup and drank and the bitterness of the caff was lost in that of his mouth.

He cast his mind back to what the woman had asked him. His voice came out like something old and rusty with edges flaking off, gone forever. "Yeah, the trip was supposed to take six septhours. Took eleven." Hideous trip. "Not many of us made it."

"Five," Ura Heather snapped.

As if he didn't recall every individual. Garrett couldn't prevent the shudder from showing this time, ripping through his body. Hot caff slopped on his thigh. He barely noticed.

More words spewed. "But your HealingHall in Gael City wasn't as good as you all thought it was. The sickness got out from there, didn't it? Despite all your warnings and all your sterilization procedures and everything." He didn't care if he sounded harsh. *No one* knew what had happened on that trip. "One of your own Healers spread it."

Heather's nostrils pinched. "A ThirdLevel Healer." A sneer from a woman who'd been born a highest Noble with best psi-magic, Flair.

"She died, too." Lark Holly sent an admonitory glance to Heather.

Blinking, Garrett recalled the two were aunt and niece.

Another concerned noise came from the beautiful SecondLevel Healer he tried to ignore. He made his eyes shift from a frozen stare; his glance swept the file again. How many times had he told this story? So many that the words were the same.

"The door was first unlocked at thirty-two minutes into the first seventy-minute septhour." Heather was pedantic. "Does that match your recollection?"

He leaned forward and glanced at the panel. "Sounds right. First three to die were Brev and Partha Sundew, HeartMates, then Avena

Blackoat. I don't remember after that." His mouth twisted. No. He would not go through this again. He'd already guaranteed himself more nightmares.

Plunking his caff down on a table, he set his feet and rose. "Don't have any more to tell you. You've got all the words about this that I have in that thick file. Either take me to the boy so I can give him a transfusion or tell me what you really want."

Frustration set on Ura Heather's face. Too fliggering bad.

As she met his gaze, her expression smoothed. "We've learned a lot about Iasc sickness, enough to enforce certain processes to keep it from becoming an epidemic. It's not enough. The herb NewBalm helps mitigate the sickness but doesn't have as good results as your blood."

Her words jarred him completely from the past and anchored him in the present and he was grateful. Maybe he would never go back there again.

A few deep breaths and he could answer her. "What do you want?"

She smiled and it was knifelike. "You survived the most deadly strain of the sickness, and"—her glance lowered to the now open folder and the sheets inside—"your case of Iasc is believed to have been the shortest on record."

He grunted. "Not many records from the quarantine clinic, I'm guessing." Everyone had perished save him.

Her lips thinned again. He didn't like her and he was sure he wouldn't like what she was going to say.

She snapped the folder shut, leaned forward. "We need more information on how you—your body, your Flair—combated the sickness. We want to reintroduce the Iasc into you."

"No," he said.

Lark Holly offered her hand to the young Healer, who looked at her but took it. Together they moved before Garrett. Two gazes to his one. Holly's violet and the other's emerald.

The SecondLevel Healer spoke. "We need your help. A little boy is sick."

He flinched and met her gaze. Soft, tender, deep. And he knew
no matter how hard he fought, he would lose this battle. The past
and the future demanded his blood.

Bile seared up his gullet, coated the back of his throat. His pulse
hammered in his temples.

"Yes," he said thickly. Only then did he recall the prophet
T'Vine's words: *You should cooperate completely with the First-
Level Healers.*

He picked up his caff and drank, keeping his own gaze hard.
"Lay it out for me."

Three

We'll do our best to ensure your survival," FirstLevel Healer Ura Heather said.

He believed her. His blood was too valuable an asset to lose.

Heather pushed his file aside; again she leaned forward, a hint of concern shading her eyes. For the project more than him, he guessed.

"We don't anticipate the project will last longer than six days, but we want you available for a full week."

Six days of hell, descent into the very Cave of the Dark Goddess and a crawl back up.

"You will be monitored the entire time."

He looked outside at the green Healing Grove, knew he wouldn't be anywhere as pretty as that in reality or delirium. Here in Primary HealingHall, his body would be cradled in luxury. The rich chamber displayed more wealth than the den of his friend, FirstFamily Great-Lord Laev T'Hawthorn.

Garrett's brows rose. "Here?" he asked.

Heather looked startled. "No."

"Oh," Garrett said softly, "you won't risk this place, your domain, eh? Just like the HealingHall in Gael City."

Heather's eyes should have bored holes through him. Again he moved to the wall and lounged against it, drinking caff. He had the upper hand now and they all knew it.

"This place is very large and busy," the SecondLevel Healer murmured. He kept his gaze on Heather, lifted and dropped a shoulder.

"I live in MidClass Lodge." He smiled. "That building is even larger and busier than here."

"That won't work as a venue, then." Ura Heather turned her gaze toward Lark Holly. "Options?"

FirstLevel Healer Holly cleared her throat. "I've contacted the Turquoise House, the House becoming a sentient Residence. TQ is between occupants and has decided to redecorate, so it is empty of all furnishings. It is intrigued with the project." Her smile showed the pity that he hadn't wanted. "TQ is also interested in GentleSir Primross himself, as a private investigator."

"Huh," he said, but his curiosity was snagged, too. Not many people were allowed in the Turquoise House. It was more exclusive than the greatest Noble Residences that had huge staffs.

Heather's lips pursed, but she couldn't hide her interest, either. "When will it be available for us four to view it?"

The younger woman squeaked. As the words sank in, he stiffened. He opened his mouth to protest, then remembered T'Vine's words and the man's haunted eyes. Garrett shut his mouth.

"Surely you don't want me—" the lower-level Healer began.

"You've already been exposed to the sickness and have shown you're smart enough to call in better Healers when the diagnosis is beyond your skills," Heather said. "You've followed proper sterilization procedures. You're SecondLevel and will be an acceptable assistant to us on this. You will monitor GentleSir Primross."

Garrett carefully put his cup down on a table, retreated behind an expressionless mask again.

He didn't like this, but now T'Vine's prophecy replayed, echoing in his mind. He wouldn't stare at the woman, no matter how often his gaze wandered that way.

Lark Holly said, "Opul Cranberry is Healer Panax's patient, and needs her."

Heather waved that aside. "Panax will be of more service by tending to Primross. You, FirstLevel Healer Holly, can supervise the child's case. When can we see the Turquoise House?"

Lark Holly's sigh was faint. "I'll scry the House that we are on our way."

"Good." Heather snapped her fingers, then smiled in satisfaction. "The glider awaits us at the main entrance." She strode from the room.

The other two Healers fell in behind her, Lark Holly commenting quietly to the younger woman, "I'll make sure that you take no harm from this project, financially or otherwise."

"Thank you," the SecondLevel Healer said politely.

Garrett strolled behind them, thinking how he could broach the matter of losing several days' worth of work to Heather. Did she expect him to donate his time as well as his blood? He supposed so.

As he brooded, he realized his gaze was fixed to the SecondLevel Healer's ass. Nice and high and round, though he couldn't see much because she had on trous and a long tunic over that. He liked the way she moved, gracefully, elegantly.

Not at all like Dinni's bouncy step. The Healer had long dark brown black hair tied back in a severe braid. Her face was roundish and he preferred pointed chins. She had a creamy complexion that showed she didn't spend much time in the sun.

Not at all like Dinni.

But SecondLevel Healer Artemisia Panax was his HeartMate.

He didn't want her.

He'd never wanted her.

Now they'd be together for as long as his sickness ran again. She'd see him at his absolute worse.

That was good.

*T*hroughout the drive from Primary Healing Hall to a mid-Noble-class area, Artemisia's mind buzzed. From the glare he'd given her, Garrett Primross wasn't happy with the plan. Who would be? She must have made a terrible impression on him since he'd barely looked at her. His animosity sent a thorn of unexpected hurt into her she tried to shake off.

She wasn't pleased, either. Caring for a very sick person developed an intimacy, and her feelings toward him were mixed—attracted but wary. She wouldn't have trouble being professional but wasn't sure how he'd react toward her.

And she'd have to leave her home. She hadn't lived away from the hidden sanctuary in Druida City since she and her Family had been named caretakers years ago.

No lover had been strong enough to break those bonds. She didn't know if that was depressing or not.

They pulled into the glider drive and the courtyard of the Turquoise House and Artemisia understood why it was called that. The outside walls were a shiny blue green. The door of the sprawling one-floor House was an equally glossy oak with bright brass latch and fittings.

Lark Holly walked up to the entrance and Artemisia followed. Primross was behind her and FirstLevel Healer Ura Heather brought up the rear. The door swung open and they stood in a bare entryway.

"Greetyou," said the House in the mellow tones of a famous actor, lilting with satisfaction.

Primross stiffened. "You speak with Raz Cherry's voice?"

"Yes," said the House. It—he—chuckled. "We came to an agreement years ago, when I first became aware of myself and wanted a male voice. I am pleased you recognized it, Garrett Primross."

Garrett made a half bow and said, "Where would you prefer me to stand so you can scan me?"

"Very intelligent!" the Turquoise House said. "Very courteous. Please move to the mainspace fireplace, down the hall ahead and to your left, first door on your left."

The man took the lead, Lark Holly appeared amused, and Heather reluctant. Artemisia's shoulders relaxed. She lived in a Residence now, one who was like a crotchety old man who had to be catered to. This House seemed much more cheerful. That would be helpful in the trying days ahead.

"You and SecondLevel Artemisia Mugwort Panax will stay for a week?" the House asked as they stood around the empty main-space.

Artemisia tried not to wince. The Turquoise House had included her real surname. Her shoulders tensed, but a sliding gaze at the others showed they appeared focused on the bare House. A week seemed a long time to her, though the sickness had lingered and been fatal for as long as three weeks.

"Yes, a week," Heather said brusquely. Artemisia wondered if the woman was trying to ease her out of Primary HealingHall. Artemisia straightened her spine. She was sticking. She wasn't flashy, but she was determined and knew how to do stubborn.

And she hoped she had a supporter in Lark Holly. Still, there were more detriments to this project than advantages.

"Ah," the Turquoise House said in a tone that had her listening closely. "I know of both individuals, Garrett Primross and Artemisia Panax."

Now it was being discreet. So Artemisia knew that her home, BalmHeal Residence, had been too chatty with the Turquoise House. How many of her—and her Family's—secrets did this House-becoming-a-Residence know? How would the House use what it knew? Would it? How ethical was it?

"You know of me, do you?" Primross said coolly as he stopped near the empty fireplace. He reached into his trous pocket and pulled out a gold coin, rolled it across his knuckles, made it disappear. "You know that?"

"Sleight of hand!" the Turquoise House said delightedly. "More!"

"Want to learn more secrets?" Primross shrugged. "Maybe, maybe not." He left the impression he'd established dominance in the relationship. Artemisia could only envy how quickly and easily he'd done that.

Ura Heather had stayed near the door. Did the older Healer wonder what her own ancient Residence might have said about her to the Turquoise House?

Even if Artemisia's home blabbed of her, it would have been complimentary. It loved her more than anyone else who lived in it, which had also kept her close.

Staring at the slick-looking walls, Heather said, "You have instituted sanitation, decontamination, and sterilization procedures, I see. Well done."

"Thank you," the Turquoise House said with an edge of irony. "It is very important that the human populace of Celta declines no further. If I can help in that endeavor, if I can save lives, I am well rewarded." There was a drop in the air pressure in the room as if the House gave a soft sigh. "Unlike any of the HealingHalls, I can monitor all the organisms within me, understand the slightest changes in my walls and beings."

"Residences are uniquely suited to do that," Lark Holly soothed. "Only one had the sickness within."

"T'Hawthorn Residence," Primross said. He leaned an elbow on the mantel as if he were already at home within the spare and sterile walls.

The emptiness would take Artemisia some getting used to. Her home was the most comfortable place she'd ever lived, including the Family estate they'd lost when she was a teen.

"Yes, T'Hawthorn Residence had a death," Lark said.

"I have spoken at length with T'Hawthorn Residence," said the House. "I need all records of the sickness from the Healers and HealingHalls transmitted to my Library."

Heather gasped. "We don't share confidential—"

"You want me for an experiment." Turquoise House's tone was harder. Artemisia was amazed at its range of expression. "I will not accept this project without sufficient data. Change the venue to a HealingHall, or your father's home, T'Heather Residence. Your Residence is interested in the sickness. We all are. Or use the starship *Nuada's Sword*. I know it has laboratories, sick bays, and sterile rooms."

"Not the starship," Artemisia said. "I don't work well there, not where Flair is diminished or suppressed." She couldn't offer her own home, BalmHeal Residence, the original HealingHall of the colonists, now a hidden sanctuary for the desperate of Celta.

Not many of those suffering from the sickness had made it to the old BalmHeal estate in time. She and her mother had had only two cases during the epidemic. Both casualties were buried in one of the sacred groves. Artemisia was sure the Turquoise House knew everything that BalmHeal Residence did. Their Residence had taken the deaths very hard.

"I'll transfer the information," Lark Holly said.

Ura Heather walked out.

"Thank you both." Lark Holly curtsied to them and swept from the room, leaving Artemisia with a man who still hadn't met her eyes. Awkward.

If she'd had regular clothes on, she'd have tucked her hands in the wide opposite sleeves, but she was wearing a work tunic with tight cuffs. She stood by the open door, but he didn't move.

"You aren't going to refuse our request?" she asked him.

"It's mostly the Heathers' request, isn't it? FirstLevel Healer Ura Heather and Lark Holly, whose mother was a Heather."

"The Heathers have always been the best Healers."

"That doesn't bother you? That no matter how hard you try, you'll never be their equal?"

Artemisia blinked. "Why should it? The Heathers are from the FirstFamilies, are descended from people who had psi power on ancient Earth. My Family isn't so old, our Flair isn't as evolved." She lifted her chin, held out her hands, and flexed her fingers. "I'm sure you've practiced your sleight of hand for a long time. If I began now, would I ever reach your level of competence? I doubt it." A corner of her mouth quirked. "Even if I had the natural dexterity you do."

He nodded. "I'm good with my hands." Then he swayed back, bumping against the mantel as if surprised at his own words. His heavy brows lowered. "I have a problem with the power of the entrenched Nobility. I also happen to agree with the Turquoise House. This situation is about saving lives, but with Heather it's all about status. The first epidemic happened on her watch as the highest Healer of Celta. Her father had to come out of retirement. I don't think she'll ever forget. If she could eradicate the disease, she'd be redeemed and go down in history as the savior."

Artemisia stared at him. Now that she looked more closely, an element of his natural intensity was anger. Another reason to be wary. "I get the impression that you don't want me to be with you in this project."

"I want you," said the Turquoise House.

"Thanks," she replied but didn't take her gaze off Primross.

He shook his head; his wide mouth thinned. "I don't, but I don't dare refuse you."

"Why not?"

"Vinni T'Vine, the prophet, visited me this morning and insisted I follow *all* the wishes of the FirstLevel Healers."

Her chest went tight. No one liked hearing a prophecy featuring himself or herself. She focused on what Primross previously said. "I don't agree that the Nobles are too powerful. I think they're doing their best."

His eyes widened. He shook his head. "You are naive."

"You're cynical. All the FirstFamily Nobles I've met have been decent people." It hadn't been the FirstFamilies who'd demanded the Mugworts' title be stripped from them, but other Nobles of their own rank, at the instigation of the newssheets.

He jutted his chin at the window facing the courtyard where the HealingHall glider was pulling away. "You think FirstLevel Healer Ura Heather is decent?"

Artemisia flushed. She'd had unkind thoughts about the lady but wouldn't admit them. "She's doing the best she can. If we're in this together, I don't want to talk politics."

He nodded slowly. "Done."

"I suggest you take a tour of my premises," the Turquoise House said. "SecondLevel Healer Panax can determine how things should be arranged best for this experiment."

"Fine," Artemisia said.

Primross's mouth twisted, but he said, "Sure."

"This is the mainspace," the House repeated. "I have a Master-

Suite and MistrysSuite and several bedrooms and waterfall rooms, a kitchen as well as many no-time food and drink storage units. I have a playspace and a den and a library."

"Give us the tour." Garrett's half bow to Artemisia held a mocking quality. "After you."

She sniffed and went into the hall, followed the House's instructions, and studied the rooms. Lovely proportions but all were set up to contain and destroy the sickness with sticky white walls and no furniture. Bare, bare, bare.

The more time she spent with Primross, the more it seemed as if she became sensitized to him. Her skin felt hot, and it wasn't the sickness. She was all too aware of his size, the way he moved, and his deeper and rougher tones that contrasted so well with the House's actor voice.

Time and again she had to yank her focus from the virile man to the stark House.

Garrett was too aware of the woman he didn't want to replace his lost love and tried to concentrate on his conversation with the slyly knowing Turquoise House. That entity hinted at more than one secret regarding itself, the woman, and Garrett.

The Turquoise House had figured out that riddles itched Garrett like a bad rash. The House dropped innuendos, ensuring Garrett was intrigued. Why, Garrett didn't know, but the House had an agenda.

So the obligatory tour wasn't over when a data stream came from Primary HealingHall, officially approving the project. Garrett's last trickle of hope that he'd be spared the whole terrible thing was squashed.

He and the SecondLevel Healer stood in a small bedroom that connected through a dressing and waterfall room to the bedroom of the MasterSuite. The view out the undraped windows was the only thing that made the place tolerable. The Healer had decided the chambers were right for the experiment. This would be her room.

Garrett glanced at his wrist timer. "I need to make arrangements for my business."

"You are a *private investigator*." The Turquoise House rolled the sentence. "A fascinating business."

Garrett grunted. "I like it well enough."

The Healer's delicately curving brows arched. "You wouldn't pursue a vocation if you didn't enjoy it."

She already sensed too much about him. Every instant he was with her, the innate bond between them grew from the wispy tendril they'd always had to a thin thread. It would only get worse.

"You will tell us of some of your cases?" the House asked. "Though that business with the Hawthorn jewels earlier this year was well publicized—a triumph for you!"

The woman blinked as if she didn't recall his greatest case, the juicy events of kidnapping, attempted murder, accidental death, jewel theft, and a goddess's curse. Garrett shouldn't have been irritated in the slightest, but he was. People were contrary.

"Maybe I'll tell some general stories. Nothing confidential." He wanted the woman to ask. But she stared around the place, frowning. She wasn't comfortable in the House and he wondered why.

No. He would *not* wonder about her. She presented no intriguing puzzle. "I'll go to Primary HealingHall and let them take my blood for the boy. Then pack my stuff," he said.

She sighed. "I must, too."

"Do you teleport?" he asked. She should be able to at her level of Flair.

"Yes," she said, not sounding offended as he would've been if she'd asked him. She didn't appear to be easily offended. Easygoing. Soft.

Not like Dinni, who'd been adamant in her refusal of him.

The Healer wet her lips and his reluctant gaze went to her wide, tender mouth. She said, "I must plan procedures with the FirstLevel Healers. We probably won't start the project until tomorrow morning. You'll be scried with the information."

"Fine." He gave her his briefest nod. Again no reaction from her at the slight. Garrett teleported away from the disturbing female and to Intake at Primary HealingHall.

four

The irritating Garrett Primross was gone. Artemisia relaxed her shoulders.

"My HouseHeart is quiet and serene if you wish to rest," the Turquoise House said.

The offer to visit its most secret room surprised Artemisia so much that she stretched out a hand to steady herself. Her skin cringed at the tacky feel of the wall.

"All organisms deposited by human contact have been destroyed," said a flat voice.

The House rushed into speech. "My apologies, Healer. The decontamination and sterilization system came with med announcements that I have not yet programmed into my own voice."

Artemisia never recalled an apology from her own sentient home. "It's very brave of you to host us, Turquoise House."

"Please call me TQ. T'Hawthorn Residence said it took no harm. I want to be able to offer my humans the very best." Strong, solid, and determined tones.

"I can't understand why you'd let me in your HouseHeart." If the inner sanctum of the HouseHeart was destroyed, the Residence died.

"I trust you," said TQ. "BalmHeal Residence and I talk a lot."

There came a cacklelike sound Artemisia couldn't place, but she knew it as punctuation. "He is very old and I am very young, but I was there when he stirred from sleep. My inhabitants at the time were with us both. BalmHeal Residence speaks of you a lot." A short silence hung. "My HouseHeart needs maintenance," TQ said, embarrassed.

"You don't have permanent caregivers?"

"No. FirstFamily GrandLady Mitchella D'Blackthorn decorated me, and will help me later. Others who have helped have agreed to have their memories bespelled so they forget details."

Artemisia rocked toward the wall again, moved to the middle of the room. "No one knows how to reach your HouseHeart?"

"Not at this time," TQ whispered.

She wouldn't say that was foolish. "I'm extremely honored."

"I believe I need a failsafe human."

She let out a held breath. "So another Residence has information on how to reach your HouseHeart and about your House-Stones?"

"Yes."

"I'll be glad to help you, and agree to memory blurring."

"Would keeping your memory be acceptable until my true person comes?"

"Your true person?"

"I have had tenants, but am waiting for my Family."

She didn't suppress her curiosity. "Are you waiting for a destined person?"

"Like humans wait for HeartMates?" His voice lilted. "No, I know the Family I want."

"Oh."

A long creak came from a distant room. "My HouseHeart is very restful and you have had a difficult morning. I am sorry I mentioned your surname."

"I don't think that will be a problem." Though Garrett Primross seemed an observant man. But she hadn't hidden information about herself. If he checked, he'd know who she was and of the Family's scandal.

"And I am sorry about Opul Cranberry's illness," TQ said.

"How do you know of Opul?"

"T'Heather Residence heard Ura Heather speaking to her father about the child. The GrandLord cautiously approved the experiment. T'Heather Residence told me."

"Ah."

"Incoming scry from Lark Holly at Primary HealingHall. Visual on your bedroom wall."

A second later the whole wall rippled, then showed a huge image of Lark Holly.

"Greetyou, Artemisia. Opul Cranberry is being prepared for the blood transfusion from GentleSir Primross. We anticipate all will be well, but Opul is upset I'll be his primary Healer." Lark smiled. She probably wasn't often considered secondary to anyone else. Artemisia was glad Lark was amused. "Can you come say good-bye to Opul? It's essential he remains calm."

"Of course."

"You can give me your recommendations for contamination spellshields and such to keep you safe, as well as the rooms you chose for the project in the Turquoise House. We anticipate starting at WorkBell tomorrow morning."

Artemisia swallowed and kept her gaze steady. "I'll be ready."

"I know you will." A warmer smile from Lark. "Primary HealingHall is lucky to have you."

They signed off and the scry faded and the wall went back to blank white. Artemisia breathed deeply. "TQ, can you scry BalmHeal Residence, please? I must talk to my parents." She was sure her younger sister, a priestess of the Lady and Lord, could set up a blessing ritual that evening.

"Of course," the House said.

"I promise I'll come this afternoon and help you with your HouseHeart."

"It can wait." His voice was soft. "We are patient beings."

"Thank you for your support in this endeavor, TQ. It will be a difficult process."

"The experiment will be fun and interesting!"

Artemisia was sure it would be fascinating . . . and terrible.

𝒜t the HealingHall, Garrett was met by a worn Lark Holly. "Thank you for returning. Little Opul needs your help. He's responding very slowly to the new medicine." Lark's expression hardened into sheer resolve. "We *will* save him. We *will not* have another epidemic."

Garrett made a noncommittal noise.

Her lavender gaze lasered in on his. "I give you my personal word on that."

He held up a palm. "This situation is not under your control."

Her breath huffed. "You're right, but we know this sickness now. We will not let it win. Please follow me to the transfusion room."

He hardly needed to, he'd been here to donate his blood so often, but he was glad to stop talking and take action.

He was placed on a bedsponge near the sick child, a young boy who stared at him with bright blue eyes in a pale face. Even his red orange hair seemed subdued.

"You're not pretty Artemisia," the boy whispered, voice rougher than a child's should be.

"No, but he will help you." Lark Holly pulled up a stool between the two beds.

"He's big."

Garrett managed a smile. "Yeah, I am."

The boy turned his head and closed his eyes and Garrett saw pain roll through him. He engulfed Opul's hand in his own. It was small and hot and reminded him of Dinni and her baby. He didn't know how to avoid the past. How many times would he be expected to relive it?

Then the child looked at him again and tugged words from him. "I'm here to help. It will be all right."

Opul's chin trembled, his lips compressed, then words tumbled from him. "I was bad and opened the box that came from G'Uncle Hulten before he died."

"Sshh." Lark Holly held out a softleaf to the kid.

He grabbed it and scrubbed his face. "Now I'm sick and I'll make everyone else sick and more of my friends will die." The boy bit his lip bloody. Lark exclaimed and touched it, Healing the small wound.

"No," Garrett said and knew he'd make more promises that could be broken by death. He squeezed Opul's small and sweaty fingers. "I got the sickness and lived and so will you."

Slow blinks at him. "Yeah?"

"Yes." He struggled to think of something to help the boy. Struggle was right. He'd struggled all through the sickness to get the bus to the clinic. "What do you want to do most?"

"GentleSir Primross." Lark Holly's voice cooled with warning that he was not an expert in this area. Healers generally wanted Iasc patients to stay quiet, relax, and rest.

He met her eyes. "I survived," he said. That was the bottom line. He'd lived when others died.

"I like to run best." Another chin wobble. "I'm going to miss the southern district race because I did something stupid!"

An idea came to Garrett, dried his throat. His glance clashed with Holly's intense stare; she watched him closely, listening hard. For something he hadn't put on the record? Who knew what worked? He reached for the tube of water and swallowed fresh liquid. "Listen, Opul."

The child's pale blue eyes looked into his own. "When the fever and shakes come again, pretend you're running a race. Know that you *have* to reach the finish line, *must* win." Like he'd had to get through the mountains.

With a little quiver, Opul's fingers clamping on his hand, the boy said, "Hard, to be sick and in a race and try to win, not stumble or fall, make mistakes."

Hard to be driving a strange vehicle and know he *had* to get to the clinic. But he'd had a goal; everyone else had been giving in to their misery, even Old Grisc.

Garrett's teeth clenched on the tube of water, pierced through it, and liquid spurted everywhere. Cold and shocking.

With a ladylike snort, Lark Holly rhymed a spell couplet and the water evaporated, even from his clothes. An odd feeling he'd brought on himself. She took the split tube away to the disintegrator and gave him another.

"You think that would really work? Thinking I'm running a race?" Opul asked.

"Having a tough goal worked for me."

Eyes wide and with trust, the boy nodded. "I'll think of that."

"A good idea," Lark Holly said softly. "Now let's get some of GentleSir Primross's strong blood and Flair into you."

Another nod from the child.

"I'll come to your next race," Garrett said.

"I live in Toono Town," Opul said. "Sometimes adult work makes it difficult to attend races."

Garrett didn't like the excuse. "You're a priority for me." He didn't have any hot cases, could use more work. If something heated up, he'd still make the time. It was rare he had emergencies, life-and-death situations.

"You're a priority for all of us," Lark Holly said.

"Even pretty Artemisia?" Opul asked. "She's not here."

"Not her choice," Garrett said. "She was assigned away."

"She'll come say good-bye," Lark Holly said.

The boy pouted, then his fingers were twisting, growing hotter. "I don't feel good. How long will I be sick?"

He didn't seem to be thinking he'd die, at least. Not that that had helped many. No one Garrett had known with the sickness had thought they would die.

"Perhaps a week," Lark Holly said.

"Let's get this done," Garrett said.

Lark Holly said, "I doubt he'll have more lucid moments.

I helped clear his mind for the transfusion and now will put him into a trance. Can you self-trance and stay grounded?"

"Of course."

Holly counted down and Garrett sank into a meditative state. He was aware of hands on him. A Flaired suction tube was placed against an artery in his arm. Hurt flashed; his blood flowed. This wasn't the first time he'd had his blood and Flair sent into someone with the sickness.

He hoped it would be the last.

Opul's pain and heat and shudders reached him and he could only endure. And know they were a precursor of worse, but he didn't want to think of that.

*W*hen *he came to, he wasn't in the same room but lying on a hard* table in a sterile place, naked. "What the hell?"

"Preparation for your ordeal to come," a ThirdLevel Healer said, cheerful enough to irritate. "Decontamination and all physical, emotional, and Flair measured."

"I don't recall agreeing to this."

"Part of the procedure."

"Hell. How's Opul?"

The Healer's round face folded into serious lines. "The sickness has him. He's thrashing around a lot more than he was. That's your fault, I heard."

He sat up. "You're done."

Her lips pursed. "Just."

Ura Heather and Lark Holly walked in.

"Where're my clothes?" he asked. They were his favorite set of leathers.

"They'll be fine," Lark assured him.

"Being decontaminated, too?" Couldn't be good for them, especially the padded tunic or boots. Dammit.

"That's right," Heather said. "You're in excellent shape."

"Good to know. Gimme my clothes."

"Incoming scry from the Turquoise House on the wall screen."

The Healers turned to it. "My clothes?" Garrett prompted. With a dark look, the ThirdLevel Healer went to a wall handle and pulled. Garrett's breechcloth, leathers, liners, and boots were there along with his pocketed belt. They didn't look any worse, but how would they feel?

"I need today and tomorrow to set up," the Turquoise House announced arrogantly. "I received the specifications for the beds and bedsponges and linens and cabinets and medical equipment. I am upgrading them to luxury and ordering them from Clover Fine Furniture. I will send the bill to Primary HealingHall."

"You won't!" Heather exploded.

"This is your project. Pay for it or cancel," the House said.

The House was doing well, especially for an entity that had no backup Family.

"The All Councils will fund the project," Lark soothed.

Heather's expression set in furrows. It would take some of the shine off the project if it was funded by all the councils. Take some of her glory if she found how to beat the sickness through his blood.

"Primary HealingHall can handle the expenses," she said stiffly.

Lark Holly lifted a brow in his direction. "Including compensating GentleSir Primross for his time."

Garrett heard the grind of Heather's teeth. Without sparing him a glance, she said, "All right."

He'd dressed fast. "My thanks. Much to do, arrange. Gotta go."

"GentleSir Primross," the Turquoise House's tones were warmer. "Please come over tomorrow morning."

Garrett nodded. "Will do. Later."

He left and strode down the carpeted hall—spell cleansed every half septhour with fragrant herbs. Primary HealingHall could handle a load of expenses.

He turned the corner and saw his HeartMate leaning against the wall outside Opul Cranberry's room.

His body surged toward her, yearning. He feared for the boy and his gut twisted. "Is the kid okay?"

Five

*A*rtemisia *looked at him with anger and his chest hurt. "Little Opul* has Iasc sickness. Of course he isn't all right." A second's pause. "The transfusion went well. Though he's more active than most patients, it appears your blood is mitigating his ordeal. We are hopeful."

"Hope is a terrible thing," Garrett said.

Her emerald eyes gleamed with understanding. "Yes."

He had to leave before more stuff fell out of his mouth. "TQ asked that I come by tomorrow morning."

"Me, too," she said with a smile—at the thought of the House and not Garrett. Damn, he was obsessing.

"See you later, then."

In the next day, he'd be using a lot of Flair teleporting and keeping his twitchy nerves in order, so he took the public carrier to his office. On the way he decided to have client scrys forwarded to the man he trusted most—FirstFamily GreatLord Laev T'Hawthorn.

The minute he stepped off the vehicle, the band of feral cats flowed toward him. Black-and-White tom said, *We have heard you will stay at Turquoise House. You will feed Us there?*

Garrett grunted. "I'll make sure you have food."

Good.

He and the cat scanned the street and alleys, much busier than that morning, which felt like years ago to Garrett.

A change of place is fun sometimes and the yard of Turquoise House is nice. We will spread the word.

"How did you hear?" Garrett asked.

The House told Us.

Garrett reached the few steps up to the building and glanced back. The cats sat at the bottom, all in a row, all looking up at him, tails curled around their paws.

He knew what they wanted. "I'll check your food trough."

It is too low; dogs and others ate.

"Since this isn't a regular feeding time, I'm checking my office, first."

More than one cat sniffed in disapproval. He ignored that.

Inside his office, the wall scry panel showed ripples of Hawthorn purple. No doubt Laev T'Hawthorn had already heard of the experiment. Garrett grimaced. He'd have to talk, and explain or something. At least the Noble lord hadn't called his personal scry pebble.

No other messages flashed so no clients had called.

Garrett took a bucket of dry kibble from storage and proceeded to the back door. More than seven animals were in the courtyard. Garrett sensed a raccoon in the bushes, which meant he must set a spell to clean the water after it left. Raccoons weren't as communicative as cats and were scarcer. Garrett was cultivating the raccoons. He didn't know of any FamRaccoons. He might get goodwill from Nobles and others if he introduced another Fam animal.

He looked at the beady eyes a few meters distant and sent, *Greetyou.*

The raccoon ran away in a hunched lope.

The cats yowled for food.

Garrett dumped the kibble along a trough and hearty slurps began. The cats wouldn't finish it all and the raccoon would return.

Back in his office, after he'd squared away for his absence, he called Laev T'Hawthorn.

The man answered immediately, with a gleam of curiosity in his eyes. "Merrily met," Laev said.

"Yeah, yeah," Garrett said.

Laev laughed, then sobered. No matter that he loved and cherished his HeartMate, his first wife had died of the Iasc sickness. The illness had also affected Laev's FatherSire's health and weakened him to die later. "I heard about a new case of Iasc and that you went to Primary HealingHall."

"Yes," Garrett said.

"And FirstLevel Healer Ura Heather has a project to clear her name of the smudge the epidemic left on it?"

"Also true. I gave Opul Cranberry, age six, a transfusion."

"You got good blood."

Garrett lifted and dropped a shoulder, sucked a breath to the bottom of his gut. "I agreed to an experiment to reintroduce the disease into me. FirstLevel Healers Ura Heather and Lark Holly will supervise the case and I'll be under constant observation by a SecondLevel Healer."

"What!"

"You heard me." The ramifications would run through that smart head fast.

"Then NewBalm isn't working as well as we all had hoped."

Hawthorn had a financial interest in the herb so his mind naturally went to that aspect first. Garrett flicked his hand. "Still early days for that medicine, young harvests. The Healers anticipate that I'll be unavailable for an eightday. I thought I'd forward any calls to you to hold."

"I don't like this idea."

"I don't much, either."

Laev tapped fingertips together. "If the Healers believe it will work . . ." A line dug across his brows. "Much to consider."

"Yeah."

"I value you."

The warmth of friendship welled through Garrett, easing his mind. He could trust Laev. "Thanks."

The man's face set into brooding Garrett didn't like to see. Laev asked, "Someone will care for you?"

"The SecondLevel Healer," Garrett said.

Laev frowned. "Who?"

Garrett realized he couldn't avoid it any longer. He'd have to say her name.

Eyes narrowed and keen, Laev asked, "Who is the Healer who will be on-site?"

Yeah, Laev had deduced Garrett wasn't telling him something about the woman. Usually the Noble wouldn't press, but there was payback. Garrett had pried a few secrets from Laev, so the guy wouldn't quit.

And, hell, he was a friend. Breath trapped inside Garrett's chest so that it ached, then he said, "SecondLevel Healer Artemisia Panax."

"I don't know her or of her," Laev said. Then his eyes widened, mouth opened, shut, and he cleared his throat. "I amend that. I know the lady."

Garrett stared, understanding that they both kept secrets that neither would reveal.

"You can trust her," Laev said.

"I know," Garrett said. The Lady and Lord wouldn't give him a HeartMate he couldn't trust. He didn't know all the ins and outs of HeartMates and didn't want to discover them, but he already knew enough of the SecondLevel Healer to respect her.

Her superiors trusted her and now he had an independent opinion from his good friend.

Laev's gaze angled past Garrett, a habit of the Nobleman's when he was thinking. "We have to beat this sickness. Ura Heather and my aunt are the main Healers on the case?"

Lord and Lady, Garrett had completely forgotten Laev was related to the Healers. That was the problem with the FirstFamilies. Each and every one of them had ties to others—by blood, alliances, or enmities.

"Lark Holly is your late father's sister," Garrett said.

"That's right." Laev's look was direct. "I love and trust her very much. You want me to call my G'Uncle T'Heather about this matter?"

"That would make everything worse."

"Very well." Laev inclined his head. "Know I will attend closely to this situation."

"It's a Healer deal."

Laev shrugged. "I have a business interest in the herb that mitigates the disease."

"I know."

"So the Healers will keep me informed. As for your business, I'll take care of anything that is forwarded to me," Laev said with relish.

"No investigating. Only rescheduling."

"Of course," Laev said blandly.

"Thanks, Laev." Garrett touched two fingers to his forehead in a short salute. "I'm leaving for home." His smile was more grimace. "The experiment takes place at the Turquoise House, day after tomorrow."

"Do you want me to come with you?"

Yeah, Garrett would like his friend near, a man in the whole mix that he could trust. But Garrett wasn't going to say so. "Thanks for the offer. No. Just keep track of the whole deal."

"I'll do that. Go with the Lady and Lord. Blessed be."

"Blessed be."

*A*fter the lovely Family ritual in a sacred grove of the sanctuary, Artemisia excused herself for bed. She didn't sleep.

Throughout the deeply touching ceremony, as she experienced the cycling energy of her parents and her sister, Artemisia realized a few things. One of the reasons she hadn't left this House for a home of her own was because of this loving acceptance. They'd all faced the hideous scandal of being accused of conspiring with the Black

Magic Cult murderers. They were innocent but tried in public opinion and found guilty. They'd gone through that time together; not many others would understand.

And her mother and father were HeartMates. She liked being around them, included in the circle of love with her sister. Both her sister and she had HeartMates and neither of them had looked for their loves.

Men tended to do that if they were older than their HeartMates and experienced the connection with a HeartMate first in the dream-quests that freed Flair—Passages. Artemisia and Tiana knew their fated mates were men, and were older than they.

The few times that she and Tiana had spoken of the matter, they'd come to the conclusion their HeartMates weren't interested in them, perhaps because of the scandal. Who needed men like that?

Tiana had focused on her goal to be the premier priestess of the Lady and Lord in all of Celta and used the Mugwort name. But her teachers and colleagues were supposed to be compassionate and forgiving.

Artemisia's peers were only supposed to be compassionate. Forgiving was a different matter.

So Artemisia went by the surname of Panax, a branch of her mother's Family of Healers who had distanced themselves from the Mugworts when the whole nasty mess had happened. She worked with an aunt, uncle, and cousin who completely ignored her.

She wondered if that would change if *she* became notable due to the experiment. If it helped her Family, that was good. Like most Families, they lived together in a large House. Unlike most Families who were not of the highest nobility, the Mugworts lived in a Residence, an intelligent House. The Residence loved her, too.

And her home was utterly unique. It was the first Healing Grove founded by the colonists and became the estate of the caretakers, the BalmHeals, who had all died out. Celta was still tough on its Earth transplants, as the Iasc sickness proved. Illness and sterility took a toll on the population—human and animal and plant. But Celtans had the length of their life and the increase of magic, psi powers, Flair, augmented. Not a fair trade as far as Artemisia was concerned. Like everyone else, she wanted it all—long life free of sickness and phenomenal Flair.

FirstGrove, BalmHeal estate, was a triangle in the northeast corner of Druida City, so two of the estate's walls were also the city walls. The concave triangular wall facing the city looked out onto only empty warehouses. The place was hidden from everyone except the desperate, the whispered secret sanctuary of Druida.

Like the rest of her Family, Artemisia was bound to the estate by blood and love. If she cut those bonds, she could never remember the location or return—unless she, herself, was desperate. She was bespelled to not tell anyone of the place.

Her Family had been stripped of their nobility and fortune and were running from Druida City when they'd been approached to be caretakers for the Residence. The best blessing of their lives.

No one knew what would happen when Artemisia and Tiana wed, if their men would be welcome at BalmHeal. If it was up to the Residence, he might be contrary and throw them all out, or grudgingly accept the new men.

Artemisia wanted a husband, but she wanted to stay in the sanctuary, too. She loved the old, crotchety Residence, her parents, the grounds that were a mixture of Earth and Celtan plants and hybrids. The sacred groves and the Healing pools were the best on Celta. No, she didn't want to leave. But she wanted a busier career outside the sanctuary.

She wanted a career, a mate—not necessarily a HeartMate—and to live in her home.

She couldn't see Garrett Primross accepting those modest goals. Like Tiana, ambition burned in him.

His image slid into her mind with the thought. Tall, muscular, powerful, with excellent Flair. Sexy. And he loved solving riddles, but he wouldn't be contemplating *her* secrets when he was infected with Iasc and wrapped in fever and nightmares.

She hoped it wouldn't be nightmares, but with his history, she suspected they'd torment him. Not that she should look at him with lust, enjoy the slow sensuality that ebbed through her in his presence. He was her patient, forbidden.

And she wasn't even sure she liked him.

Artemisia Mugwort Panax. Her name jerked Garrett from a doze near dawn. He'd curled up on his bedsponge as if he were a kid, so he stretched long and hard, thinking.

He'd heard the name of Artemisia Mugwort during his investigation for Laev T'Hawthorn . . . and Artemisia's younger sister was the best friend of Camellia D'Hawthorn, Laev's HeartMate. A small mystery solved. There was something else, but his mind had alerted him to the new day. The last day before he was infected with the horrible sickness. His stomach tensed.

Better make the most of it. He'd hired someone to spellshield his office and was due to meet him in a septhour. He'd send that bill to Primary HealingHall. He wasn't sure who provided the Healing-Hall's budget; it wasn't funded totally by the councils of Celta. He thought Nobles who wanted to use the facilities paid an annual tithe and the Heather Family plowed gilt into it. Didn't matter much as long as he got reimbursed, but his curiosity encompassed everything.

He was glad that the Turquoise House had decided on luxurious linens and furnishings. Not that Garrett would appreciate them when he was thrashing around with the sickness.

He had other tasks: clearing space in his no-time food storage so he could add his fresh food, dragging out his oldest clothes to wear, finding a damn nightshirt. He didn't want to examine why he wasn't comfortable being nude with the SecondLevel Healer. Dozens of small errands he had to take care of, including updating his will.

Splat! Something soft and squishy hit his window. He glanced at the long smear of blood and winced. Dead mouse head. The feral cats were hungry.

Now he had to clean the window.

*A*rtemisia arrived at the Turquoise House an hour before WorkBell, was greeted enthusiastically and informed she was the first to arrive. Which had her relaxing; that was irritating because she'd told herself she was perfectly calm.

"Come in!" TQ said. "I have camp chairs and a table in the mainspace by the window. My people like that window best. I also have an old drink no-time ready to be deconstructed."

He sounded insistent, so she let her steps take her to the small seating area and the window out onto the gardens. She halted when she saw several cats chasing each other in the back grassyard. An orange mother cat followed by a small kitten avoided the others and paraded, tails up, to a cobbled space. Moving so she could see the pair, Artemisia noticed an area complete with several bowls of food and a small fountain.

TQ said, "My friend and your Residence, BalmHeal, says you prefer warm half caff and half milk?" As it spoke, the no-time drink unit extruded a shelf with a steaming china mug. Artemisia took it, though she'd already had three cups that morning. "Thank you," she murmured.

"I have received all furniture and equipment on our list. A holo wall mural artist came yesterday afternoon. We practiced and I can sterilize the entire room and not affect the art!"

"Wonderful. I like murals for my patients."

"I have heard Opul Cranberry progresses well through the sickness. It appears the duration will be significantly shorter than anticipated."

She'd already checked and was relieved. "Yes."

"Because of GentleSir Primross's potent Flair-imbued blood," TQ pointed out.

"Yes."

"He is a tough man and an interesting individual," TQ continued with admiration.

Easier to agree. "Yes."

"Here as requested, TQ," Garrett called.

Six

Artemisia tensed again at Garrett's voice, then forced her muscles to ease.

TQ broadcasted, "We are in the mainspace. Some of our cat friends have arrived to stay with us."

Artemisia said, "I don't have cat friends." Then she realized TQ spoke of himself and Garrett. The guy had cat friends. Yes, he was interesting. And when he walked into the room, his impact made her catch her breath. He had a very intense aura and too much of an effect on her. She'd hoped she'd been imagining that.

He wore standard trous and tunic of cotton in a deep brown that accented the light amber color of his eyes. The clothes didn't show his musculature, but Artemisia knew he had a good body.

TQ said, "Hot, strong black caff, GentleSir Primross, your preference. Please take the mug to the GentleSir, Artemisia."

"Call me Garrett, TQ." A corner of his mouth lifted.

Artemisia picked up the new mug with liquid hotter and darker than her own. His mug was thick, manly pottery of dark green. He looked at her pretty floral mug with light-colored caff, then his own. His lips quirked deeper but flattened into a line when their fingers brushed. "Thanks."

Did he feel the same sizzle of affinity that she did? She thought so, and he didn't welcome it. She didn't, either, though if he'd been at least nice the previous day, she might have. She'd noticed his slights but ignored them.

He was her patient, forbidden to act on any attraction, though a less vulnerable man she'd never seen. But that was now. Tomorrow he'd be at the mercy of the sickness . . . and her. She swallowed. She didn't want to watch him suffer.

"Artemisia, about that matter we discussed yesterday?" The House addressed the Healer in rich tones while Garrett sipped the best caff he'd had in days. He watched her over the rim of his cup; obviously she and the House had bonded more after he'd left. He shouldn't have been irritated that the House might prefer her, but was. Competitive and stupid.

"Yes?" she asked. She was aware of him; even though she turned and walked to the window, her body angled toward him.

"I have decided to offer Garrett an invitation. No doubt he has kept many secrets."

"Oh," she said, her glance sliding to him. He remained impassive, but curiosity began to itch along his skin.

"Yeah, no doubt I have secrets and keep them." Garrett was antsy enough to pull out a coin and run it between his fingers. Showy to others and fun for him, the action did double duty.

The Healer stared at Garrett with wide emerald eyes, studying him, measuring him for the first time. His body reacted to her scrutiny, his chest expanded, his abs tightened. His feet shifted to widen his balance a little—women could deliver the most awful blows. And his cock grew heavy. He didn't want that and was damn well going to keep her focus on his face. So he smiled.

Her eyes widened and her mouth curved, but she compressed her lips. As if she didn't believe that smile of his. Smart woman.

"Do you keep secrets?" she asked.

"Love secrets. I keep them if I think that's the right thing to do. And for the right person." He let his voice chill.

Her chin lifted. "Fine. TQ, you deal with this guy. I want to check on the furnishings."

"I will explain to Garrett." TQ's voice was smooth on top, with a warning underneath. The House had learned to use its actor's voice well. "Artemisia, the furnishings are fine, exactly as ordered, and Clover Fine Furniture delivered on schedule."

"Maybe I want my own pillow," the Healer said.

"It would have to go through decontamination often, I'd think," Garrett said. He continued to roll the coin. Occasionally it would flash and her gaze would go to it.

"My pillow won't be harmed, I don't think. It's a feather pillow." Artemisia walked from the room.

There was a slight hiss from TQ. "You have irritated your Heart-Mate."

Yes, that he knew Artemisia was his HeartMate was one of Garrett's secrets. He flinched. "How do you know?"

"Everything my inhabitants have whispered of, I know," TQ said.

Which made Garrett want a list of those who'd lived in TQ. Must be a record somewhere and he'd find it, later. But now he was stuck for a week with the Healer.

"I keep secrets, too," the House said. "And I know you're a discreet man."

"Don't suppose you'd give me a list of the people who've stayed with you?"

"No. And I have my own secrets, naturally." The House made a sound like clearing a throat—which he didn't have, and which the actor who'd given him the voice wouldn't have done at this moment. It showed weakness. TQ was definitely his own entity, and not a human male. "My HouseHeart chamber needs maintenance. I asked Artemisia to help. I want this done before the Healers' project."

"Which is why you aren't ready today." Garrett slipped the coin into his pocket. His lust had subsided. Good. He could still smell the woman in the room, though.

TQ said, "Correct. I had considered requesting your help, too."

Fascination blazed through Garrett. He nearly trembled with it. He'd never been in a HouseHeart, the most important place of a sentient House. The HouseHeart reflected the Family. But the Turquoise House had no Family, so Garrett himself might be able to infuse a bit of himself into the long-lived being. That would be a satisfying goal in itself, a tiny legacy of himself in stretching infinity.

After his loss of Dinni, he'd discovered that he'd needed to make a mark on the world. Something more than just surviving the disease. This could be a true contribution.

"You are reconsidering your offer?" His throat was hot with desire to learn, to see, to discover.

"You do not treat Artemisia well, though she is your HeartMate. Humans are very odd."

"HeartMate and HeartBonding is odd."

"I have seen HeartBonded people."

Garrett wondered if the House had actually had a HeartMate couple exchange the bond sexually within its walls. How much could the House sense? Garrett's mind veered to an image of a naked Artemisia screaming her passion. Shut that down!

"Why do you treat Artemisia as you do?"

"My business."

"How am I to help my people, help *you* during this time, if I don't understand you? How am I to learn?"

The plea socked Garrett's gut.

Dammit, now he couldn't speak because his throat had tightened. He coughed. "We're private here?"

"Artemisia is making arrangements to get her pillow." There was a slight pause as if TQ's attention focused elsewhere. The House wasn't omnipresent, then. "I do not think that her pillow will survive the decontamination processes. When the pillow arrives I will measure it in all ways. If the object does not last, I will replace it with an exact copy."

"Things aren't always interchangeable. The pillow you provide, no matter how it seems like a match, won't be *her* pillow."

The air around him pressed against him, TQ's attention sharp. "Did you lose someone dear and irreplaceable? A woman?"

Garrett didn't answer.

Silence throbbed. Garrett shook off the rough mood and went over to the window that looked out on the rear grassyard. Beautifully landscaped, of course. One or more of TQ's residents had been a gardener. Smooth green turf, colorful flowers shifting in the slight breeze before bushes staggered in front of small trees, then tall trees, keeping the yard private. All of the feral cats he knew, and others he didn't, snoozed in the sun.

The yard looked too manicured, as were the formal gardens and fountain of the inner courtyard of MidClass Lodge where he lived. He preferred a natural tangle of plant life like he'd found on his travels outside cities.

"The records of the Gael City HealingHall state a young woman with a baby asked you to accompany the driver of the quarantine vehicle to the isolation clinic in the mountains."

He jerked, remembering. Dinni had begged. Her husband had been one of the men to find the infected fish and had died. Her baby had been sick. She'd looked fine except for sorrow and worry.

Garrett's throat closed. He couldn't answer, pretend this didn't matter.

"*Her* records at that HealingHall state that she had told the Healers she would scry a friend—an old lover—who she was sure would help with the driving, and that you grew up together."

There wasn't even a sturdy chair he could sit on, only two little rickety ones. He hitched a hip on the wide windowsill. His chest hurt.

"I have lost people, too," TQ said softly. "One or two died here despite all I did to save them. You lost the woman, Dinni Spurge Flixweed."

"Yes," Garrett forced out. "I lost my first love, my first girl."

Footsteps echoed in the quiet and the Healer paused at the door, expression irritated. Then her head tilted as she picked up the atmosphere. The woman seemed more sensitive empathically than most.

Why would it take so long to get a pillow? A messenger service could 'port anywhere in moments if she gave them visual clues. Another thing for Garrett to figure out later.

She crossed her arms. "Have we considered the situation?"

Garrett's past swept away with the lure of seeing a forbidden place, a HouseHeart.

"I will allow GentleSir Garrett Primross into my HouseHeart with the usual proviso that a spell will be applied to his memory so it will fade, and if he gives us his Vow of Honor that he will record no details."

Not so easy an access as Garrett had expected. Disappointment shadowed his thoughts, but he would know that he'd been in a HouseHeart, had made a contribution that would live after him. He'd know it in his very bones, and that would be good. "I agree."

"This experiment will be stressful for all of us, but especially you two humans. I believe time in my HouseHeart will be good for you before we begin this process."

Artemisia's arms uncrossed and her shoulders lowered, a genuine smile lightened her eyes. "It's wonderful you will allow me in your HouseHeart. Thank you."

"You are welcome here, Artemisia. You will always be welcome," TQ responded. The House didn't add permission for Garrett. He shrugged the caring away.

A chuff of air came, followed by TQ's words. "There is a secret passageway from my southwest corner. At the end of that hallway, there is a trapdoor in the floor, under the carpet. I will tell you the secret poem. I am very good at telepathic communication, but my people must be better attuned to me than you currently are."

After all the information, the woman let out a long breath.

Garrett said, "Right." When they reached the first hallway, she turned the wrong direction.

Gritting his teeth, knowing it was a mistake, he took her elbow in his fingers. Pure desire flashed through him. Maybe the more he resisted temptation, the more his lust would mount, would rage within him. Too bad; he wasn't going to change. She wasn't the woman he wanted.

But three years had passed since Dinni's death and his grief and loss were waning, like bright moons coming from shadows that had been cast upon them.

Artemisia stopped and looked up at him.

"Wrong way."

"Oh." Her smile was quick and meaningless. She turned and Garrett had to force his hand to drop. Her elbow wasn't even that sexy.

He lied.

She hesitated at the cross corridor.

"Left," he said.

"Thank you."

There was a good-sized window at the end of the hall. No one would expect a hidden entrance to the HouseHeart to be there.

"The moles of Celta and Captain Ruis Elder of the starship *Nuada's Sword* helped me excavate a proper concealed passage and secret HouseHeart," TQ said. "Then Mitchella D'Blackthorn and I decorated it *ourselves*."

"Sounds wonderful," Artemisia said.

"It *is*!" TQ said.

The Healer caught sight of the change in the plush and patterned carpet before Garrett. He searched with his Flair and he found that the hole was narrow. "You have a problem with claustrophobia?" he asked.

"No, nor darkness or dankness."

"I am not dark or dank!" TQ objected.

"No. You aren't," she agreed absently, passing her hands over the area covered by the rug.

Garrett was struck with the idea that she knew about House-Hearts, this woman who was not one of the twenty-five FirstFamilies who had most of the intelligent Residences. From sheer curiosity, he'd made a list of sentient buildings and there weren't more than a dozen that didn't belong to the FirstFamilies, descendants of the colonists who had funded the trip to Celta. What did she know? And how?

Taking a moment to clear the desire from his senses, shutting down even the thin thread that pulsed with molecules between them, he used his Flair and caught tendrils of mystery wisping around her like fog.

"What's the spell and the password?" she whispered.

Following logic, he understood that TQ knew more about the woman than he did, and so must the Healers. He was being left out. Nearly intolerable.

On an inner breeze, TQ recited:

Home is where the Heart is
My HouseHeart is Home,
Is Me,
Home, Home, Home
For the right Family
Us

Garrett had expected a cheerful little jingle. "That doesn't make sense."

"I wrote it," TQ said with dignity. "I like it."

"It makes sense to him," the Healer murmured.

"Yes, Artemisia," TQ said.

Softly, repeating the emphasis exactly as TQ had, she said the spell.

The carpet and floor lifted straight up, the rectangle attached to the ceiling, then illusion covered it.

Illusion on the floor, too, as if the carpet remained. The spot rippled, and Garrett figured if TQ didn't want them to see that warning, he wouldn't have. "Good safety measures. Even if someone knows the words, they won't see the opening unless you allow them."

"That is correct," TQ said.

The Healer stepped forward, frowned as she peered down. Garrett came up until his body almost touched hers, looked to the floor—and beyond to a dark hole. "Light?" he prompted.